Queer Obscenity

Queer Obscenity

Queer Obscenity

Erotic Archives in Dictatorial Spain

Javier Fernández-Galeano

STANFORD UNIVERSITY PRESS
Stanford, California

Stanford University Press
Stanford, California

Printed and bound by CPI Group (UK) Ltd, Croydon, CR0 4YY

Library of Congress Cataloging-in-Publication Data

Names: Fernández-Galeano, Javier, author.
Title: Queer obscenity : erotic archives in dictatorial Spain / Javier
    Fernández-Galeano.
Description: Stanford, California : Stanford University Press, 2024. |
    Includes bibliographical references and index.
Identifiers: LCCN 2024012332 (print) | LCCN 2024012333 (ebook) |
    ISBN 9781503638754 (cloth) | ISBN 9781503639508 (paperback) |
    ISBN 9781503639515 (ebook)
Subjects: LCSH: Gay pornography—Political aspects—Spain—History—20th
    century. | Gay erotica—Political aspects—Spain—History—20th century. |
    Homosexuality—Political aspects—Spain—History—20th century. |
    Obscenity (Law)—Spain—History—20th century. | Censorship—Spain—
    History—20th century. | Spain—Politics and government—20th century.
Classification: LCC HQ76.965.P67 F48 2024 (print) | LCC HQ76.965.P67
    (ebook) | DDC 700/.4538086640946—dc23/eng/20240403
LC record available at https://lccn.loc.gov/2024012332
LC ebook record available at https://lccn.loc.gov/2024012333

Cover design: Daniel Benneworth-Gray
Cover art: Detail from a 1965 file adjudicated at the Barcelona Vagrancy Court.
Source: Arxiu Judicial Territorial de Barcelona i l'Hospitalet de Llobregat
Typeset by Newgen in Latino URW 9.75/14

To Andy

CONTENTS

Acknowledgments   ix

Introduction
Reflections in the Mirror   1
*The Politics of Obscenity in
Twentieth-Century Spain*

1 Curators of Pornography   17
*Scandal and Censorship in Primo de Rivera's
Spain (1923–1930)*

2 Dildos and Lubricant   47
Material Culture versus Nationalistic Rhetoric

3 "Plastic Objects of Obscene Configuration"   81
*From Ordinary to Extraordinary Legal
Framings (1950–1975)*

4 Burning the Normal, Preserving the Queer   109

5 Running Mascara   145
Trans Visual Archives in the 1970s

6 "Frosted Glass"   173
   The Sexual Politics of the Democratic Transition

   Notes   205

   Bibliography   241

   Index   255

ACKNOWLEDGMENTS

This book was made possible by archivists and librarians that care for and disseminate the source material. I have met very dedicated archivists, including Laura Pérez Vega in Sevilla; Enric Nogués Pastor, Alba Blasco, Carlos Tortajada, and Victor Pons in Valencia; and Anna Ollé Rubio, Meritxell Soler Cos, Joaquín Martínez Perearnau, and Francesc Xavier Gayan Felez in Barcelona. My editor, Margo Irvin, took this book in the correct direction with her kind firmness. Cindy Lim made the submission process smooth. Since Zeb Tortorici and I share our love for the obscene, Cole Rizki and I our fascination for haptic/visual archives; our ongoing dialogues are at the foundation of this book.

The peer reviewers were exceptionally constructive and on point, and some of my best colleagues/friends gave me additional feedback: Cole Rizki, Javier Cuevas del Barrio, José Antonio Ramos Arteaga, Amy Kerner, Daniela Ferrández Pérez, and Geoffroy Huard. My mentors/friends make academia more inhabitable: James N. Green, Jennifer L. Lambe, Àlvar Martínez Vidal, Federico Finchelstein, Francisco Vázquez García, Enric Novella, Rafael Mérida Jiménez, Richard Cleminson, Gema Pérez Sánchez, Isaias Fanlo, and, finally, Robert Douglas Cope, who passed away in 2019 but will always be a role model for me. Santiago Joaquín Insausti and Moisés Fernández Cano have accompanied and advised me as I struggled to put together the pieces that make up this book.

Wesleyan University and Universitat de València were my communities as I wrote this book while navigating the precariousness of academia. I acknowledge funding from the Juan de la Cierva postdoctoral program and the Andrew W. Mellon Postdoctoral Fellowship. I belong to the research groups "Memorias de las masculinidades disidentes en España e Hispanoamérica" (PID2019-106083GB-I00); "El problema de la alteridad en el mundo actual" (HUM-536); and "La clínica de la subjetividad: Historia, teoría y práctica de la psicopatología estructural" (PID2020-113356GB-I00).

Finally, and most importantly, my parents, Teresa and José María, taught me what it means to love someone for who they are. Chiqui, Curro, and Pablo, my siblings, make me laugh every day; our quirks make life more fun. Gracia is my *hermana*, there is no distance that can separate us. Andrew T. Creamer, Andy, you are simply the best; you make me see any flaw in my writing in ways that make me feel able to fix them (except when you get cover letter, you know what I mean). Andy's smile, soft belly, and beautiful voice are the invisible syntax of this book.

Queer Obscenity

Queer Obscenity

INTRODUCTION

Reflections in the Mirror

THE POLITICS OF OBSCENITY
IN TWENTIETH-CENTURY SPAIN

On the night of 25 August 1972, three neighbors huddled together and peered through the window of a private house in their small village. In a mirror hanging on the wall the neighbors claimed they saw reflected back two young men having sex. Pierre Bourdieu refers to the "mirror effect" that takes place when those who document their observations expose themselves.[1] In this case, the words of these neighbors and the authorities would betray their pretense of offense and lay bare their crude prying and loathing. This book exposes subjects, primarily state agents, who have violated the erotic intimacy of others. Whether one operates in the epistemic mode of objectivism (the window) or subjectivism (the mirror), there is no escaping the realization that the glass "is never immaculate. There are scratches on it, blind spots, curvatures. [. . .] There are no innocent immediacies of reception."[2] I aim to foreground these imperfections, desires, and biases as modes of archival mediation.

The peeping neighbors alerted the authorities, and the young men were arrested and sentenced for public scandal. The defendants appealed this ruling, arguing that their neighbors had demonstrated an "unhealthy curiosity" when they deliberately violated their intimacy and expectation of privacy; however, Spain's Supreme Court dismissed the appeal, stating that it was the defendants' responsibility to take every precaution so that no one would find what they were doing. The magistrates considered the three neighbors' testimony, in which they recounted how scandalized they felt by the sight of two men having sex, proving that their suspicions and motivations to spy on them were legitimate. In other words, the Supreme Court legitimated voyeurism for the sake of policing obscenity.

This book is a history of obscenity in Spain that traces a surveillance mode dependent on documenting intimacy and preserving transgression. The authorities produced archives that were discursively and materially aimed at conferring masculinity based on varying degrees of touch. Supposedly "real men" (as both consumers of mainstream pornography and state agents) would preserve their masculinity by *seeing without being touched*. Alternatively, state agents perceived "deviant" subjects as those who—through visual, spoken, or written evidence—*remained touched by the visibility of their transgression*. Authorities put transgressive desires on the stage in the witness stand and state archives to keep them off-scene—the authorities themselves became "unwitting pornographers" when "bringing *on* the obscenity in order to keep it *off*."[3] The Supreme Court magistrates established that the "heinous vice" (*vicio nefando*) of homosexuality, referring to private consensual acts between adults of the same sex, was not criminal *per se*. However, if anyone other than the participants became aware of these acts, then they became a crime.[4] The Supreme Court, and state authorities more broadly, imposed obligatory invisibility on nonstraight subjects while contradictorily investing state resources to make their transgressions visible.[5] Treating police officers, judges, and forensic doctors as prying observers, and the judicial files and legal compendia as a derivative form of obscenity (one more explicit and transgressive than most contemporary print culture) is not only theoretical positions I adopt, but they also emanate from contemporary subjects' acts of resistance, perspectives, and critiques.

A file initiated in 1963 at the Málaga Vagrancy Court, for instance, includes amateur photographs of Black men and a White man having oral and anal sex, which were confiscated from a Moroccan national. He had been arrested while traveling on a train. When left alone in his cell, he tore up the photographs he had in his possession. However, the authorities, discovering the pieces, invested time and effort to skillfully reassemble them and tape them together in the manner of a jigsaw puzzle.[6] One can imagine police officers hunched over and holding each piece up to the light, examining it, and then trying to fit each minute photographic trace back together into coherent images of black men performing oral sex on each other and penetrating a middle-aged white man whose face is out of frame. This is one example of how state officials carefully curated and preserved materials that, in their view, reflected and enticed revolting desires, as proof of defendants' antisocial tendencies. This pretense was rooted in a reactionary ideology that equated the Spanish nation with virility. As the Supreme Court ruled in 1969, "[H]omosexuality is an obscene practice that is especially rejected by our culture, more tolerant and open towards relationships between people of different sex."[7] According to this sentence, the contraposition of openness toward "straight" sex, whether procreative or not, and the treatment of homosexuality as obscenity was central to Spanish mores.

In a 1963 speech in front of his colleagues, Judge Luis Vivas Marzal discussed in detail why and how homosexuality could be penalized without being a crime. At the core of his argument lay the essentialization of

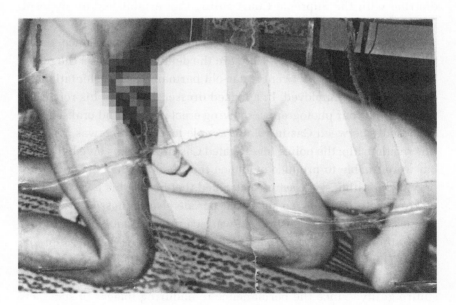

FIGURE 1. Photograph included in File 93/1963, showing a scene of anal intercourse between two anonymous subjects and the tape that authorities used to reconstruct the photograph. The image has been slightly edited. Printed with permission by the Archivo Histórico Provincial de Sevilla, fondo documental Vagos y Maleantes, Sig. 8935.

nonstraight sex as a form of obscenity that disturbs Catholic morality *even when it remains unknown and unseen by the public.* In other words, Vivas Marzal articulated the concept of "public scandal" redefining the social, constructing an imagined viewing public or requiring the judicial to produce/become the public as prying observers. Vivas Marzal considered how homosexuality could be catalogued as public scandal when "carried out in the dark, in closed premises, discreetly and stealthily."[8] Public scandal must thus, in his words, "transcend" to register as such. In Spanish this verb is polysemic; "transcend" might mean that it affects people other than the participants or that it is "relevant" for the body politic. For Vivas Marzal, homosexuality is always relevant because he characterized it as gross indecency. The Supreme Court, for its part, inconsistently delineated between sin and crime, producing a "highly variable" precedent that left ordinary judges beset by "bitter doubts." Vivas Marzal cited Supreme Court rulings that would support the "radical conclusions" that homosexuality without the public's knowledge could not be penalized as scandal.[9] However and curiously, he concluded his diatribe with the Supreme Court ruling that established an opposite interpretation.

Not coincidentally, this 1961 ruling had to do with audience, reception, visibility, and visuality. Here are the details of the case: the police heard that Casimiro, a twenty-year-old barman, lived "ostentatiously" despite being unemployed. In a locked dresser drawer in his room, the police found four photographs, showing erect penises and oral sex acts, supposedly between Casimiro and a male lover. No one was aware of this relationship; the police investigated Casimiro for his lavish lifestyle but were unable to produce evidence that his lover had economically provided for him; and Casimiro clarified that he and his lover used the camera's self-timer device such that no one else witnessed the scenes in question. For these reasons, he was acquitted of public scandal; the prosecution appealed, however, and elevated the case to the Supreme Court. The latter overruled the initial ruling, concluding that the fact of the photographs being meant to persist was precisely what made Casimiro guilty: "since the permanence in enduring images of such acts constitutes the grave transcendence that the Law condemns, and there is no need to further reason that the act reproduced in the aforementioned photographs is offensive to modesty and good customs."[10] In other words, a photograph could take the role of an offended witness because photography has the power to capture and prolong the transgressive acts through its material circulation and reception as forms of consumption. Yet it was the police who amplified this power by ensuring the long-term preservation of homoerotic materials (photographs in the case of Casimiro as well as movies, letters, and literature in other cases) in police and state archives. The state's curatorial politics around erotica are uncanny: they catalogued the forementioned photos as the quintessential moral violation yet, by doing so, they preserved the images to establish the premise that nonstraight sex is deplorable because it lives on through its material traces.[11] Vivas Marzal concluded that, no matter what the legal doctrine established, there ought to be no "sympathy" for these violators and their "propagation of evil."[12] This book explores the manifold transgressions that moved judges like Vivas Marzal to be so hyperbolic.

In Spanish the words *vicio* (excessive depravity) and *marica* (and its derivatives *maricón*, *maricona*, and so on) mark the territory of erotic "deviation" that authorities mapped through their arrests, exams, confiscations, and rulings. On the one hand, *marica* historically refers to "subjects assigned male at birth who adopted a feminized persona through sexual practices, embodied and spoken languages, and social interactions, including relationships with masculine men, situational gender switching, and subcultural codes."[13] There is no letter for *marica* in LGBT+, yet maricas' ways of making visible gender and sexual transgression are central to queer and trans genealogies.[14] *Marica* is a slur appropriated by those it was meant to stigmatize as a way of signifying a refusal to adopt sanitized labels external to their own experience. There are resonances, then, between queerness and *mariconería*. I often use *marica* in this book, with the cautionary note that there is no true way of accessing the interiority of defendants in order to confirm their self-identification.[15] On the other hand, *vicio* is defined as an appetite so excessive that there is no way of satisfying it.[16] *Vicio* overlaps with but also outstrips same-sex desires: those who experience it (*viciosos*) are considered unredeemable, as they revel in transgressing and in passing it along to others. Males who posed for and preserved homoerotic photos were treated as *viciosos,* but so was an elderly gentleman who organized slide presentations of canonical art with nudity or a poet who dared to publish an erotic piece in a Catholic bulletin.

Interestingly, as the cases above highlight, the materials that police and state archives ultimately preserved are examples of erotica rather than pornography. In other words, we don't find mainstream hard-core pornography in the police archive. Indeed, the distinctions I make between erotica and pornography are based on how they were used by historical actors in ways that pertain to this book's central argument: while the legal definition of pornography responded to formal economic market dynamics—what sells—I use erotica to denote non-marketed intimate materials (photographs as well as letters, postcards, and recordings), which have their own intimate economies outside of formal market-based logics.[17] This distinction ultimately speaks to why I was able to find the erotica of maricas but not mainstream porn preserved in judicial archives. The term *obscenity* was used to cover the whole spectrum, from mainstream hard-core to public awareness of nonprocreative sex.[18] The centrality of Catholicism in nationalistic ideologies in Spain translated into the particularly harsh reaction on the part of the authorities to desecration through sex, which is part and parcel of the obscene.[19] In sum, the politics of obscenity had two sides. Transgressive art, desecration, homoeroticism, and cis and trans women's visual and bodily autonomy were radical gestures that undermined authorities' tacit recognition of a "legitimate" consumer of porn: an adult Spanish male, affluent, politically obedient, and, ideally, married.[20]

While both homoerotic images and mainstream porn were considered obscene, they led to distinct sentences and preservation policies. Francoist authorities implicitly established that maricas were "too close" to their personal erotica, irreversibly touched and infected by it, in following the Platonic and Augustinian traditions for which "touch was the basest of senses."[21] In these cases, "images readily assume an intimate relation to the psyche and even to the body of the beholder."[22] By contrast, for "straight" men the emphasis was on sight as a tool of knowledge and domination that maintains distance between subject and object. Consuming porn that aroused heterosexual drives, often as a ritual of male bonding, was compatible with procreation as a duty to the nation. Unlike erotica, once mainstream porn was destroyed, consumers remained untouched by it; the creators and entrepreneurs, not so much. The state sanctioned "the visual economy of pornography: the gender-pleasure arising from the production of masculinity," using philosopher Paul Preciado's terms.[23] Preciado refers to how *Playboy* positions its readers as voyeurs who can enjoy the "male pleasure of seeing without being seen" by "looking through a peephole, a crack, or a window into what had previously been a private space."[24] *Playboy*'s philosophy bears an uncanny parallelism with the Supreme Court sentence that sanctioned the neighbors' decision to look through a window and, more broadly, with state agents observing and documenting "deviance" while paradoxically distancing themselves from it through these same acts of observation and documentation.

Conversely, I aim to queer the archives produced by the reactionaries who were in power in Spain for most of the twentieth century by juxtaposing their unacknowledged permissiveness toward masculine peccadilloes or "slight offenses" (including mainstream porn) with the material, visual, and textual traces of transgressive cultures.[25] Queering involves a nonessentialist reading, one that is attentive to the performative configurations of subjecthood and power positions, to underline the absurdities, contradictions, and tensions in judicial transcripts. Courtrooms are "little theaters" where the law puts on a show even when the public is not allowed in. Following Michelle Castañeda, the theatrical presentation of the law's cruel contradictions becomes "strange" in the sense of "parodic, nonsensical, and absurd."[26] The prosecution of public scandal involved citizens' obligation to narrate for the state, producing a documentation that originates in aurality yet buries it below layers of bureaucratic language. The absurdity of the law consists in mediating those facets of subjects' lives that feel more intimate, sexual, and unspeakable, forcing subjects to verbalize them on the court bench to translate embodied experience into a dry text full of jargon, interjections, the use of the third person, and the occasional *lapsus linguae*.

By targeting scandal—both as a violation per se and as an aggravating circumstance—courtrooms operated as a magnifying glass for history, leaving us a fragmented erotic record that overrepresents subversive material culture and texts while obliterating objects aligned with dominant gender regimes and hegemonic masculinity. This is a radical intervention in the history of obscenity and porn, which has primarily revolved around print culture in liberal legal frameworks. From its inception, the academic subfield that historicizes obscenity has maintained the core premise that modern pornography came into existence during the nineteenth century through restricted access, in that the general public was denied access to pornographic materials and literature, reserved for an elite class of white men.[27] Rather than magnifying subversiveness, print culture often toned it down. For example, eighteenth-century British literature gave voice to female characters who related genital sexuality in their own terms, but over the course of the nineteenth and twentieth centuries those passages were redacted in multiple republications.[28]

In contrast, Spanish authorities staged, echoed, and projected transgression in order to evaluate and judge it, taking the position of the scandalized spectator as a procedural precondition for the crime. I focus on dictatorial periods (the Primo de Rivera and Franco regimes), when authorities that had a fraught relationship with modernity implemented reactionary programs in the face of mass politics.[29] They responded to drastic changes in sexual mores during the twentieth century by mediating the erotic through archives and the courts: they fragmented novels and recited explicit passages out loud to ritualize defendants' degradation and purge obscenity from literature (reinscribing it in judicial records and the state's publications); they touched homoerotic photographs, letters, and drawings while feigning disgust; and they destroyed sexually explicit materials to protect defendants who kept a straight personae. Whereas courtroom archives were originally conceived as architectures of containment, I show how the poetics of touch—visual, haptic, and material—generate intoxicating and unbounded intimacies with erotic objects.[30]

My reading methods take the dramatization of moral exceptionalism in courtrooms under reactionary regimes to be the paradoxical hotbed for obscenity, through an economy of the senses that moves between stigma and the potential of repair. Here the Spanish *tocado* (touched) is closer to the sense in which authorities aimed to touch or affect defendants by using their testimonies and material culture to shame, wound, or stigmatize them.[31] By curating and archiving defendants' explicit images of gay sex or queer authors' literature, reactionary authorities intended to keep them wounded and within reach. The acts of confiscation also meant that creators and transgressive communities could no longer enjoy the haptic qualities of their own erotic possessions; where touching an image of someone you desire, care for, or had sex with is a potent experience of affective connection with one's erotic past. State policies mobilized the senses to surveil and discipline: saturating the courtroom's soundscape with voices that conveyed repentance or producing reports about how dildos and sex toys felt when police officers touched them. The judiciary had to move across media: from visual and moving images to textual descriptions of "obscenity," constantly translating embodied actions into text.

I translate across media as well to reimagine how the archival materials that I have gathered touch on marica, queer, and trans affects. Inspired by microhistory, I move between the verbal, the visual, and the haptic through the texture of sources.[32] As an additional mediation layer, I translated the quotes from originally Spanish sources into English (often including both versions so that readers can compare them). In the last instance, this book can be read as a compendium of objects that have in common their fragmentary nature, the fact that they were singled out and extracted for preservation because of their subversiveness. When gathering them both at institutional archives and beyond, I became aware of how the police acts like Walter Benjamin's collector: "What is decisive in collecting is that the object is detached from all its original functions in order to enter into the closest conceivable relation to things of the same kind."[33] The material culture studied in this book is often untraceable; what remains is a constellation of objects (physical or textual) related through their punitive consequences. In many cases, consumption of these materials mediated by sympathy or identification with the transgressors is what made them scandalous and obscene—something to keep in mind when reading the next chapters.

In writing this book, I consulted over 1,400 files from courts in Madrid, Barcelona, Granada, Sevilla, Málaga, Bilbao, Las Palmas de Gran Canarias, and València. These records are held in different types of archives, from court and provincial archives to the national administration's central archives. To obtain access to these records, I had to present pleas to courts and government agencies at the national and regional levels. Many archives do not have a catalogue on their collection of vagrancy and dangerousness files. Most often, researchers must request special access by demonstrating their credentials and committing to maintain defendants' anonymity.[34] For this reason, I use random pseudonyms when referring to defendants judged at Vagrancy and Social Dangerousness courts, and I only incorporate photographs that were authorized by archives' supervisors. Furthermore, in most archives I was only allowed to transcribe, a time-consuming task that I occasionally expedited by dictating the contents of the files aloud.[35] Apart from these files, I have also consulted the public scandal files from the Audiencia Provincial de Madrid, held at the Archivo Histórico Nacional (AHN); the Supreme Court sentences;

reports on the activities of the purging commissions appointed in 1937 (held in the archives of several universities); the proposals and minutes resulting from the 1970 debate on pornography in the Cortes; censorship files; the historic films at the Centro de Documentación Cinematográfica of València; the Biblioteca Pública Arús nude photographs collection; and the Biblioteca Nacional's collection of historical newspapers, among others.

With all these documents I draw a sort of navigational chart to historicize obscenity throughout the twentieth century.

Narrative, Interventions, and Chapters Outline

After World War I, Spain experienced significant urban expansion along with the radicalization of the working class, resulting in drastic regime changes. Lieutenant General Miguel Primo de Rivera's regime came to power through a relatively nonviolent coup d'état, having enlisted the support of Spain's King Alfonso XIII. This regime lasted from 1923 to 1930, showing close ties with fascism but putting entrenched social privileges at the forefront.[36] In a deeply hierarchical system, obscenity was judged according to the consumer's status. In fact, the king himself was a pornographer who commissioned hard-core films for his private entertainment, films that have survived to the present day. Liberal principles, including freedom of speech and egalitarian citizenship, had a significant role in public debates and the legal status of obscenity in the United States, the United Kingdom, Germany, and France—the most studied countries for the interwar period—but had limited impact in Spain.[37] The 1920s and 1930s were the "golden era" of *sicalipsis* (popular erotica) in Spain.[38] Writer Gonzalo Torrente Ballester (1910–1999), who came of age in the Primo de Rivera dictatorship, remembers how when he was young, "pornography was tolerated: it was basic, low-price pornography, requested with shame from the owner of the newsstand where it was sold, and surreptitiously read, borrowed, and commented."[39] The first chapter interrogates the particularities of the restricted toleration of obscenity in a proto-fascist dictatorship.

I argue that authoritarian policies deeply shaped material culture through the ritualistic fragmentation of artworks in courtrooms and judicial archives. Starting in 1922 expert lawyers in the United States achieved two major shifts in obscenity cases: the recognition of artworks' unity, so that the entire book had to be evaluated, and establishing the "tolerances of the average adult" as the criteria to judge obscenity.[40] The opposite took place in Spain. The Supreme Court ruled that elites' *morality* was the criteria for which to determine public scandal. Prosecutors selected literary works' most offensive passages to be read aloud in courtrooms, and judges incorporated them into their rulings—they brought erotic novelettes to the scene to mark them as obscene. As a by-product of this ritual, passages dealing with gender transgressions and homosexuality are well preserved in judicial transcripts at the Archivo Histórico Nacional, while the novelettes to which they belonged were censored and destroyed.[41] Fragmentation was the foundation of an authoritarian policy that spectacularized obscenity to confine it. Out of these confines, explicit works were implicitly tolerated if they aroused male heterosexual drives and/or stigmatized non-normative sexualities and genders. While in other countries, like France, increasing toleration for obscenity was openly justified on the grounds that sexual knowledge prevented perversion,[42] Spanish authorities covertly sanctioned men's access to obscenity but treated sexology as subversive. Male privilege was justified through the notion, deeply grounded in Spanish society at the time, that men can exercise multiple roles with different degrees of exposure and reconcile their family responsibilities with occasional sexual escapades.

During the Spanish Civil War (1936–1939), fascist lawmakers passed new laws that, in an act of historical revisionism, established a direct relationship between obscenity and the Second Republic's progressive policies. The revisionist legislation erased the memory of popular erotic cultures that had thrived under the Primo de Rivera dictatorship. The second chapter contraposes state discourses with material culture from the Civil War to the early 1960s, complicating the interpretation that popular erotic cultures vanished with the Second Republic.[43] In the earlier Francoist period, official propaganda imagined Spain as a pure Christian nation and blamed obscenity on Spain's "enemies": communism, liberalism, and freemasonry, among others. Fascist laws were enacted to empower state agents to systematically screen and purge books from the collections of public libraries by setting on fire anything labeled as obscene or politically subversive. The reality was more complex, as district commissions, tasked with screening and selecting the books to be destroyed, lamented over their logistical challenges, including short deadlines and lacking human resources. Eventually, national authorities had to compromise and recognize that obscenity was subjective. Some libraries with collections of obscenity, such as a series of homoerotic photographs housed at a freemason library in Barcelona, survived the purge by ending public access.

After World War II, the Franco regime had to acclimate to a new international order by downplaying its fascist elements and gradually approaching the Western powers. Starting in the mid-1950s, tourism became essential for the regime's economic policies, which required leniency in the local implementation of antiobscenity laws and the Vagrancy Law.[44] The town of Torremolinos, in the Mediterranean Costa del Sol region, came to epitomize this trend. The authorities confiscated porn, dildos, contraceptives, and aphrodisiacs from Spanish elites and international visitors. The police set out to strengthen gender hierarchies that deprived women and maricas of any agency in sex, but material culture betrayed an enduring interest in erogenous stimulation and nonprocreative sex. The treatment of non-Catholic and racialized defendants animated controversy—both in the courts and in the local press—on whether fascism or top-down modernization defined the regime. There was uncertainty around the Franco regime's geopolitical positioning amid the racial and postcolonial conflicts of the Cold War. In response, Francoist authorities claimed an equidistant position between the primitivism they attributed to racialized populations and the excessive permissiveness of the Western world.[45] Francoist Spain was both a clientelist nation in its relationship with the United States—as the Franco regime ceded military sovereignty to the United States and lifted its trade barriers—and, historically, a European metropolis involved in racial colonialism.

Up until the early 1960s, obscenity in Spain followed the tradition of underground stag films: it circulated clandestinely or was produced by amateurs for self-consumption, and it remained confined to brothels and other restricted spaces. However, over the course of the 1960s and 1970s, hard-core pornography would become fully visible in the United States and other countries. This phenomenon channeled anxieties over urban decay, deindustrialization, and social upheaval while also epitomizing the "progress" of the Sexual Revolution of the 1960s.[46] Chapter 3 traces how the Spanish Supreme Court responded to the increasing visibility of pornography from 1950 to 1975 and legislators' initiatives to curtail this trend. By the early 1970s, magistrates' belief that Spaniards enjoyed a naturally superior morality gradually gave way to their disbelief and apprehension that pornification was out of control. Magistrates were personally invested in maintaining a hierarchy between modes of consumption that concerned the formation of gender/sexual identities. They established a de facto gradation of pornographers' legal liability depending on their role in the staging and (de)formation of gender. Pornography consumed as a male rite of passage and expression of masculinity was treated leniently, whereas homoerotic materials, desecration, and youth countercultures were not. Likewise, the use of sex toys was considered too obscene to be recorded, while explicit testimonies on maricas' pain were incentivized and recorded. These rulings implied that (since their sexual fulfillment was intrinsically obscene) suffering was the only decent thing maricas could do.

As the ordinary framework of the Penal Law proved to be insufficient to offset the expansion of the pornography business, Francoist legislators (*procuradores*) incorporated it into the extraordinary framework of the *Ley de Peligrosidad y Rehabilitación Social* (Law of Social Dangerousness and Rehabilitation), which replaced the Vagrancy Law in 1970.[47] Fascist *procuradores*, especially women like Pilar Primo de Rivera (Miguel Primo de Rivera's daughter), argued that late capitalism's technical sophistication had provided the perfect alibi for porn. While up until the 1960s the regime conceived obscenity and communism as entangled evils, in the 1970s many Francoist lawmakers and opinionmakers saw contemporary communist regimes as a model of effective moral policing. During the Cold War, the Franco regime prided itself in its indisputable anticommunist credentials to seek an alignment with the West. Yet, as hard-core porn became mainstream in the West, many *procuradores* advocated for Spanish exceptionalism, that is, Spain's uniqueness as a developing Catholic nation versus free-market hedonism and Third World politics.

The fourth chapter juxtaposes the prosecution of homosexual defendants and the preservation of their erotica under the Vagrancy Court (1954–1970) with the destruction of mainstream pornography and lenient treatment given to its consumers under the Dangerousness Law (1970–1978). Judicial authorities handled blasphemy in movies as distinct from mainstream porn, more like homoeroticism in terms of the transgression they posed. Contemporary press coverage cemented the notion that foreigners (particularly racialized people and northern Europeans) and some Barcelona citizens played a major role in the porn industry. Similarly, press articles associated maricas' erotic consumption with spectacular criminality and, particularly, with the destruction and trafficking of religious art. Mediatic representations thus perpetuated the normative image of the average Spanish male citizen, threatened by, but not involved in, the entangled transgressions of pornography, desecration, and homosexuality. Judging by the content of judicial files, the maricas' erotica was predominantly homemade and mainstream pornography imported. While the law theoretically targeted those who traded in obscenity and not consumers, the actual target was the subcultural networks that facilitated the circulation of transgressive visual and cinematic culture.

I read confiscated photographs to suggest that defendants' embodied language challenged authorities' perspective: defendants incorporated the codes of international physique culture, eroticized sexual receptiveness, and invested homoeroticism with the aesthetic traits of timeless classicism. The dense network through which homoerotic images circulated in Spain was exposed to the authorities during police raids as a result of third parties' complaints and in relationship with other criminalized behaviors (blackmail, sex work, theft, etc.).[48] On the one hand, when defendants were arrested or exposed, it was in their best interest to destroy their personal homoerotic photographs. State violence moved its victims to erase their own material culture. On the other hand, the burning of mainstream pornography in Social Dangerousness Courts was the authorities' way of preventing its circulation (among state agents as well) and protecting normative defendants' "right to be forgotten." Male defendants who presented themselves as both normative breadwinners and childishly helpless to the allure of foreign pornography struck a chord with judges. In other words, masculinity emanated from the capacity of male subjects to tutor women and minors while incorporating the regime's sociopolitical tutelage.

In the fifth chapter I analyze the curation of visual archives of trans subjectivity by the Franco regime, focusing specifically on the experiences of four trans women who were prosecuted in the early to mid-1970s. Based on the definition of photographs as "material performances," I reconsider recent debates about the ethics of turning away from forensic documents, delving into the ethics of research on trans visibility in contexts of criminalization. The examined evidence demonstrates the disproportionate targeting of working-class trans women as well as the centrality of the *paseo* (stroll) in their daily struggle for belonging. Likewise, their confiscated photographs show a community posing in natural or public settings using different techniques to highlight the eroticism of their bodies. Trans women's representational strategies centered joy, sisterhood, and intimacy as tenets of a livable life. By focusing on the relationship between the state's curatorial practices, in the past and in the present, and trans visual archives as an index of trans women's physicality, relationality, and aesthetics, this chapter builds on and shifts the field of transgender history in Spain and unites oral history and visual studies.

The sixth and final chapter investigates the transition from Francoist moral policing to the eroticization of democracy. From the 1970s to the early 1980s, media representations were a testing ground for the moral principles that were to define Spanish society in its relationship with Western democracies. In the early 1970s, Francoist opinionmakers aligned with antipornography activists in countries like France, the United Kingdom, and the United States, focusing their efforts on modernizing the image of their cause while maintaining a sense of moral panic. These opinionmakers argued that decency and decorum were majority values that transcended ideological divisions, appealed to an antipornography consensus that brought together the Pope and the international leftist intelligentsia, and expressed their admiration for communist regimes' moral policing.[49]

Despite efforts to the contrary, after Franco's death the paradigm of the inoffensive standard consumer of pornography (a well-off straight man who endorses moderate politics) gained ground in Spain. Before and during the political transition, the *destape* ("uncovering") referred to the exhibition of sexual acts and nude bodies that had hitherto been censored.[50] In this last chapter I show the backstage of state policies that propitiated the *destape,* emphasizing the agency of editors, judges, performers, small business owners, activists, and consumers whose interests put them at odds with each other. The historiography on sexual liberalization in Spain has focused on establishing its role in the modernization and democratization of mass culture through erotic films and magazines.[51] I take a more intimate turn by looking at anonymous porn consumers. The materials confiscated from them are an entry point to discuss the continuities and ruptures between the preservation of forbidden desires under a dictatorship and a democratic regime that made itself tangible for citizens through new possibilities for sexual experimentation.

Throughout the 1970s, censors targeted media representations of political and sexual transgression, which they saw as intertwined. All the while, legal and judicial frameworks gradually incorporated mainstream pornography—first soft-core and then hard-core—as a legitimate, if ideally invisible, consumer market. Since the late 1970s, obscenity was no longer an "extraordinary" object of regulation but rather fell under ordinary criminal law. Rulings issued at the Barcelona Dangerousness Court focused on the issue of porn's visibility and physical access restrictions, while publishers boldly challenged the application of the penal law in Supreme Court cases. The interplay between top-down and bottom-up processes shaped the outcomes of this period. *Playboy*'s disappointing sales in Spain showcase the population's lack of interest in respectability, cultural alibis, and international beauty models and suggests that the cult of men's sexual autonomy (which undergirded *Playboy*'s success in the United States in the 1950s) had been sanctioned in Spain throughout the century. In other words, in terms of the relationship between obscenity and masculinity, the democratic transition made explicit and open—even spectacular—what for decades had been implicit and secret.

ONE

Curators of Pornography

SCANDAL AND CENSORSHIP IN
PRIMO DE RIVERA'S SPAIN (1923-1930)

The Centro de Documentación Cinematográfica of València holds a unique collection of films produced in Barcelona in the early to mid-1920s, during the Primo de Rivera dictatorship. The three films were commissioned by none other than King Alfonso XIII, who apparently screened them at private soirées for his closest circle of associates.[1] The narrative of the films sexualizes the structural power dynamics at the core of the late monarchical regime. Corruption is the central theme in *El Ministro* (The cabinet minister), which begins with a man losing his position as a civil servant in the state bureaucracy and then follows his wife as she has sex with a cabinet minister in exchange for her husband's reappointment. The scenography in the film suggests that respectability is an artificial pose. The wife wears a fur coat, a crucifix on her chest, and a veil over her hair when she enters the office of the cabinet minister, but she does not wear any underwear. There are unexpected notes of realism in the film: the penis of the main actor is often flaccid and requires constant stimulation; the "wife" shows the most pleasure when her acting partner performs anilingus on her but slaps his hand when he tries to hold her by the nape during oral sex; they dance before climax and cuddle on a sofa at the end of the scene. The hypocrisy carries through to the conclusion of the film, as the husband complicitly chooses to believe that nothing unseemly has happened between his wife and the minister.[2]

Similarly, *Consultorio de señoras* (Doctor's office for ladies) portrays an upper-class household where the lord and lady of the manor alternatingly relate to their servants as such and as sexual partners. The maid is particularly focused on the lady's desires, as she abandons her lord before he reaches orgasm to attend to the lady's call and sexually satisfy her. The lady's facial gestures are central to the film and convey her pleasure, always attained outside of marriage and most intensely when the maid performs oral sex on her and licks her nipples. As Mireille Miller-Young argues in her study on black women in early stag films, "gestural acts" demonstrate performers' agency and "erotic subjectivity, complex personhood, and forceful social critiques" in the face of a dominant gaze that reduces them to the status of a fetish.[3] In the case of the films produced for Alfonso XIII, the way in which actresses rolled their eyes in pleasure in scenes that dispensed of any male presence gesture toward the male fetishization of lesbianism but also to its transgressive erotic intensity.

The concluding scene in *Consultorio de señoras* returns to the theme of complicit hypocrisy, with the lord of the manor masturbating as he observes through a peephole while his wife has sex with the maid and a male servant.[4] The third film in the collection is titled *El confesor* (The confessor) and centers on a priest who takes advantage of his position to force women into having sex with him. Among the three films, this is the most explicitly violent in its depiction of sexual abuse by religious authorities, much in line with the anticlerical literature that had sparked republican movements in Spain since the nineteenth century.[5] There are multiple elements of scenery and the actors' performing style that interconnect the three films, including the same pieces of furniture appearing in their set designs (mirrors, in particular, are repeatedly featured in sex scenes, as actors look into them to signify the pleasures of self-voyeurism); the same cast of actors, who switch roles from one film to another, alternatively occupying positions of social domination and submission; and cinematography (a common shot foregrounds the actors' facial expressions of pleasure). In the context of an incipient professionalization of the pornographic film industry, actors were often recruited in the brothels of Barcelona. Their bodies were diverse in terms of size, shape, and form—which is a more realistic reflection of bodies than the sculptural ones that predominate in the mainstream pornographic films of today—and their stage presence betrays their lack of familiarity with filmmaking techniques, as they often unintentionally stare at the camera.[6]

In watching these films, the lingering question is whether the explicit sexualization of the ruling elites' moral double standards resulted from the king's commission—to derive pleasure from identification through narrative plots in which the highest social echelons (the films' audience) had secret sexual affairs, as a sort of self-satire—or from a decision by the filmmakers, the brothers Ricardo and Ramón de Baños. In any case, the narratives of these films mirror the sociopolitical context of their production, which, in its blatant legal sanction of status inequalities, shaped the creation and distribution of pornography. For instance—in contrast with Alfonso XIII's pornography patronage and screenings—Atilino, an illiterate and blind peddler from Zamora, was accused in 1918 of selling obscenity (treatises on sexual issues, titillating almanacs, and written works by Catulle Mendès and Giovanni Boccaccio, among others). His

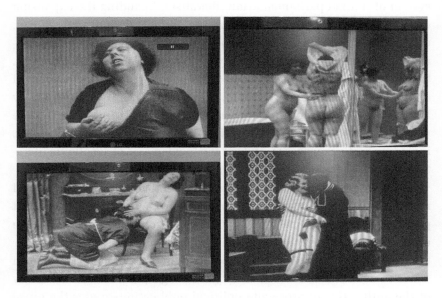

FIGURE 2. Scenes from the films produced by Ricardo de Baños and Ramón de Baños for King Alfonso XIII. The original films are held at the Centro de Documentación Cinematográfica de València, València, Spain.

case eventually made it to the Supreme Court. He was unfortunate enough, while on his sales route, to run into the mayor of the city, who browsed and was offended by some of his inventory. Even though Atilino was selling materials previously approved by the government authorities in Barcelona and lacked "malice" according to the findings of the court of Zamora, the Supreme Court magistrates ruled that his case had to be reopened to adjudicate his liability.[7]

This chapter explores the sociopolitical terrain in which pornography both brought together and set apart the livelihoods, sexual entertainment, and judicial treatment of people in different positions of power (from the king to the peddler) and includes an analysis of the roles of policymakers, bureaucrats, judges, prosecutors, publishers, merchants, editors, literary authors, illustrators, and police officers involved in negotiating the boundaries of obscenity. I argue that status differentials shaped the preservation of pornography in archival records. The Primo de Rivera dictatorship during the reign of Alfonso XIII brought about a harshening of the legal framework for the persecution of obscenity. As Piro Subrat emphasizes, the dictator rose to power based on an agenda to confront the perceived threats undermining the Restoration (1874–1931) system of limited parliamentarian liberalism, including the expansion of anarchism, working-class movements and Catalonian nationalism, constant insurrections in the Moroccan protectorate, and the instability of partisan politics. After two years of complete military control, the dictatorship in 1925 ceded part of its power to a new governmental civilian party (the *Unión Nacional,* or National Unity), still headed by Primo de Rivera. According to Gloria G. Durán, starting in 1926 there were systematic raids and censorship of antigovernmental publications, including erotic magazines, and yet the "golden era" of sycalyptic literature continued under this regime.[8]

In 1928 the government passed a new penal code that incorporated measures and concepts inspired by Italian fascism.[9] This was the first penal code in Spanish history that codified homosexuality under the umbrella concept of public scandal.[10] The new code was also stricter than previous ones regarding obscenity, which came to be defined in terms of sexual arousal and nudity, although preserving the leeway of the authorities to prosecute political publications under the guise of antiobscenity campaigns.[11] Under the new code, those dedicated to distributing, advertising, or trading with "drawings, illustrations, paintings, prints, images, ads, emblems, photographs, films or other obscene objects" were to be sentenced to imprisonment (between four months and two years) and monetary fines (up to 10,000 pesetas).[12] Despite the new regime's claimed investment in Catholic and family values, the authorities' moral double standard and permissiveness toward entertainment for heterosexual men produced an image of hypocrisy. In 1928, the government banned the First Eugenics Conference that was taking place at the School of Medicine in Madrid. A Royal Order issued on 22 March 1928 discussed how, as a public event, the conference had become an act of "propaganda against childbearing of pornographic rejoicing" that undermined "Christian morals and society's ethical foundations."[13] If the conference was to continue, attendance had to be restricted to scientific experts. As Maite Zubiaurre and Subrat point out, the harsh policing of contraception as pornography contrasted with the permissiveness toward cabarets and erotic shows attended by Primo de Rivera himself.[14] The dictatorship's policies regarding public morality implicitly established that contraception was more "pornographic" (in the sense of threatening to the Catholic values of the Spanish nation) than an entertainment industry that incited the heterosexual libido of males.

Duplicitousness and inconsistent moral standards sanctioned by the state are the central theme of this chapter, which traces these inconsistencies through press articles, the rulings of the Supreme Court, and the rulings issued by the Audiencia Provincial de Madrid (provincial high court of Madrid) and preserved at the AHN. For the period of the Primo de Rivera regime, the AHN catalogue contains 153 entries related to cases of public scandal from the Audiencia, of which I have consulted an extensive sample. Different instances of state power simultaneously censored and preserved obscenity, revealing gaps and contradictions between the text and the implementation of the law and significant difficulties in confiscating, tracing, and destroying pornography. This was partly due to an incoherent policing system by which erotic novelettes could simultaneously receive an official governmental stamp while incriminating their distributors as culprits of public scandal. What is more, because of the stenographic rituals and procedural requirements established by the courts, judicial sources and legal compendia became obscene in and of themselves, while access restrictions allowed authorities to ignore this reality.

The production and consumption of pornography was constitutive of and shaped by inequalities of socioeconomic status, gender, and sexuality that determine the configuration of privilege by the law.[15] As I will demonstrate in the first section, "feeling scandalized" was itself codified as a privilege that only a certain class of "cultivated people" enjoyed.[16] Throughout the studied period, the question of whether dubious materials were meant for consumption by "cultivated" or "plebeian" sectors remained a central factor in setting the boundaries of obscenity.[17] However, sexual explicitness was overall considered appropriate if it contributed to draw the boundaries of stigmatized sexual behavior. Authorities and opinion-makers were lenient toward explicit materials if these aroused the male heterosexual libido and deterred same-sex desires. The haunting potential of these desires thus accounts, at least in part, for implicit permissiveness.

This chapter first delves into the scaffolding of state policies and the strategies of resistance and archival paradoxes that derived from those policies' contradictions. Then it focuses on the penetration of homosexuality, transgression, and scandal into judicial archives, particularly those produced at the Audiencia Provincial de Madrid and preserved at the AHN. Finally, it illuminates the role of personal connections in facilitating the preservation of explicit materials, concluding with a brief reflection on the contingencies and inextricable mysteries of archiving.

Conflicting State Policies, Subterfuges, and Archival Recording

From 1870 to 1928, the penal code stipulated monetary fines and short imprisonments (up to ten days) for those who commercialized erotica, under the clauses referring to public morality and scandal. At the same time, "pornography" remained a malleable concept that ranged from erotic postcards to textbooks on hygiene and neo-Malthusian approaches to contraception.[18] The Supreme Court and local authorities tried to confront the vagueness of the legal definition of pornography through innumerable memos and rulings. Carmen Cubero Izquierdo argues that the proliferation of bureaucratic memos and official discourses against pornography never amounted to an actual state effort to eradicate it. According to her, from the late nineteenth century to the early twentieth century, "the pornographic phenomenon suffered relative low levels of repression."[19] Still, the Supreme Court jurisprudence provides the official interpretation of the ideologies undergirding the state's prosecutions of obscenity. In 1888, the Supreme Court magistrates established the requirement to incorporate the lens of socioeconomic class in adjudicating cases of public scandal, which encompassed pornography. On 12 July of that year, they ruled that the "concept of scandal refers to the offense that the knowledge of certain facts or events [*hechos*] produces in the feelings of modesty and moderation that are proper of cultivated people [*personas cultas*]."[20] Including the term "cultivated people" assumed that only the upper and middle classes had the right and faculties to feel offended. In other words, feeling scandalized was a class privilege. And scandal was both subjective—insofar as it derived from individuals' feelings—and supposedly objective, insofar as it entailed evaluating and abstracting the collective moral values of the propertied classes.

The events that led the magistrates to define scandal in such a way are themselves—at least in the way they were represented by the authorities—illustrative of a significant gap between the mentalities of disenfranchised poor people and the dominant classes. In fall 1885, a preacher arrived at a village in the Andalusian province of Málaga. Through his preaching, he was able to get the villagers involved in a millenarist movement. To prepare themselves for the coming end of the world, his congregants abandoned the iconography of the institutional Catholic Church and created their own image of Jesus Christ. A photograph of this sect's statue of Jesus wearing a wig was later submitted to the courtroom as incriminating evidence. According to the court records, the baby Jesus, wearing a gold necklace and a watch, had appeared to one of the believers in a field of fig trees and announced the end of the world. Later the Virgin Mary, wearing only a black dress and "huge diamonds," appeared and explained to the same man how to save a little boy's soul. Local women played a fundamental role in this movement, leading prayer sessions and collaborating on rituals to save souls from purgatory. One local woman in particular took a much more proactive role in the movement by preaching to her family and neighbors, encouraging them to confess in preparation for the end of the world. One night they set a fire and burned their furniture, clothes, and pigs. Then, they got naked and flogged each other around the fire. Finally, they set fire to a farm while the woman celebrated a wedding between two of the movement's followers. The Guardia Civil came the next day and, finding multiple injured naked people in the village, reported the events to the municipal judge.[21]

Beyond the factual basis of this bizarre narration of events included in the ruling of the Supreme Court, the defendants appealed the charges of public scandal on the grounds that the villagers and participants had not felt scandalized. Hence, it became necessary to create a new juridical concept. If actual "cultivated" people were to be absent ever again in episodes and places like this village in Málaga, the penal code still contemplated the fiction of an abstract concept of modesty shared by the elites, whose authority the judges could cite to distinguish the tasteful from the scandalous (e.g., such as the court's view of the millenarists' public acts of arson while in the nude and their worship of a baby Jesus flaunting a gold watch).[22]

For every exercise of authority, there is a subterfuge.[23] In the case of obscene literature judged at the Audiencia emphasizing the failures of the state, transferring liability to more vulnerable actors, and posing as a moralizer were three common subterfuges. First, different actors implicated in the commercialization of pornography became aware during the judicial proceedings of blatant inconsistencies in the implementation of state policies, although the state's obvious inefficacy did not necessarily lead juries to be more lenient. For instance, Baltazar, owner of a press kiosk, claimed in 1932 that he only sold erotic novels that had been officially authorized by the government, but they were confiscated by the police anyway.[24] Indeed, the manager of Editorial Fénix confirmed that the Press Department (Negociado de Prensa), part of the General Direction of Security (Dirección General de Seguridad, or DGS) of the Ministry of Governance, had "stamped" the novels according to the Print Law.[25] It would seem then that—despite the hyperbureaucratization of the editorial industry—the system was misleading, as the civil servants of the Ministry of Governance had officially stamped the novels, only for police officers to confiscate them as scandalous at the gates of the Ministry headquarters. The courtroom issued a call for the DGS to clarify this puzzling situation. Instead of the Press Department, it was the Pornography Department of the DGS that undertook the inquiry. Some other novels confiscated at Baltazar's business (*La venganza de Menéndez, La Marquesa de Sade, El bolo de Bolonia, Limpios de polvo y paja,* and *Sirvo para todo*) had been published by Ediciones Lidia, but the civil servants at the Pornography Department were not able to find anything in their records related to this press.[26] In other words, there was a unit within the state structure dedicated exclusively to keeping track of the business of pornography. When this unit failed to fulfill its role, things got even more confusing. Adolfo Durán, director of *La Lidia*, a Spanish bullfighting magazine, was called to testify and denied any connection between the publication that he led and the mysterious Ediciones Lidia.[27] The investigation had clearly reached a dead end. Regarding other books that had been stamped by the civilian government of Madrid, the later clarified that this stamp did not mean authorization but was simply a formality, a way to "exercise control over all kinds of publications."[28]

It is understandable that someone like Baltazar—and small businessmen on the ground generally—would not have fully grasped the intricacies of this state management model, in which selling books stamped by the government could still be a crime. Baltazar had to pay a fine of five hundred pesetas, serve four months of arrest, and was deprived of his electoral rights.[29] The court bailiff burned the thirty-nine novels confiscated at Baltazar's newsstand.[30] Baltazar fell victim to a Kafkaesque system in which different state agencies—the civilian governments, the Ministry of Governance, the DGS, the district attorneys, and the Press and Pornography Departments, among others—all had a say in the publication of erotic novels while simultaneously trying to transfer responsibility from themselves to other agencies. For instance, while recognizing that they had stamped the "scandalous" novels, the civil servants in the civilian government pointed out that they had shared copies with the office of the district attorney, which apparently did not pursue any action. Yet there is no record of this office discussing its own role as they prosecuted Baltazar for selling novels they had received prior to their commercialization. As Hannah Arendt argues: "In a fully developed bureaucracy there is nobody left with whom one can argue, to whom one can present grievances, on whom the pressures of power can be exerted," but "the rule by Nobody is not no-rule."[31] Baltazar was arrested, tried, and imprisoned by civil servants who refused to be accountable for their own role. The location of the arrest is significant; he was selling the novels at the very neuralgic center of national governance. In other words, given that large state agencies oversaw but did not prevent the distribution of "pornography," it became the role of police officers to contain the visibility of this industry, at least in those places where the exhibition of pornography had become a flagrant challenge to the letter (more than the praxis) of the law.

The model for transferring the active role in censoring "pornography" to police officers—while clearing large agencies of any liability—had a correlate in the management and contractual models implemented in publishing houses. Press directors usually transferred any legal liability to authors. The latter were generally quite poor, judging from the fact that they were often granted exceptions by the court because of their incapacity to pay monetary fines.[32] For instance, on 19 September 1925, the Ministry of Governance issued an order to the postal service so that every copy from the book series *Novela pasional* (Passionate novel), published by Prensa Moderna, would be confiscated. As a result, a postal service employee confiscated a copy of *Más allá del vicio* (Beyond vice) in the Andalusian city of Almería.[33] Back in Madrid, a typographer named Pedro testified that he had printed the novel on the orders of the director of Prensa Moderna, Luis Uriarte Rodríguez.[34] However, Uriarte—identified as a thirty-two-year-old married journalist—declared that any liability fell to the author, Juan Caballero Soriano.[35] The latter had used the pseudonym "Pedro Morante" but admitted that he was fully and solely responsible for the charges of public scandal, adding that his intention had been "making art known in its beautiful literary forms" (*dar a conocer el arte en sus bellas formas literarias*).[36] Possibly, this deposition resulted from a prior agreement with the press director. In other words, part and parcel of being an author of erotic literature was accepting the condition of fugitive. Much of the judicial records and evidence included in the files of the Audiencia of Madrid refers to authors' constant attempts at escaping law enforcement agencies so as not serve their sentences, even after admitting to their culpability. In this 1925 trial, for instance, Caballero Soriano was declared "a rebel" because he did not appear at the courtroom to hear his sentence.[37]

Alternatively, there were "brokers," for lack of a better term, whose role was to assume the legal liabilities of the editorial houses. In 1926, Luis Uriarte hired Julian José De la Mata for the specific position of "director of publications of a gallant character" (*director de las publicaciones de carácter galante*). Thus, when the Audiencia called Uriarte to testify on the publication of *La Desflorada* (The deflowered)—which was the 105th issue of the series *Novela pasional*—he simply submitted a letter by De la Mata in which the latter had accepted a job offer from Uriarte. According to the letter, De la Mata would oversee the acquisition of the original illustrations and texts—or write them himself using a pseudonym, if necessary—and would be paid 25 pesetas for each published title. Most importantly, De la Mata stated in his letter that he would be "solely responsible for all the effects that could derive from the publication of such originals. Likewise, I take charge of housing the management of such publications in my own personal residence."[38] As a legally binding document, this letter had obviously been signed by De la Mata on the instructions by Uriarte, whose main goal was to exculpate himself by generating judicial evidence that he could present to the courtroom whenever the erotic novels were prosecuted. For this same reason, the letter stipulated that De la Mata would accept any responsibility for novels published in the month following his hypothetical job renunciation. In other words, once there was a criminal case against any of these novels, De la Mata had no way to escape the liabilities that Luis Uriarte had paid him to accept.

Luis Uriarte's cunning use of contractual relationships to protect himself resurfaced in multiple court cases, as De la Mata forcefully came to realize the legal implications of the letter he had signed. When De la Mata eventually decided to renounce his position in 1926, Luis Uriarte reminded him through a formal letter—which he submitted to the Audiencia as well, to be considered as judicial evidence—that De la Mata would remain liable for the collection for the following month.[39] Called for his deposition at Court, Luis Uriarte justified himself—"as the Managing Director, he can't take care of the proper management of each publication, which has forced him to appoint several [assistant] directors."[40] Despite De la Mata's official leadership position, the ultimate responsibility was assumed once again by the author, Segundo Ildefonso Uriarte Pujana, who confessed that he had just intended to "bring bread to his home" (ganarse el pan para su casa).[41] The established order of things seemed to be, then, that the equation between authorship and liability would generally serve to protect editorial entrepreneurs, who built additional firewalls through contractual relationships with brokers.[42] Eventually, during the Second Republic, a conservative secretary of justice issued a new press law that set the record straight regarding this intricate issue, establishing that authors, editors, printers, and directors of presses would all be considered accountable for the publication of pornography.[43] This contrasted with every other article of the law, which was dedicated in its entirety to calibrate different actors' liability and insert them into a clear hierarchy of accountability.[44]

Still, the Supreme Court had issued a ruling in September 1885 that gave legal validity to a third subterfuge, most used by authors of erotic literature. According to this sentence, "as far as the penal code is concerned, the novel that has a known tendency to censor vice [*vicio*] does not offend morality, good costumes nor decency, no matter how crudely some scenes are narrated in it."[45] In other words, sexual explicitness was appropriate if it contributed to draw the boundaries of legally and socially condemned behavior. In this case, the examined novel was Eduardo López Bago's *La pálida*, part of a tetralogy aimed at representing prostitution as the "most evil crime perpetrated against nature and humanity."[46] While López Bago's moralizing intention was indisputable, over the course of the early twentieth century this piece of Supreme Court jurisprudence would be cited and instrumentalized by authors whose moral stances were more ambivalent. As Gloria G. Durán argues, discussing "deviation from the norm" was a way of emphasizing that norms are socially constructed rather than natural and unchangeable.[47] The most significant example—which I will later analyze in more detail—is Álvaro Retana, who gave voice to those at the margins of sexual normativity, particularly bohemian maricas, while keeping a facade of moral condemnation. Alberto Mira reads Retana's work as paradigmatically "camp."[48] Other examples, while less known, also point to the potential loopholes in the legal scaffolding of anti-pornography policies. In 1925, the defense lawyer of author Artemio Precioso cited the precedent that apparent condemnation neutralized the potential public scandal.[49] However, this legal defense strategy did not work. The tribunal selected passages of Precioso's novel *Por qué engañan ellas* (Why do women cheat) to be read in the courtroom as part of its sentence, which includes five pages of such passages, written from the perspective of an unrepentant adulterous woman. The final scene in the transcript involves an "assembly" of liberal women openly discussing the meaning of free love, the hypocrisy of men, and the "enchantment and beauty" of breaking social norms.[50] What was at stake in these courtroom debates was whether the narrative voice of moral transgressors in the novels undermined their authors' statements about their moralizing intention to the point that those statements became irrelevant. The recording of fictional transgressors' perspectives and first-person accounts into state records was a collateral effect of the resolution of this debate by means of analyzing evidence.

At the same time, national authorities realized that by prosecuting obscenity they were paradoxically recording it in state archives and official publications. To confront this issue, the government issued a Royal Order on 12 November 1927 that affected judicial proceedings related to "pornographic publications." Following this order, every judge and jury, including those at the lowest levels, were accountable for communicating their sentences directly to the district attorney (*Fiscal de la audiencia provincial*) and the general security director, specifying as clearly as possible "the means used for disabling or destroying the copies, pamphlets, books, postcards, photographs, etc."[51] Likewise, local judges should keep the central authorities informed about "the place where these are kept, and the people in charge of their custody, and later of each agreement that entails a transfer of place or person in charge of custody."[52] The ultimate goal of this policy was to collect systematic statistics to prove the efficiency of governmental action aimed at preventing the propagation of obscenity. The text of the law did not contemplate the possibility that the collected data would illuminate gaps or flaws in implementation. Instead, local reports would be centralized to effectively prove that the policy for the destruction of pornography was working nationwide.[53] Even within this simple tautological frame, the Royal Order failed. The General Direction of Security presented its grievances that, in the year after the order was published, in only one case (adjudicated by the municipal court of Jaca) had local judicial authorities followed it by reporting on the handling of pornography in accordance with the order. As a response, José Oppelt García, attorney general of Spain (1928–1930), decided to take care of this matter, sending a memo on 16 February 1928 to district attorneys nationwide, instructing them to collect the data demanded by the Royal Order and open disciplinary files on any individual who might have been neglectful in implementing it.[54] In brief, there was a significant gap between the text and the implementation of the law regarding the destruction of pornography, due to negligence among other possible but unmentioned factors (including public servants' interest in keeping the confiscated material).[55]

In addition, the measures that the government took to reshape public narratives on sexual mores constructed through judicial rulings operated in two inconsistent ways. On the one hand, the rulings of the Supreme Court were censored from 1927 to prevent the recapitulation of obscenity in state sources. The rulings for cases involving "pornography" adjudicated after 1927 usually include a sentence clarifying that some text has been effaced according to a *Real Orden* (Royal Decree) issued in August of 1927 ("According to the Royal Decree of 22 August 1927, the transcript of the text of *Resultando* [proven facts] has been suppressed").[56] The cited decree includes the following preamble:

> The *Gaceta* has been publishing with certain frequency, as some recent issues demonstrate, rulings in which the narration of those events [that the court] considers to be proven necessarily is of such repugnant realism and forces [the use] of a lexicon of such nature, that it upsets not just every cultivated spirit, but even the strongest stomach, undermining public decency, as it becomes possible to read in an official newspaper what would not be allowed in any other print without a strong governmental penalty.[57]

According to this preamble, in a peculiar turn of events, the *Gaceta de Madrid* or *Gaceta* (1697–1936)—which, for centuries, functioned as the official nationwide bulletin for news concerning public interest and the state bureaucracy—had become a vehicle for the publication and reading of obscenity. An average reader of the *Gaceta* might have opened it expecting to read the daily announcements of official appointments and legislative changes and found, interspersed among those, "indecent" texts. The *Gaceta* was in such cases both a binding corpus of legislation and an obscene publication. For instance, the same year that the Royal Decree put an end to the republishing of obscene judicial transcripts, the Supreme Court had reproduced in one of its rulings the contents of the novelette *La ciudad del vicio* (City of vice) by Luis Elias Cabanzón. The most explicit scene of the novel described a threesome. An old man called Tuso runs his mouth over the body of a woman called Mariquita while La Carmelo pours champagne over Mariquita's body. Based on the preserved fragment, La Carmelo seems to be an androgynous character. During the threesome scene:

> *La Carmelo entonces corrió hacia su cuarto y volvió con un consola-dor de goma atado a la cintura, que se erguía, rojo y triunfal, como saliendo de su sexo. Tuso jadeaba inútilmente sobre Mariquita, besándola en la boca. Fue necesario que la Carmelo lo cabalgara y que hundiese entre sus anchas posaderas el falo de goma para que el*

*lanzase su gran grito, exultante de júbilo, al recobrar plenamente su
virilidad y poder hollar como él era hollado [. . .] con los ojos vidriados
y extáticos de morfinómana, Carlota, el alma de la casa contemplaba
aquel cuadro con una irónica sonrisa.*[58]

La Carmelo then ran to the room and came back with a rubber
dildo attached to the hips, which stood up, red and triumphant, as
if emerging from La Carmelo's sex. Tuso was uselessly panting over
Mariquita, kissing her on the mouth. It was necessary for La Carmelo
to ride him and to get the rubber phallus deep into his wide bottom
for him to roar, exhilarated with joy, as he recovered his virility and
was able to penetrate as he was being penetrated. [. . .] Carlota, soul
of the house, contemplated the tableau smiling ironically, with her
morphinomaniac, glassy, ecstatic eyes.

Although I have not been able to locate the republication of this
ruling in the *Gaceta*, this judicial transcript—describing an old man
who is unable to have sex with a woman until another person pene-
trates him with a dildo, while a morphinomaniac woman contemplates
the scene—is a good example of the material that the Royal Decree described as unsuitable for the *Gaceta*. As the Decree explained, there had
been norms in place to prevent the republication of obscene rulings at
the *Gaceta*. However, the magistrates of the Supreme Court confronted
a very particular dilemma in this regard. Since their rulings constituted
legal doctrine and up until the enactment of the 1927 Decree they had to
choose between either publishing their rulings in full in the *Gaceta* or
not publishing them (hence suspending their doctrinarian effects), magistrates had been choosing to republish censored obscenity. The Decree
formally invoked the king's authority (let's remember his own penchant
for porn) to "appeal" (*encarezca*) to the Supreme Court to be more vigilant, while giving it the possibility of publishing expunged versions
of its rulings. Therefore, censorship became integral to the archival
recording of the Supreme Court's interventions to police obscenity.

On the other hand, the recitals of obscene works continued in the audiencias throughout the 1920s and 1930s, leaving for posterity a fascinat-
ing record consisting of the transcripts of those fragments or paragraphs
that juries and judges had considered to be the most explicit, offensive,
and scandalous. In the United States, by contrast, judges "refused to

allow obscenity, including the title of obscene works, to be read into the record" up until the 1930s.[59] In Spain, if judges decided that a work was not obscene even before the ritual of reading selected passages took place, then it did not pass the threshold of preservation by inclusion into judicial files. Instead, some of these works occasionally entered the spaces of preservation for "legitimate" literature. For instance, Artemio Precioso was charged and brought to court at the Madrid Audiencia in 1927 for his work *¡Lavó su honra!* (She cleaned her honor!). The judges concluded that the novel, while crudely representing a case of adultery, framed this issue in a language and moral perspective that were far from being obscene.[60] Hence, the file does not follow the pattern of including fragments of the novel.[61] Instead, the work can be consulted in its entirety at the National Library.

The cases of illustrations deemed inoffensive by the Audiencia are complex, insofar as the judicial authorities described them to support their rulings, hence transmuting them from a visual image to a textual register. In 1928, in the case against illustrator Enrique Estévez, the file reads, "the cover represents two girls laying on the grass, one beside the other, one of them has uncovered her chest and the other is leaning her hand towards it. Next to them a third girl simulates a satyr, as she is plucking some roses."[62] Judges, deciding that this image could have illustrated the cover of a non-obscene work, acquitted Estévez. However, since the author of the text had become a fugitive (so there exists no ruling in which to include selected passages), the novel itself remained on the margins of the law and has not been institutionally preserved. We are left only with a vague description of its cover.

These complex preservation policies resulted in archival records that, on the one hand, intriguingly gesture toward the absence of obscenity in the rulings of the Supreme Court and in cases of fugitive and clearly "innocent" defendants.[63] On the other hand, the same vigilant attitude did not extend to other archival records produced by provincial audiencias. As a result, the AHN contains, through the records of the Madrid Audiencia, a publicly accessible repository of the same sorts of texts which were censored by virtue of the Royal Decree, allowing us to read obscenity through the gaze of those actors who were implicated in judging it but also in curating it so as to keep only those passages that are most enticing and transgressive.

Transgression and Scandal at the Audiencia Provincial de Madrid

Searching for obscenity in the AHN retrieves a bulk of relevant records which originated in the Audiencia Provincial de Madrid (Madrid's high court) in the 1920s and 1930s. Still aware that something obscene was taking place in this Audiencia, prosecutors proposed alternative measures to impose decency in the courtroom. For instance, on 21 February 1933, when a jury was formed to judge *El mal amor de María Teresa* (The bad love of María Teresa), an erotic novel by Segundo Ildefonso Uriarte de Pujana, both the prosecutor and the defense lawyer agreed upon "public morality reasons" because of which the trial should proceed behind "closed doors."[64] In this case, the fragment of the novel that was selected to be recited in the courtroom as evidence of public scandal dealt with a young woman recovering from a night of intense sexual activity: "María Teresa had another aspect to her. A woman who looked a little sad and defeated by a night of love [. . .] The ardent nights of young women! Nights when thoughts travel far looking for a compensation for loneliness, and they call sleep upon them through bodily fatigue."[65] In this case, Pujana was acquitted, probably because the juries who heard the selected passages did not find them to be obscene enough to merit a sentence. By contrast, a few days earlier Pujana had been convicted in another of his recurrent trials for public scandal. This time, the passages from the "scandalous" novel (*Las primeras armas,* [The first weapons]) were much more explicit:

> Eduardo's finger moved faster. Margarita, for her part, also accelerated the fast-swaying movements of her hand. Soon, an intense and maddening spasm took over both maneuverers [. . .] with the unsuspected magnitude of the enjoyment. Margarita felt a dense, warm liquid moisten her hands. In turn, Eduardo noticed that the finger he had hidden in the intimate corners of the beautiful [woman] seemed to be impregnated with a fluid, warm liquid. Eduardo's member began, little by little, to lose faculties. But Margarita's caresses soon made it recover its primitive ardor [. . .] instantly the manly member rose with the same enthusiasm of the first time [. . .] Margarita's hand went over Eduardo's bulging member with the same speed as before.[66]

There might seem to be an easy-to-establish correlation between content and sentence in these two cases—the character of María Teresa vaguely reminiscing a night of sexual activity would have been less scandalous than a very explicit description of ejaculation by genital stimulation between Eduardo and Margarita, in which the latter proves to be an experienced and generous lover who also looks for her own sexual satisfaction (thus challenging the traditional construction of femininity). In fact, in 1933 another jury concluded that Pujana's *La Encerrona* was scandalous, and the passage that was read as evidence narrated the moment in which two lovers, Víctor and Paquita, orgasmed simultaneously ("The two bodies were convulsed by swift and violent torsions of orgasm").[67] Judicial records like this, in which orgasmic pleasure is so central, belong to an erotic popular culture defined by "corporeal and spiritual ambiguity, prepubescent erotic promiscuity, and endemic bisexuality."[68] Ambiguity, promiscuity, and bisexuality appear once and ever again as central themes in the multitude of cheap erotic novelettes that were sold by the thousands in Madrid and other Spanish cities, confiscated by the police, and read in courtrooms. For instance, the first file related to public scandal that I consulted at the AHN includes the following transcript of a passage of the novelette titled *Caprichos de Lesbiana* (Caprices of a lesbian):

> Then their mouths and genitals [*sexos*] merge with each other, and Lolita's skillful tongue looks for shelter along with Beatriz's tongue and caresses it, and wisely and ticklishly goes to her palate [. . .] Beatriz faints first, and her charming eyes [. . .] penetratingly fix on those of Lolita, as if they were also trying to merge with each other, like the rest of her body, full of bliss, in an insurmountable and voluptuous sensation, while she babbles: This is! This is it! This is what my flesh has longed for, but I was not able to reach! My life! My life! I enjoy so much with you! The blonde one was riding and riding [. . .] She is already at the threshold of that sensation, and sobs, while the erotic jolts shake her body, making her surrender, paralyzing her, making her babble meaningless words, feverish words, growls of a satisfied beast [. . .] Oh baby baby! [. . .] then there is the silence, full of ruminated happiness, of passion. They rest but the flame has not died, it will re-inflame the insatiable flesh of those two women.[69]

This passage's significance lies not so much in its literary value as in its very vivid cinematic recreation of a sexual encounter between two women who kiss with their tongues, "ride" each other, and excitedly talk to each other (using the unrealistically wordy phrases penned by the author) to reach an orgasm. The author's style addresses the reader's capacities for visualizing the scene through the colloquiality of some exclamatory phrases and the description of specific body parts (tongues and genitals) "merging" with each other until the female protagonists are shaken by orgasm. As Maite Zubiaurre argues, "sicaliptic fiction sheds a more positive and less lethal light on lesbianism. In fact, it displays lesbian pleasure as an opportunity to understand, and to teach, how the female libido works."[70] Although the author of this novel was male, the women described in this scene fixate on each other and find extreme pleasure while fully dispensing with any male presence. Puzzlingly, these sorts of passages were read and transcribed in the records of the courtroom, as pieces of evidence that had to be attentively heard by the juries. Consequently, judicial files became obscene literature in and of themselves.[71]

In the first decades of the twentieth century, literature merged with "pornography" in terms of both policing and daily consumption. As a journalist complained in *El Criterio* in 1892, pornography threatened to "completely infect the crystalline and pure river of Castilian literature."[72] Lily Litvak situates erotic novels as a central component of the spirit of experimentation and hedonism that characterized urban life in Spain between 1920 and the outset of the Civil War in 1936. In these years, many women embraced modern signs of emancipation by wearing short skirts, smoking, drinking, and driving their own automobiles. Jazz music, cocktails, and cocaine were among the elements comprising Madrid's frenetic nightlife scene. For Gloria G. Durán, women's agency in this period of modernization became evident in their role as consumers and performers in music halls, taverns, and theaters, where they validated gender diversity.[73]

A certain degree of sexual freedom was a sign of the times. In this sense, Cubero, Litvak, and Zubiaurre agree that the circulation of erotic images and publications was less clandestine that one might expect under an authoritarian regime.[74] Newsstand owners came to argue that the proliferation of the commercial distribution of obscenity amounted to its de facto normalization, which made judicial repression close to untenable, especially since the bureaucratic system of press censorship and policing was plagued with inconsistencies. In July 1932, a police officer warned Baltazar (whom we have encountered before) that he should not sell certain obscene books in his newsstand, which was situated in Puerta del Sol, right in front of the Ministry of Governance. The officer confiscated the books, letting Baltazar know that he would receive a summons to testify in court, but he decided not to arrest Baltazar at that moment because his presence was necessary for the running of the newsstand.[75] This decision, in and of itself, suggests that the commercialization of erotic novels was so extensive that some police officers did not see the need to immediately arrest those who benefited from this business. Indeed, Baltazar boldly admitted in front of the court that "those novels were in his newsstand as in every other one in Madrid, to be sold on commission. They acquire some through the Management of the magazines and others are brought by the foremen in charge of delivering newspapers and novels. The unsold copies are returned to the Management."[76] This business management model entailed a constant back and forth among publishers, brokers, and newsstand owners, which suggests that the commercialization of erotic literature was, if anything, at a border zone between a clandestine and normalized phenomenon.

In this context, authors such as Antonio de Hoyos and Álvaro Retana contributed to the visibility of homosexuality and gender nonconformity, both through their literary works and their public behavior.[77] This visibility coincided with, and was facilitated by, the commercial high point of the serials of short novels. Publishers targeted the working and middle class with these serials, which peddlers sold in cinemas, cafés, and on the street. The dynamic literary style of serials was well suited to the consumer habits of moviegoers in expanding cities. They were very affordable and had enticing, colorful illustrations on their covers. *Colección Pompadour,* for instance, presented itself to the readers by declaring its intention to publish novels that "study love in all is gracious nudity and bravery, without pseudo-prudery. Pages of passion, lust, vice if you may; but cleansed of any gross word and scented with the living essences of art and beauty."[78] The most popular novelettes had runs of up to three hundred thousand copies. The titles of the collections of erotic literature included *La Novela pasional, Imperio* and *Frú-Frú,* which became the target of judicial prosecution by the courts of Madrid.

At the same time, book reviews in mainstream newspapers offered an excuse for journalists to discuss the point at which homosexuality became pornographic, and they generally agreed on a clear maxim, which aligned with the Supreme Court jurisprudence. If authors treated homosexuality as a moral or pathological issue, their words were considered inoffensive.[79] However, if they refused to characterize gender and sexual nonconformity as an "issue," then their works were to be treated as pornography. As Richard Cleminson and Francisco Vázquez García have well documented, in the first years of the century sexologists established a causal relationship among onanism, homosexuality, and racial degeneracy.[80] In this line, the Attorney General sent a memo in 1904 so that his subordinates would "persecute pornography so that we are not turned into a decadent people. [. . .] Disciplinary measures will be imposed upon those who are negligent in performing this important endeavor."[81] A 1916 article on childrearing recommended parents to keep their children away from movie theaters and "pornographic works" authored by "degenerate spirits." According to this article, boarding schools were a "pernicious" space where children learned to masturbate, "being, as well, one of the causes of homosexuality, especially ladies' schools, where they often celebrate the cult of Sappho with all pomp."[82] By contrast, in 1930 a reviewer praised *Ananga-Ranga,* a fifteenth-century Indian treatise on eroticism: "it has a deep moral aspect, insofar as it fights [. . .] homosexuality and infidelity."[83] Explicit discussions of sex were not considered pornographic if they were inscribed in the fight against homosexuality.

The implications of this maxim were often under dispute, since authors and publishers developed strategies to make sympathetic representations of homosexuality permissible. Ogier Preteceille, a French-born translator who would play a significant role in the Spanish Socialist Workers' Party apparatus in the 1930s, wrote in 1928 the review of Radclyffe Hall's *The Well of Loneliness.* Preteceille perceptively reported on all the measures that had been originally taken in England to avoid accusations of pornography. The advertising of the novel was "extremely discreet," and the selling price was higher than usual so that common readers could not afford it, which provoked a debate on the underlying premise that poor people were more prone to be corrupted. The novel received unwanted attention when the *Sunday Express* denounced it as immoral and was censored by the Home Secretary. Preteceille described it as "a highly moral book, since it addresses, without pornographic complacencies, an existing, real, undeniable issue: that of sexual inversion in women." For Preteceille, the tone of the novel was, in fact, so argumentative, and Hall so set in presenting female homosexuality as a pitiful condition, that its literary qualities were sacrificed. As a progressive intellectual, Preteceille believed that censorship did nothing but increase the public's interest in unsavory issues ("At the Champs Elysées, Oscar Wilde's shadow will smile bitterly. He is starting to taste his revenge."). Yet Preteceille also valued discretion, seriousness, and exclusionary pricing policies as means to prevent inappropriate publicity on homosexuality.[84]

Álvaro Retana's novelettes were the opposite of serious and discreet. His "frivolous" style made him the target of antipornography diatribes. Emilio Carrere Moreno (1881–1947), a poet and journalist who ended up supporting the fascist side in the Spanish Civil War, wrote an article in 1923 about the widespread reaction against the expansion of pornographic literature. Carrere categorically believed that this literature was not art. According to Carrere, Retana's work was a "cynical display of pathological preferences." Literature could only deal with the "pitiful issues of homosexuality" through a "socio-medical orientation" that Retana's work lacked. In other words, it was precisely Retana's refusal to pathologize homosexuality that antagonized Carrere, who fashioned himself as a vanguardist bohemian intellectual. Retana represented "lesbians, hermaphrodites, and fags [maricos]" in a way that was—according to Carrere—"frankly pernicious, the seed of a vice that can seduce those whose nature is prone to horrible deviations from the normal type." Carrere argued that the success of a "systematic pornographer" such as Retana indicated racial degeneracy, as his "crowd" of fans was formed by those who found masculine clothing "fastidious" (a euphemistic reference to homosexual men). In Carrere's view, it was fundamental to protect authors' freedom from bourgeois puritanism and recognize the ethical and aesthetic values of naturalist literature, but that should not be an excuse for people like Retana and his genre/gender (género can be translated as either).[85] The French genre also has both meanings, revealing that "the disciplinary enforcement of genre distinctions has likewise functioned to maintain gender hierarchies."[86] The antipornography backlash that occupied many pages in mainstream newspapers since 1920 (particularly in La Esfera and La Voz) translated into a harshened judicial prosecution of literary authors.[87] Carrere and Retana both fell prey to this policy, in an act of poetic justice by which both the antihomosexual moralizer and his "deviant" nemesis had to appeal to the Supreme Court to demonstrate that their works were not pornographic.[88] Both of their files are now housed at the AHN.

The 1928 Supreme Court case on Carrere refers to the novelette *La cortesana de las cruces*. The proceeding of reading obscene passages took place at the Audiencia on 16 March 1928, including the description of the male protagonist indulging in his fetish of having sex with dead-looking women. The defense lawyer argued that Carrere "had not trespassed the line that divides realism in art and pornography." The contentious issue was to establish where that line was, since Carrere himself believed that sympathetic portrayals of homosexuality were intrinsically pornographic. The Audiencia concluded that Carrere's novel was pornographic and sentenced him to four months in prison for public scandal. At that point, the defense lawyer appealed to the Supreme Court on the grounds that the procedures for demonstrating and judging the pornographic character of literary works were, in themselves, misleading and disrespectful with the wholeness of art. The lawyer argued that "to break the unity of the literary construction to select traces or fragments that accommodate to the ruling veils the author's true intention."[89] To illustrate this argument, the lawyer rhetorically asked what the consequences would be of applying the same criteria to the pornographic reliefs in the ashlars of many cathedrals, like the one in Zamora. Would a judge be justified to order the burning of the whole Cathedral to put an end to the obscenity of these reliefs? Despite the grandiloquent tone of the comparison, there was some substance to this argument; the rulings focused on the adverse reaction that reading aloud explicit passages could provoke among "decent" people, rather than on an evaluation of the literary work in its entirety. Carrere—who fashioned himself as an advocate of artistic freedom and sexual openness—fell prey to the same censorship that he supported for Retana.

The AHN holds multiple Supreme Court files against Retana for public scandal, but many of them are not available to researchers due to poor preservation conditions. Given Retana's status as one of the most prolific and influential authors of queer popular literature in Spain in the first half of the twentieth century, this is quite inexplicable.[90] The file against Retana for the publication of the novelette *Crueldades del Amor*—judged at the Audiencia of Madrid in 1927 and appealed to the Supreme

Court—is one of the few that remains accessible. As was common procedure, the authorities selected, recited in the courtroom, and transcribed
into the archival record the passages of the novel that best represented
its obscene character. In this case, those passages referred to a relationship between two men, one of whom was jealous and infuriated by his
partner's decision to take a female singer (*tonadillera*) to a dance. This
was their dialogue:

> But babe, don't be crazy. How could I refuse, without any justified reason,
> to take Ninon to the dance at the Real after I volunteered to do so?
> What do you mean without a cause? I am indisposed, I can't leave the
> house, and it's of very bad taste that you go have fun with that dis-
> gusting woman. Yes, yes, disgusting!
> Sure, you don't understand these things. If it was a bullfighter, you would
> probably recover from your indisposition and come with us.[91]

As their fight progresses, the man who wants to go dancing admits that
he feels attracted to women but has decided to have an "intimate" relationship with his jealous partner because the latter is a well-connected
aristocrat. In fact—the story in the judicial transcript goes on—the am-
bitious partner continues his erotic/professional career, specializing
now in "riding" (*cabalgar*) powerful but lonely aristocratic women.
The characters of the novel—promiscuous aristocrats and their confes-
sors, singers of couplets, and the tailors of bullfighters, among others—
contributed to draw an image of worldly social circles with overtones of
colorful Spanish culture.

There were also lesbian characters. María Cruz, after experiencing
a traumatic sexual assault by her own brother, "abominated men's love
and the feeling of repulsion towards the *macho*'s pleasure got her closer
to Jacinta."[92] In total, more than six pages of the ruling are dedicated to
reproducing Retana's sympathetic portrayal of homosexual people in the
bohemian and aristocratic milieus of Madrid.[93] As noted in the previous
section, the Supreme Court jurisprudence potentially justified sexual explicitness for the sake of moralizing. This was the legal loophole that the
defense lawyer tried to use, arguing that the novel had "the manifest tendency of censoring vice without offending morality."[94] Getting to know
vice was the best way of escaping it, according to the lawyer. Indeed,
Retana formally framed his own works in terms of the disavowal of

abnormality and vice. In his introduction to *A Sodoma en tren botijo*, for instance, Retana wrote: "the reader who is truly healthy in body and spirit has to experience, like I do, the legitimate pride and joy in his normalcy, and will sympathize with the unfortunate victims of His Majesty the Vice."[95] However, the Audiencia ruled that "the abovementioned novel must be conceptualized as pornographic, as it reveals the author's tendency to exhibit vice [*exponerlo*] more than censoring it."[96] According to Alberto Mira, Retana was a unique figure who tried to reconcile "severe, domestic heterosexuality" with a literary career that centered on "giving homosexuality a voice" and highlighting that "gay camp" (encompassing flamboyant effeminacy) is pleasurable.[97] Retana's authorial voice is one of the main reasons why his disclaimers did not convince the judges. As Mira argues regarding these disclaimers: "They are part of a camp performance to keep the ambiguity that would become one of the trademarks of camp in repressive times. Retana is, in this sense, the Spanish Liberace: he is having his cake and eating it too."[98] While he posed as heterosexual, Retana's narrative style was clearly queer, as he gave his characters freedom to be camp and participate in urban homosexual subcultures.

Trying a different approach to exculpate Retana, his lawyer escalated his case from the Audiencia to the Supreme Court, alleging a break of procedure (*quebrantamiento de forma*). The Audiencia had accepted a medical certificate from the editor Luis Uriarte so that he did not have to go to court to testify regarding Retana's claims that Uriarte had published the novel without his permission. Retana's lawyer appealed the ruling given that Uriarte's testimony was one of the main pieces of evidence on which he had planned to build his defense strategy. However, the Supreme Court dismissed the appeal on the grounds that there was not enough evidence that Uriarte's testimony in court would have affected the ruling issued by the Audiencia.[99] There is no way to establish whether Retana's claim that the novel was published against his will was true. Certainly, that would have been in keeping with Luis Uriarte's conniving strategies, analyzed in detail in the previous section. In addition, Retana—who had already been in prison in 1925 for public scandal —might have changed his mind after writing the novel and decided that it was too risqué, which would have fit within his career and public persona, which were always marked by a delicate balance between conformity and transgression.[100] However, it is also possible that Retana's statement was false. In any case, the novel was eventually published and censored, leaving powerful traces of literary transgression and camp at the state archives.

Likewise, the definition of scandal extended beyond the explicitness of sexual pleasure into the politicized domain of natalism and birth control, among other areas of social controversy. For instance, in June 1932, the owner of a newsstand, situated in front of the National Bank of Spain, was arrested for selling "pornographic books." Along with novels that were commercialized and intended as sexually enticing or entertaining, there were other books characterized by their pedagogical and political interventions. *¡Huelga de vientres! Medios prácticos para evitar las familias numerosas* (Wombs on strike! Practical means to avoid large families) was written by Spanish anarchist medical doctor Avelino Luis Bulffi de Quintana and first published in 1906. It proposed a neo-Malthusian approach to family planning among the working class, in the idea that birth control would help to alleviate poverty. Bulffi collaborated with prominent figures of international anarchism, including Emma Goldman, Sébastien Faure, and Francisco Ferrer Guardia. According to Bulffi, uncontrolled reproduction exclusively benefited the bourgeoisie by providing a low-cost labor force. Hence, he endorsed women's emancipation and contraception in sex for pleasure's sake only.[101] The particular edition of the book sold at the newsstand in Madrid was published in 1925 in Buenos Aires by La Protesta, which was the major press outlet for the Argentine anarchist movement.[102] The defendant claimed that he had been selling the confiscated publications because editorial brokers forced him to distribute them in order to maintain his business. There is no ruling in this file. Yet, that erotic novels and anarchist sexological treatises were distributed by the same channels and exhibited side by side speaks to the politicization of "voluptuous" pleasure (i.e., nonreproductive practices) in a context in which transnational activism converged with local small-scale business in expanding the range of available options for working-class people to manage their own sexuality.[103]

Elite Connections

On the opposite pole of the socioeconomic spectrum, members of the regime's elite families could enjoy the delights of obscenity, as state agents who tried to prosecute them were instead penalized for their initiative.

In addition, that these elite individuals were unlikely to be charged with public scandal had the collateral effect of preserving obscene materials in their entirety, since they could not be catalogued and destroyed as pornography without questioning the innocence of the implicated elite actors. This is the reason why issue 214 (16 March 1928) of *Muchas Gracias* was preserved in its entirety as part of a file of the Madrid Audiencia. The cover is an image of a nude flapper girl (short hair, slender figure, dark makeup, self-assured posture) wearing only her tights and covering her chest with a fur adornment. On 26 March 1928, the prosecutor sued the publication to sequester the molds and published copies. That same day, the judge informed the postal service so that they would confiscate every copy in transit. Roberto Martínez Baldrich, who was both an illustrator and fashion designer, testified on 11 April that he had drawn the cover image, which in his opinion did not undermine good customs. Baldrich's creations are paradigmatic of the androgynous fashions that provoked widespread social concern in the Roaring Twenties as the most visible manifestation of the crisis of traditional gender roles. He was also the son of none other than General Severiano Martínez Anido, who was serving at that moment as the secretary of the interior, the highest national authority for issues of public order. Martínez Anido was a prominent hawkish figure of the dictatorship, known for the violent methods that he had used to repress anarchism in Barcelona.[104] Trying to locate the defendant in the easiest possible way, the subpoena was presented at the headquarters of the Secretary of the Interior in Puerta del Sol, since Roberto also worked as his father's personal secretary (he used his maternal last name to sign his creations).

It would merit a separate study to fully unpack Baldrich's contradictory position between military fascism and modern fashion and erotica. His father, who dabbled as an amateur classicist painter, always overshadowed Baldrich's career. The latter joined the military at different points of his life, and during the Spanish Civil War and World War II collaborated with the Spanish fascist forces, allegedly spying for them in France. At the same time, he always admired the libertine lifestyle of cabarets and the modern flapper fashion and advertising drawing styles imported from North America. In published interviews and profiles by contemporary journalists, it becomes clear that doubts always persisted that his professional success was due to his father's patronage.[105] Likewise, press articles reflect a constant tension between Baldrich's interest in enticing female bodies—he was even implicated in the founding of the erotic magazine *Color* in Barcelona in the early 1920s—and the awareness that these images could be deemed pornographic. A 1928 article in *Nuevo Mundo*, for instance, highlighted the "naughty intention" (*picara intención*) of Baldrich's artwork, whose "models were born out of contemporary Spanish life, of that Spanish feminine life that is reminiscent of modern gallant Parisian women, who are drawn to the intimacy of the artist's studio."[106] Baldrich drew "little women of arousing abnormality in their enticing feminism" and avoided the "ambiguous androgyny of decadent feuilletons." The real women who inspired these images, the article continues, frequented "the orgy of cabarets" and were "semi-nude female devils who laugh at man but end up his melancholic victim." In these passages, the journalist nationalized Baldrich's art and the phenomenon of the flapper girl—who, in Spain, should be arousing in her abnormality but not disturbing in her androgyny, and ultimately submissive despite her apparent feminism. The journalist also made it clear that it was due to these women's own initiative (and responsibility) that their bodies were ever more central in massively consumed erotica. Further dissipating any doubts on the morality of Baldrich's drawings, the journalist stated that they belonged to the genre of "joyful and ingenious gallant audacities, which are separated from pornography by aesthetic hygiene" and did not intend to "please the plebes' low instinct," like obscenity did.[107] In other words, whether images were meant for consumption by "cultivated" or "plebeian" sectors remained a central factor in setting the boundaries of obscenity.

In the same way that the press protected Baldrich's artistic reputation, the court bailiff who handled the subpoena had to pay a monetary fine and apologize for his indiscretion: "[It was] never his intention to bother or humiliate in any way the abovementioned Sir [the secretary of the interior], to whom he shows all due respect."[108] There was an invisible hand (namely, top-down instructions that the secretary's family was untouchable) that protected Baldrich at every step, leaving its traces in newspaper articles and judicial records. In parallel, none of the implicated authorities questioned that the magazine was obscene. The governor of Madrid acknowledged that the magazine showed "taints [*salpicaduras*], remnants of the freedom with which these publications used to operate" before the dictatorship but justified the actions of his subordinates claiming that the sequestered issue was even more obscene before it was partially censored, "as it included completely inadmissible texts and images."[109] Indeed, among the confiscated materials housed at the AHN, this magazine stands for the explicitness and playfulness of its visual and textual contents. Yet, probably because of Baldrich's family connections, the charges were dismissed. The investigating judge (*juez de instrucción*) concluded that there was no legal liability since the publication had passed governmental censorship—this factor by itself was not usually considered exculpatory, as I have already demonstrated—and the confiscated drawings were "somehow joyful" but did not offend good customs.[110] While the law mandated that obscenity be destroyed by the authorities, in this case this law could not be implemented without collaterally tainting the name of the secretary of the interior via his son and personal secretary. Since the judge did not even allow for the charges to escalate into a case, the standard procedures for handling this sort of evidence were not discussed. In other words, the preservation of this magazine at the AHN is almost certainly the indirect result of the endemic political corruption by which the regime's elite families used the state apparatus for their own personal purposes. Baldrich also allegedly benefited from this system by obtaining, according to historian Paul Preston, "the [national] monopoly of rat extermination."[111] Moreover, according to the press, Baldrich's artwork contributed to domesticate and nationalize modern feminism, reducing it to a set of aesthetic and erotic values that enticed heterosexual men without undermining in any way their dominant position. In the last instance, this sort of art did not offend the powers that be.

The role that personal connections played in the preservation of Baldrich's artwork brings us back to the materials at the very beginning of this chapter, the films produced for Alfonso XIII. How were they preserved? The films were found by the director of the Valencia film archives, the late filmmaker José Luis Rado, who spread the story that they had been kept in a convent for decades.[112] This story, republished in innumerable press articles on the anecdote of the monarch dabbling as pornographer, could have been true. After all, the clergy maintained a prominent role in the censorship apparatus of the Franco regime, so an ecclesiastical censor could have accessed the films and decided to keep them at a convent. However, there is no evidence to support this version of the story, which might be factual or Rado's way of embellishing a chain of events that might have been more profane or detrimental for someone else. Hence, contingency (the hypothetical censor's decision to smuggle the films into the convent) and secrecy (the true chain of events) appear as fundamental elements in the preservation of the verboten. In other words, to shed light on the (dis)continuities between the early decades of the twentieth century, the Franco regime, and its aftermath we must pay attention to contingent personal decisions and different layers of (in)visibility as central factors for the archiving and preservation of obscenity. The next chapter delves into those decisions and the contrast between people's material culture and the regime's nationalistic rhetoric.

Conclusion

Authorities and state agents assumed the very role of pornographers by collecting obscene and queer literature (and, in the case of the monarch, by commissioning hard-core films for personal consumption). Obscenity is inextricable from the positions of creators, consumers, and the state authorities and from the latter's responses to cultural democratization.[113] These responses betray how the authorities' interests and shortcomings contradict the image that they wanted to project in official statements. This chapter argues that status inequalities during the Primo de Rivera dictatorship shaped decision-making in different courts and, consequently, archival preservation. Instead of taking official statements and legal codes at face value, I juxtapose different sorts of materials (from erotic novels and press articles to the Supreme Court rulings) to trace how defendants carved spaces of resistance and pleasure at the interstices of contradictory state policies. Following this approach, in the next chapters I transition into the Francoist period and analyze the relationships between sexual intimacies and international politics, and institutional archiving and intangible affects. In the implementation of state policies, the principle that emerged was that art and pornography were distinguishable from each other, not through the aesthetic qualities of objects but rather depending on whether unproper audiences (women, maricas, and young people) were exposed to and enticed by explicit images, otherwise deemed harmless if exhibited in museums. Despite censorship, obscenity kept circulating through underground networks that merged homemade and amateur techniques with the preservation of erotica from previous decades and the importation of illegal publications.

TWO

Dildos and Lubricant

MATERIAL CULTURE VERSUS NATIONALISTIC RHETORIC

The following objects were found: a leather suitcase, a rubber dildo that imitates a phallus with hair, two rubber breasts, a rubber male doll, representing a man with an erect penis; another female doll depicting a woman with hair on her Mount Venus; another doll imitating a woman; six wooden eggs; three rubber tubes of different length and caliber; two pairs of shackled handcuffs; a camera [. . .] a statuette made of clay, I would rather say of bone, which represents a pregnant girl.

Fueron hallados los efectos siguientes: una maleta de cuero, un consolador de goma, imitando un falo, incluso con vello, dos senos de goma, un muñeco de goma masculino, representando un hombre con el pene erecto; otro muñeco femenino representando una mujer con vello en el monte de venus; otro muñeco imitando una mujer; seis huevos de madera; tres tubos de goma de diferente longitud y calibre; dos pares de esposas grilletes; una maquina fotográfica [. . .] una estatuilla de barro, digo de hueso, representando una niña embarazada.[1]

This passage is taken from a report on the register that the police conducted on a house in Madrid on 25 June 1958. The police had "vehement suspicions that photographic or other sorts of evidence could be found" in the registered apartment, which would help them demonstrate that the defendants were implicated in sex trafficking. The report pays significant attention to issues of materiality, suggesting that it was elaborated while the objects were being examined. The last sentence in particular—"a statuette made of clay; I would rather say of bone" (*digo de hueso*)—is written in Spanish in a conversational tone that conveys the immediacy of the textual recording of the examination, rather than deliberate decisions pertaining to the content of the report. Police officers' interest in the materiality of sexual cultures mirrors the practices that took place in this apartment. Dolls and dildos were made to look more real by adding hair that could have been human or animal in origin. Hair is "detritus matter that matters"; when severed from a body and touched accidentally or unwilfully by someone else, hair "becomes abject, evoking feelings of disgust, unease, and forced intimacy."[2] The officers who examined these dildos were intimately involved with and recorded hair's erotic afterlives.

Lynn Hunt points out that a "new experience of sex" emerged in Europe in the early modern era through the intellectualization of sex, libertinism as "a mode of thought and action" that questioned traditional authority, and the use of sex aids such as dildos and pornographic readings.[3] Anjali Arondekar argues that rubber dildos represent the entanglement between structures of colonial economic extraction and the global circulation of pornography. Rubber originated in South America, but in the nineteenth century British colonizers turned it into a major Indian export. Feminist scholarly debates on the symbolism of the dildo have oscillated between emphasizing its formal proximity to the male phallus and positively assessing its role in lesbian sex. Arondekar points out that the Indian rubber dildo was discussed in the nineteenth century in terms of its functionality and its role in providing pleasure with little attention to its aesthetic qualities.[4] Francoist police officers, for their part, preferred to focus on the technical description of dildos' materiality while disregarding the details of their practical uses. In line with Arondekar's attention to archival absences, Spanish officers' refusal to acknowledge dildos as functional objects speaks volumes about their perception of sex toys as a threat. Similarly, in the archival records analyzed in this chapter, there is an underlying anxiety about Spain's geopolitical positioning that expresses itself in the treatment given to defendants.

Obscenity—as an expanding business and a central trope in contested representations of national mores—became paradigmatic of Spanish citizens' creative ways of crafting their own material culture while also importing illegal publications and incorporating international iconographies into their sexual fantasies. In 1939, General Francisco Franco—leading a multifarious coalition of fascists, Catholic conservatives, and nationalist military officers—defeated the middle-class progressives and the socialist, communist, and anarchist workers who supported the Second Republic during the Spanish Civil War. Franco's victory gave way to a systematic campaign of extermination of political opponents, through summary executions and labor camps. A press law of totalitarian aspirations was passed in 1938, officially putting the press to the service of the most reactionary vision of the Spanish nation.[5] Newspapers published under this law provide a vivid impression of how journalists tried to influence public opinion in an institutional framework that did not recognize freedom of expression.

In the aftermath of World War II, the international community censured the Franco regime, and the population suffered from conditions of political repression and food shortages.[6] By the mid-1950s, Francoist policies of economic autarchy had proven to be a failure. At the same time, the United States and its Cold War allies demonstrated an interest in Spain's strategic position as the gateway to the Mediterranean. Hence, liberal democracies suspended their condemnation of *Franquismo*'s fascist roots and offered the dictatorial regime a path of normalization through a military alliance against communism that opened Spain to international investment and tourism. Through a series of legal reforms, the Franco regime rebuilt its institutional framework in the mid- to late 1950s, which in the 1960s allowed it to consolidate a model of economic development based on mass tourism, cheap labor, and state repression. Catholicism remained the official state religion, and the clergy maintained its monopoly over education, censorship, and public morality.[7] In this context, the regime codified "homosexuality" among its list of dangers to society when it revised the Vagrancy Law in 1954, thus asserting its authority and capacity to reconcile the agendas of socioeconomic modernization and Catholic-nationalist indoctrination. The targeted individuals were to be interned in "special institutions" (most often common prisons), displaced and exiled from their hometowns and surveilled, totaling up to nine years of sentence.[8] Under a political system that enshrined masculinity as a duty to the nation, the Vagrancy Law became an instrument for enforcing gender normativity among the poor. The very archival classification of these files within the legal framework of "vagrancy" points to the state's focus on the sexuality of "non-productive" social sectors, namely domestic migrants who had been excluded from the expansion of the formal economy. Homosexuality was an umbrella category that included "any kind of sexual and gender deviation: prostitution, transgenderism, [and] effeminacy."[9]

In parallel, antiobscenity policies indirectly fostered homemade production, which was imaginative but occasionally problematic (as with the fetishization of underage women in the materials confiscated in 1958).[10] The police report lists pieces of clothing that were alternatively foreign ("three Hawaiian skirts") or deeply inscribed in Spanish Catholicism ("a girl headdress for the first communion day"). Likewise, the report intuited that a young woman had posed for nude photographs. A man, also arrested, had "pen-painted on the photograph an ejaculating penis [and a text] that says: 'I like your milk to enter through my pussy and my mouth. I'm a whore, the only thing I like is to fuck and suck cocks, and to get fucked in the ass.'"[11] The report went on for many pages describing the amateur photographs, most of which showed underaged women, a female model called Emma, and the defendant; international magazines with articles on diverse topics (including "Love and Magic"); titillating stories written by the defendant; drawings with handwritten texts (like "an ink drawing depicting a penis at the time of intercourse, and below the word 'fuck'"), which served to publicize the prices of sexual services such as oral and anal sex, ejaculation between the thighs, on the chest, in the mouth, etc.; and a film projector and wooden tripod. Quite likely, the defendant ran a business that combined multiple sorts of media. As Zeb Tortorici suggests in his study of the trajectory of Spanish-born entrepreneur Amadeo Pérez Mendoza, who dominated the pornography trade in Mexico City in the 1930s, "the transnational circulation of erotica and pornography between Europe and Latin America" operated through bookshops that, covertly, also functioned as smaller cinemas and printing workshops.[12] In Franco's time, this business model went underground, moving from bookshops to private apartments but maintaining the multimedia strategy to profit from the economies of scale and a loyal customer base.

Finally, the police report included a long list of erotic novels published decades before: Pierre Louys's *Las aventuras del rey Pausel* (1901), Alfred de Musset's *Gamiani, ou deux nuits d'excès* (1833); Pierre de Bourdeille Brantóme's *Las damas galantes* (published in Spain in 1907);

Las once mil vírgenes, by Pablo Luna, Manuel Fernández Palomero, and Ernesto de Córdoba (published in 1909), and other titles in French (*Sexes en folie* and *Deuce douzais*) and Spanish translations. The collection also included books on sexual "deviance," such as *Las desviaciones sexuales*, *Los homosexuales*, and *Carnet de una invertida*.[13] The erotic literature that had circulated in Spain before the Francoist period did not suddenly vanish into thin air when the new political regime banned obscenity. Many of these books remained in the hands of private collectors. In addition to the preservation of pornography from previous decades, anyone in possession of a camera could create new amateur explicit materials for self-consumption and commercialization. In 1943, for instance, a court of instruction in Huelva heard a case involving a man called Rodolfo and a woman called Martirio who had been taking photographs of each other for their own enjoyment. It seems that these events had taken place in 1936, the year that the Civil War started, but its judicial effects lingered for years. Rodolfo was a thirty-year-old miner, and Martirio was a twenty-six-year-old dressmaker. According to the ruling, they established "love relationships" when she was nineteen, which:

> Initially were normal, but after a short time they started to show their lascivious carnal appetites, against what is normal by nature, performing acts like he introducing his genital organs in her mouth, and he introducing his tongue and lips in her genital organs; acts that they performed in public sites. [. . .] Using a photographic camera in public sites, close to Huelva and its boulevards, Rodolfo obtained several photographs of Martirio (who willfully posed because she was blinded by her deep love for him) who lifted her skirt to show her genital organs; showed her breasts and her gluteal region; while Martirio also obtained photographs of Rodolfo in the nude and showing his erect penis.[14]

At some point, Rodolfo decided to punish Martirio out of jealousy and made copies of these photographs, which he sent to multiple people in the city, including Martirio's parents, which led to an investigation for public scandal. This was "revenge porn" *avant la lettre,* which "involves publicly releasing pictures of a person's sexual activity [. . .] to provoke widespread shaming."[15] According to Ganaele Langloisa and Andrea Slane, these "personal acts of revenge within a misogynistic culture of violence and sexual abjection" have escalated into new "economies of reputation" and "the automated management of subjectivities through information networks" in the internet era.[16] While Langloisa and Slane focus on the question of agency in algorithmic capitalism, the economy of subjectivity consisting in enjoying one's self-image while risking exposure originated when photography became affordable. Martirio and Rodolfo navigated this economy by deriving pleasure and intimacy from images, but Rodolfo eventually turned to sexual violence to denigrate Martirio through shame-based community values.

They were both convicted for this course of events, but the court considered her love "blindness" (*obcecación*) and his "outburst" (*arrebato*) as mitigating circumstances, which betrays the gendered judicial categorization of defendants' motivations. For the court, it was understandable that a woman would surrender herself for love and that a man would punish her out of possessiveness and rage.

Apart from amateur photographs for personal use, there is only sparse evidence that bookstores and newsstands owners sold erotica in the 1940s. To do so, they developed techniques of secret communication inspired by espionage. In 1946, Alberto was accused of selling "foreign propaganda" in a newsstand in Gran Vía in downtown Madrid. The "propaganda" might refer to any international newspaper, since at that point the Franco regime was ostracized by the international community of Western democracies because of its sympathies toward Nazism during World War II. Along with these newspapers, Alberto sold obscene materials, which suggests that there was a certain overlap between erotica and anti-Franco international publications. Saúl, a forty-seven-year-old married bookstore owner, allegedly had supplied Alberto with pornographic postcards and illustrations. When the police registered Saúl's bookstore, they found ninety-eight pornographic illustrations and an "American cypher" (*clave americana*), namely a piece of paper with holes and instructions on how to rotate it (this paper is included in the judicial file). By using this cypher, Saúl could write messages only for other people in the know.[17] Through the development of secret codes like these, politically subversive news and erotica continued circulating in Spain as the country suffered from international isolation.

The Francoist authorities, for their part, projected the discourse that the sexual excesses of the Second Republic ended once and for all with the end of the Civil War, as the new regime "purged" libraries with fire, banned the publication of erotic literature, and imposed strict moral

DON JOSE MARAVER SERRANO, RELATOR SECRETARIO DE SALA DE LA AUDIENCIA
TERRITORIAL DE MADRID.

                         CERTIFICO: Que al folio dos del sumario número
doscientos setenta y cinco de mil novecientos cuarenta y tres del
Juzgado número catorce de los de instrucción de ésta Capital se-
guido por escandalo público o contra   existe la
llamada Clave americana, que es como sigue:

       CLAVE AMERICANA de facil manejo para hacer incomprensible un
escrito, a no ser que se lea con la misma o igual clave.- Serie A.
Convinación numero 8-1

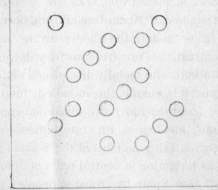

       Modo de usar la clave.- Se coloca la clave sobre el papel que
se ha de escribir, sujetándola por el agujerito ventral con una punti
ta (chinchita), que servirá de eje, y haciendo de manera que el lado
de la estrella vaya a parar en la parte superior, en s ntido horizont
y de cara al que escriba; una vez en ésta posición primera, cuidando

FIGURE 3. File page showing the clave americana ("American cypher") and the instructions to use it. Ministerio de Cultura y Deporte, Archivo Histórico Nacional, File 234bis, Legajo 86, Fondo Tribunal Supremo, Sala de lo Penal.

policing on the borders. However, judicial files demonstrate that political rhetoric and daily practices followed different logics, as confiscated materials betray a persistent interest in sexual experimentation, which the regime treated as antithetical to national mores.

Purged by Fire

On New Year's Day 1957, General Francisco Franco gave a speech in which he identified the enemies of the Spanish nation that aspired to become "the perfect society" under his rule.[18] The "forces of evil" were those sectors that—through a "demonic, insidious, hypocritical, coldly calculated work"—were trying to install in Spain "secularism, an equivalence between truth and mistake, materialism; suppressing moral restraint, undermining the principle of authority, [promoting] libertinage, the degradation of customs, pornography, the release of passions, and making an apology of deadly sins" *(el laicismo, la igualdad entre la verdad y el error, el materialismo, la supresión de los frenos morales, el menoscabo del principio de autoridad, el libertinaje, la degradación de las costumbres, la pornografía, el desate de las pasiones y la apología de los pecados capitales)*.[19] According to Hunt, pornography's "shock value" has rested in its "materialist underpinning" since the eighteenth century.[20] By contrast, the Franco regime from its inception built a rhetoric of Spain as a Catholic and socially disciplined nation by identifying a polymorphous absolute enemy, the so-called "Jewish-masonic-communist conspiracy" *(contubernio judeo-masónico-comunista)*. In the minds of the regime's ideologues, this international conspiracy was embodied in the secularizing policies of the Second Republic. For Francoist thinkers, secularization (a central tenet of Spanish liberalism) aspired to de-Christianize Spain by arousing people's materialistic and sexual urges.

This vision permeated the earliest legislative actions of the military forces that rose against the Second Republic in 1936. On Christmas Eve 1936, the seditious government based in Burgos issued an order that made illegal the "trade and circulation of books, newspapers, brochures, and all sorts of pornographic prints and illustrations and dissolving literature."[21] The report on this legal order was elaborated by the Commission on Culture and Education appointed by the military junta. They justified the measure by describing the "diffusion of pornographic literary" as "one of the most effective weapons" used by the "enemies of the nation" (that is, by the Second Republic and its progressive supporters). Through pornography, these enemies of "religion, civilization and family" had taken advantage of the "docile intellect of young people and the ignorant masses" to cultivate "revolutionary ideas" that brought disgrace over Spain.

The fascist and Catholic thinkers that were shaping the new regime's cultural policies saw the erotic literature of the earlier decades of the century (discussed in the previous chapter) as a central element in the radicalization of Spanish politics. Or, more simply put, pornography was one of the factors that led to the Civil War, and to prevent this "tragedy" and "bloodbath" from repeating itself, the rebel military government banned pornography as well as "socialist, communist and libertarian literature." To criminalize together erotica and left-wing publications was the authorities' way of attributing sexual depravity to progressive movements and vice versa. From the passing of this order, publishers and owners of bookstores and newsstands were given forty-eight hours to hand the now-illegal materials to the military authorities, which would deposit them in public libraries and the archive of the Treasury (*Hacienda*), where they would remain inaccessible to the public.[22] In 1937, the Commission on Culture and Education revised and radicalized this policy by appointing district "purging commissions"—formed by representatives of the military, the Church, the fascist party, Catholic parents, and librarians and university officials that supported the military—that would identify "revolutionary propaganda" and pornography in libraries of all sorts and proceed to destroy it.[23] Bureaucratization, as a means to incorporate the different "nationalistic" sectors into a cultural consensus, marked a rapid shift from restricted access to destruction as the official strategy to neutralize the appeal of erotic/subversive literature and erase it from archives and libraries.

The reports of the purging commissions provide a vivid impression of the haste, improvisation, and lack of human resources and knowledge that governed the implementation of the policy of destruction of "deviant" literature amid the war.[24] The Ministry of National Education circulated a memo in June 1938, recognizing that "the enormous and difficult task" of classifying all the books in public-access libraries was taking much longer than expected, since the books were in all sorts of languages and required a careful reading. Some books had been easy targets for the commissions, including "anti-religious and pornographic works, and works that propagate dissolving ideas aimed at the popular masses." Beyond these "objective" criteria, most books had to be evaluated subjectively, since the Ministry considered that books had a proper audience and were dangerous if read by someone else. The memo provided examples of improper content for specific readers, such as a housemaid looking at the illustrations in an anatomy treatise. This example implies that renditions of nudity for medical training and treatment became inappropriate, likely obscene, if glimpsed by a working-class woman. Walter Kendrick argues that pornography as a debate materialized consubstantially with the notion of an "inflammable reader who might get the wrong impression from hygienic and art-historical 'pornography.'"[25] Given the impossibility of contemplating and preventing all the potential scenarios of impropriety, the Ministry gave the order that commissions submitted their final reports, returned books to their libraries of origin, and dissolved in thirty days.[26]

The operations of the commission at the Granada university district demonstrate the connection between book purges and the physical extermination of progressives in Spain. The president of the university was the reactionary Antonio Marín Ocete, appointed by the military authorities. Significantly, Salvador Vila Hernández, the legally elected university president, and five progressive professors (who had voted to demote Marín Ocete in 1936 because of his repressive handling of student protests) were all shot by fascists and crossed out from university records, raising suspicions about Marín Ocete's role in their killings.[27] Along with him, the commission was formed by literature professor Tomás Hernández Redondo, archivist María Pardo López (the only woman on the Commission; she served as secretary), two Catholic priests—Rafael García y García de Castro (appointed by the bishop of Granada, a position he would eventually occupy) and Manuel Fidalgo (appointed by Falange, the fascist party)—army pharmacist Juan Casas Fernández (appointed by the military) and Diego Palacios Ruíz de Almodóvar, representing family heads.[28] One of the assistants appointed by the president declined because of his workload, and Manuel Fidalgo was appointed to replace a Falange member who was at the front lines of the Civil War. Recruiting these commissions was a complicated task because of the war and the potential members' lack of interest. Tensions between fascism and the Catholic Church dissolved in the praxis of state violence and censorship, with the fascist party appointing a clergyman to represent it in the management of libraries. The conclusions of the commission amount to an excuse for its superficial evaluation of libraries: "For works that are purely [aimed at] entertaining reading, such as novels, theater plays, etc., it was impossible to form criteria given the variety of opinions on this matter and, in addition, because there is an enormous quantity of them in each library. It was more than impossible to examine in detail each of these works in the short period granted to the Commission."[29]

Fascist lawmakers envisioned a totalitarian machinery that would relentlessly purge all libraries, but reports elaborated on the ground suggest that not enough human resources and time were dedicated to implement this vision. The Commission made a list of books they recommended to withdraw from libraries in the provinces of Granada and Málaga and the city of Melilla, based on members' previous knowledge of these books and their "subversive or dissolving ideas." While the list of libraries subjected to this purge is quite extensive, including villages' libraries, schools, and clubs dedicated to hiking, personal libraries were not evaluated. Since "pornography" was for the most part housed in personal libraries, it was not targeted by purging commissions to the degree that the law implied. Many libraries did not have a single book worth purging, according to the Granada Commission, and there were multiple villages that had no public library.[30] Rafael García y García de Castro was tasked with examining books on which the Commission did not have a clear, established opinion and reported on which ones should be withdrawn, including *La mujer en el cristianismo* (Woman in Christianity), the history magazine *Figuras de la raza* (Figures of the race), Ferdinand Ossendowski's *El hombre y el misterio en Asia* (Man and mystery in Asia), Martin Ludwig Schlesinger's *El Estado de los Soviets* (The Soviets' state), Giovanni Papini's *Hombre acabado,* and a collection of books on education in Scandinavia, Russia, and Germany.

The Commission purged literature that discussed self-reflective Catholic beliefs (as in the work of Papini, who was then a fascist sympathizer) and the politics, education, and human geography of other countries. At the same time, these books might have remained accessible to the public in other university districts if individual members of the purging commissions applied different criteria. The end goal for the Granada Commission was to isolate Spaniards from the rest of the world and prevent critical thinking in fundamental matters like religion. The model that the

Commission praised was the library of the military officers' club in Melilla (*casino*), whose content was "Spanish to the core" (*españolísimo*). For
the purging commission, military libraries provided a model insofar as
their contents exalted nationalistic values, Spain's imperial mission, an-
tiliberalism, and a conservative interpretation of Catholicism.[31] In other
words, the ideal was militarizing libraries. The list of books withdrawn
from school libraries in the Valladolid district similarly showcases the
new authorities' anti-intellectualism. International authors like Goethe,
Dostoevsky, Tolstoy, Kant, Freud, Rousseau, Victor Hugo, La Fontaine,
Flaubert, Balzac, Engels, and Ibsen and Spanish authors like Machado,
Pérez Galdós, Espronceda, Larra, Pardo Bazán, Blasco Ibáñez, Valera,
and Unamuno were all purged.[32] Not only political radicalism but also
canonical literature, social critique, and inner life were deemed dangerous. The model citizen envisioned through these purges was disciplined
and public-facing, with no interest in interiority and independent thinking beyond the triad of religion, nation, and family.

In this line, the records of the Zaragoza Commission reflect a deliberate attempt to erase the politics of utopia, aestheticism, and fantasy from
public libraries. The list of books targeted by censors in this region include authors who denounced social inequity and questioned dogmatic
worldviews: Dostoevsky, Tolstoy, Flaubert, Balzac, Nietzsche, Engels,
Poe, Rousseau, Darwin, Balzac, Dewey, Dickens, Kant, Flaubert, and
many others.[33] Looking at these lists, one gets the impression that censors
fantasized with public libraries where any intellectual tradition rooted
in the Enlightenment, or even the Reformation, had been erased. In fact,
they occasionally used all-encompassing formulas that betray both their
intellectual idleness and visceral animosities: "any non-Catholic bible,"
"any play" by Chekhov, "any novel" by Pérez Galdós, and "any work"
by Oscar Wilde.[34] Singling Wilde out as a figure who ought to be fully
obliterated from Spanish libraries bespeaks a desire to estrange art from
life. Wilde turned his own persona into an object of awe, took to its ultimate consequences the bohemian cult of art for art's sake, refused to
conform to Victorian society's rules of discretion, and pursued utopia as
the compass of his work.[35] While fascists' hatred for Wilde is a corollary
of his historical role in catalyzing public awareness of the "unspeakable
sin," the repeated appearance of *Peter Pan y Wendy,* the Spanish translation of J. M. Barrie's *Peter Pan,* in the Zaragoza censors' lists caught me
by surprise. I had not previously thought of *Peter Pan* as a potentially

subversive or obscene work. On the contrary, the Second Republic had incorporated *Peter Pan* in its public programs to increase literacy rates and reading habits among children.[36]

Fascist censors' motivations and criteria remain obscure in the records, but *Peter Pan* has a patent significance for queer imaginaries in Spain. By withdrawing the book from public libraries, the fascist authorities were depriving readers of a utopian fairy tale that questioned the suffocating triad formed by adulthood, gender dimorphism, and expediency.[37] Terenci Moix (1942–2003) is the gay writer whose novels guided me through adolescence. He titled the volume of his memoirs dedicated to puberty *El beso de Peter Pan*, because this figure represented the tensions among adult society's alienating demands, (homo)sexual awakening, fairy tales, and the queer resistance to growing up. For literary scholar Robert R. Ellis, Neverland becomes a political gesture in Moix's oeuvre as "a means through which sexuality is produced and queer praxis temporalized."[38] While Peter is often seen as androgynous or asexual, Ellis recasts Peter's "swaggering effeminacy" within Moix's homoerotic imaginary: fairy dust serves to fly away to a land where one can form queer bonds beyond straight hegemony. Leela Gandhi theorizes the politics of immaturity as an affective repertoire that undermines taxonomic order—childhood means indeterminacy, playfulness, open-ended possibility.[39] Performance scholar José A. Ramos Arteaga suggests a reading of *Peter Pan* as a "hymn to childhood's anarchy," lost when one adjusts to daily regulations: "Barrie describes how the lost boys gradually lose their ability to fly because they go to school, learn to make calculations, and become useful men."[40] The story's allegoric arc might have antagonized censors in charge of implementing the new regime's ideology. The authorities infantilized citizens who were forced to accept the state's moral and political tutelage, while masculinity was measured by subjects' performance of their civic, family, and labor duties. Flying amid fairy dust, playing as a form of queer bonding, and reading as an act of (political) fantasy did not have a place in fascist-controlled libraries.

Despite state schemas to purge libraries of obscenity and queer imaginaries, some homoerotic photographs survived through access restrictions and the intervention of powerful politicians. The Biblioteca Arús is a majestic nineteenth-century library situated in one of Barcelona's most exclusive neighborhoods. When visiting it, one first passes multiple references to freemasonry, then ascends the elegant marble stairs, passes a replica of the Statue of Liberty, and finally enters the reading rooms, which feel frozen in time, with their tenuous light, scratchy wood desks, and double-height shelves. Rosendo Arús y Arderiu, a wealthy freemason and progressive intellectual, passed away in 1891 stipulating in his will that his fortune would be dedicated to opening a library for the education of the working class. The original founding deed occupies a prominent role in one of the reading rooms. Point 6.B of the deed reads: "The Library will always be free, and no genre of books will be excluded based on social, political, or religious reasons. The gates can only remain closed to criminal or clandestine pornographic publications."[41] Despite the very explicit statement that the gates would remain closed to pornography, the library holds the Gomis Collection, a series of photographic nude portraits that—while allegedly intended to provide models for academic artistic training—were also prone to a potential reading as erotica.[42] Celso Gomis Mestre collected these portraits, which became available for public consultation upon his death in 1915. Gomis was born in 1841, received his degree in engineering in Madrid, and in the late nineteenth century played a major role in organizing local anarchist branches of the International Workers Association, being closely associated with Catalonian nationalist circles as well.[43] Gomis's political leanings transpire in his framing of his collection, which he wrote by hand in Catalan on the first page of the first volume: "It is my will, in making this donation, to leave it for artists alone, and not to those who harbor bourgeois appetites."[44] In this will, Gomis established a sharp contraposition between nudity for the sake of art and for the sake of satisfying bourgeois depravation. Gomis implicitly recognized that these images were prone to entice sexual appetites that, in his view, tainted their pure aesthetic value. Moreover, Gomis's deed was hard to implement in an open library where anarchist workers mingled with middle-class freemasons and Catalonian nationalists. Maybe this clause was meant to make the donation of the Gomis's collection compatible with the library's founding deed.

The collection consists of photographs that Gomis selected and cut from the publications of Amédée Vignola (1862–1939) for the purpose of pasting into his own albums.[45] In this way, Gomis's curatorial activity is what constitutes and gives value to his collection, which does not include any original material but rather a unique and selective assemblage of Vignola's works. Vignola had a perplexing career in which he cultivated genres as disparate as "political caricature, nude books and Catholic pastoral movies." Vignola symbolizes the contradictions that French society experienced at the turn of the twentieth century. As a Catholic militant, he authored satirical illustrations that were virulently opposed to the sociopolitical agenda of the Third Republic. Yet he also took advantage of secularizing policies to publish nude photography books and magazines under the pretense of an interest in art and ethnography, conveyed by the titles of his publications. Starting in 1907, in his final career stage, he worked for La Bonne Presse and became a prolific producer of Catholic pastoral films.[46] The way in which Vignola's publications were read and consumed as scarcely veiled erotica when originally published in France gainsays Gomis's statement that his collection of photographs was to remain *untouched* by erotic appetites, since these were intrinsic to their very creation. Most of the photographs show nude women, but a few of them contain scenes that offer the potential of a homoerotic reading.

On one of the pages, Gomis assembled three photographs of male nudes, creating (intentionally or not) a scene of models gazing at each other, as if they had been together in the studio. On the photograph at the left, the facial expressions and body disposition of two ephebes communicate that they are both fixated on and scared by the view of something that is out of their photographic frame (image below). Their gaze is directed toward the genitals of the model in the adjacent photograph, a muscular man who extends his arms and legs and shows his buttocks to the photographer.[47] Finally, the photograph on the right shows two adult male models, who are also cautiously looking at something out of frame. Since in this case they look frontally at the camera, their genitals are covered by a white silk chiffon that evanesces into air. This aesthetic resource appears throughout the collection every time the photographs covertly suggest the presence of male genitalia. Female genitalia, on the contrary, are fully exposed in the photographs, as if the artistic framing of the collection was enough to deactivate the obscenity of vulvae but not the phallus.[48] The erect penis marks the boundary between soft-core and hard-core even today, which Kelly Dennis attributes to "the taboo of homosexual desire as well as the specter of male inadequacy."[49] On a different page, a photograph shows two male models adoringly touching the body of a third one, whose figure dominates the image (image below). The latter is standing, elevating his chest, and tensing and extending his arms, as if he were ready for combat. One model is on his knees in front of him, his buttocks facing the photographer, and his hands on the chest of the standing model. The remaining model grabs the nape of the model in combat position, as if he was urging him to calm down. The theme of the scene, the disposition of the models, and the classicism of their bodies is reminiscent of some of Jacques-Louis David's best-known paintings, including *Oath of the Horatii* (1786) and *The Intervention of the Sabine Women* (1799). In both paintings, and in the photograph at the Gomis collection, warmongering provides an alibi to explore the aestheticism of the male body (with the muscles of chests, arms, and buttocks taking prominent space), while the dynamism of the scene and its theme contrast with the bodies' monumental, static qualities. As Paul R. Deslandes argues, the invention of photography brought male bodies under closer scrutiny and emphasized muscularity and dynamism as defining traits of male beauty.[50] Photographs of male wrestlers epitomize this aesthetic strategy, as the positions that wrestlers adopt in their ritualized fights have homoerotic readings based on their similarity with sexual positions.

How did the homoerotic photographs in the Gomis Collection survive the libraries' purge? The Biblioteca Arús, given its established historical association with freemasonry and working-class movements, was an obvious target. In fact, the library even preserves a document from the anti-freemasonry department of the Barcelona Police Department (*Negociado antimasónico*) requesting that the mayor of the city, Miguel Mateu y Pla, provide them with a list of dubious books. However, the mayor, a close friend of General Franco, used his personal and political connections to save the collections housed at the Arús. At the same time, the library board decided that, under the new regime, it was in the library's best interest to shut its gates to not call unwanted attention over its politically subversive collections. The head librarian died days before the fascist troops entered Barcelona, and from that moment in 1939 the library remained closed until 1967. During those years, a concierge who lived in the building guarded the books, and only people who received an explicit permit from the city government could consult them.[51]

The parallelism with Kendrick's "secret museum" as the origin of modern pornography is uncanny and goes to prove that there was nothing random in the simultaneous preservation and sequestering of the Arús Library and the Gomis Collection. Kendrick argues that, before the modern era, sexual explicitness was not conceived as pornographic but

FIGURE 4. A photograph, taken by the author, of one of the rooms at the Biblioteca Pública Arús. Printed with permission by Biblioteca Pública Arús.

was rather inserted into other genres with clearly delimited functions in the maintenance of social hierarchies: the satirical, the mystical, and the hygienic.[52] Lewd behavior emulating representations of sex was considered a threat when associated with "lower" social strata and low bodily impulses that did not attend to reason. Sex's lack of representational

FIGURE 5. One of the pages from the Gomis Collection showing three photographs of male models. Printed with permission by Biblioteca Pública Arús.

autonomy served to contain that threat. In the modern era, however, sex became a force of its own, while access to all sorts of texts and images was democratized. Kendrick illustrates, through the story of the obscene artifacts unearthed in Pompeii, how containment in this new era entailed figurative and physical barriers. The secret museum for the Pompeii artifacts and the inaccessible Arús Library are similarly trapped in an oxymoronic space; their closed gates symbolize an effort to curate and preserve the power of representation while containing the "low," but the need for gates indicates in itself an irreversible withdrawal to a defensive position, almost an implicit recognition of defeat.

Francoist Rhetoric and Policies on Spanish Moral Exceptionalism

Francoist supporters justified the destruction of erotic/subversive publications on the grounds that the new regime had assumed as its role the protection of "vulnerable" people, including women and racialized colonial subjects. After Spain's defeat in the 1898 Cuban War, Guinea Equatorial and Morocco were crucial for "the formation of a public imperial imaginary." Benita Sampedro studies the "colonial library" in Guinea as "sites from which the seemingly irreversible power of colonialism can

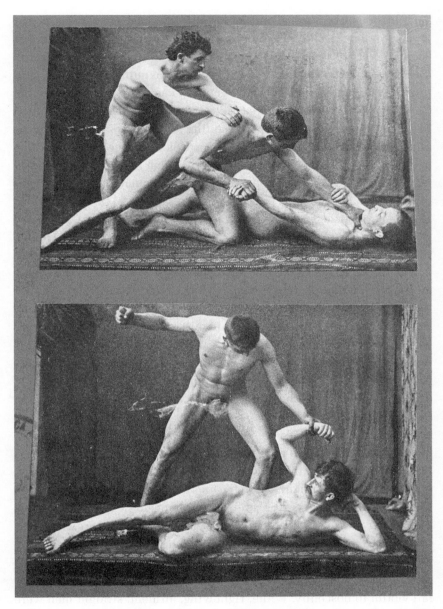

FIGURE 6. One of the pages from the Gomis Collection showing two photographs of male models wrestling. Printed with permission by Biblioteca Pública Arús.

simultaneously be enacted and contested."[53] Sampedro molds her theory
on colonialism in the bookshelves by demonstrating how Catholicism,
economic profit, racial formations, and imperial fantasies intersect in
a variety of texts. For instance, Miguel de Unamuno, one of the most
prominent intellectuals in early twentieth-century Spain, argued that
Guinea was the territory where Quixotesque Castilians could turn their
lives into an adventure novel, "inhabiting no less than a textualized reality."[54] Spaniards imagined the African colony as the territory where
text and reality could become one and the same thing, "a laboratory in
which to put in motion metropolitan utopias, frequently under the aegis
of educational or religious projects and programs."[55] In this line, *Guinea
Española*, published by the Claretian missionaries, in 1940 celebrated
the opening of a new library in the colony. To provide some background,
the author of the note explained that before the Civil War "erotic novels,
pornographic books, and scandalous postcards" were sold in the colony
and "besieged the spirit" of both Europeans and native Africans, substi-
tuting "matter for the spirit and gross shame for ideas that elevate and
dignify human personality." For this missionary, the Francoist forces
had acted as saviors by bringing back morality to the center of colonial
policies: "the glorious movement [. . .] has erased all of that [obscenity],
purifying with fire."[56] Fire was an antidote to the pornographization of
Spain and its colonies that erased the traces of the previous world (the
Second Republic) to create a new one.

Like colonial subjects, women were claimed by the new regime as
beneficiaries of its moral guardianship. The Patronato de Protección a la
Mujer (Foundation for the Protection of Women), created in 1941 to discipline and redeem "immoral" women, took as its mission "the persecution
of traffickers in obscene publications, repressing pornography, and doing
everything that tends to protect defenseless women who are victims of
insidious, scummy plots."[57] By identifying the potential victims of pornography as women, colonial subjects, and the "ignorant masses," state
laws also indirectly built the image of a subject who was not as prone to
fall victim to obscenity. White, right-wing, affluent, straight men were
tasked with "protecting" everyone else from sexual depravity, and this
mission legitimated their monopoly over political institutions. Spanish
reactionary authorities were not truly innovative in this regard; the
protection of the "weak" (young, poor, and female) was one of the main
discourses that European liberal states had used since the nineteenth

century to legitimate antiobscenity measures and affluent adult men's political privileges.[58]

Up until the early 1960s, Francoist opinionmakers associated pornography with communism and liberalism, merging both ideologies through the conspiratorial theories endorsed by the regime. A journalist writing for *Sabadell* in 1957 stated, "I, being Catholic, can't accept the freedom of the press that exists in the United States, neither as a Spaniard."[59] He argued that this freedom led to pornography. Also in 1957, influential fascist journalist Jesús Suevos attributed the fall of Senator Joseph Mc-Carthy to a "masonic-pornographic conspiracy of silence." According to Suevos, McCarthy had been able to unveil "crypto communists," traitors to their homeland and the Western world. However, the mainstream press was able to turn his own party against him, because there was a "global monopoly of information" in the hands of "liberals, masons, progressives, and pornographers."[60] Based on the notion that pornographers were waging a global war on traditional morality, press articles in Spain reported on obscenity in countries under different political regimes to give the impression that only Francoism was successful in maintaining public decency. In Leningrad, a league of young communists had organized an exhibition of "pornographic photographs, neckties with obscene drawings, and other objects that are of common use for the local youth."[61] Even in neighboring Portugal—where a right-wing dictatorship allied to Francoism had been in power for decades—the press was too liberal in republishing comical illustrations from France and "suggestive" photographs that were almost pornographic.[62]

If every country except for Spain had been invaded by pornography, then the opening of Spanish borders to international tourists became particularly problematic for moral policing. The state sub-secretary on tourism (*Subsecretaría de Turismo*) published a brochure in 1964 to inform international visitors about Spanish policies that could affect them. The brochure described how border controls operated: "At customs, depending on the civil servant's mood, he will ask you if you have anything to declare or politely beg you to open your luggage. In the latter case, start to tremble if you intended to pass cocaine, diamonds, or pornographic postcards."[63] The government's publications spread the fiction that border controls prevented any moral contagion from the rest of the world. However, judicial transcripts tell a different story. Particularly in touristic towns, the presence of international visitors profoundly transformed local mores counting on the permissiveness of Francoist authorities. Torremolinos is emblematic among those towns as an icon of early cosmopolitanism and space of shelter for maricas, gay, and transgender people.

Libertinage in Torremolinos

Letters build a language of intimacy and a space for authors to perform their own camp and sexualized personae. The use of letters as judicial evidence is a violation of privacy, aimed at transmuting pleasure into shame, camp into inversion, friendship into corruption. The obscenity of the archive lays both in the state's unashamedly documenting its own violence and in the contemporary reading of the letters as lewd material. A file from the Vagrancy Court of Granada housed at the Málaga Provincial Archive contains an entire corpus of private letters from the 1960s.[64] The history of the letters captures how the tension between pleasure and violence is at the genesis of these "obscene" archives. Marina (not her real name) committed suicide in Barcelona in 1966. She was bisexual and believed she was pregnant and had a venereal disease that she did not want to pass to others, nor was she willing to give up sex. Along with her dead body, the authorities found her farewell missive before overdosing herself with pills and sixty-eight letters (evidence 12 to 80) from her closest friends, four maricas who lived in Andalucía.

These friends playfully referred to themselves with female nicknames like *Francisca, la hija del sol viviente* (daughter of the living sun) and felt emboldened in the same facets of marica culture that authorities most despised. They enjoyed flamenco, jazz, and Hollywood movies. They mocked Catholicism—the author of one of the letters crafted an image of himself attending the Holy Week processions as a devout lady, to see the "ridicule" of a Jesus Christ impersonator riding a donkey (the authorities highlighted the letter as evidence of "atheism")—and turned to their own autonomous spiritual rituals, allegedly celebrating spiritualist sessions that the authorities underlined in the letters as evidence of a sort of heretical cult.

The letters contain drawings, photographs, and collages through which the authors materialized camp aesthetics, discussing their dresses, erotic icons, and fashion trends (they loved anything *Yeyé* and were not fond of long hair on men). In one letter, the author plays with the idea of transcribing for Marina an illustrated erotic novelette that he is reading, but eventually he gives up and asks Marina: "use your imagination, add a friar on top of a woman cook, think that Carmencita is naive [. . .] do the sum and the result is 'through the keyholy.'" This caustic rendering of the novelette intuits that it could belong to one of those 1920s/1930s serials discussed in the previous chapter. The main tropes are voyeurism; the clergy participating in cross-class, semi-abusive sex (an anticlerical trope that traverses the century); and the allure of female innocence. The preservation of pre-Franco-era erotica (or its themes, at least) well into the 1960s forms an intellectual tradition that, under the surface of National-Catholicism, infused some continuity to antiauthoritarian sexual politics.

Parodic rituals and the praxis and soundscape of friendship were also at the core of these political views. Marina's friends read her letters out loud as a group. In other words, the letters were written through aurality, for an intimate yet shared reading that bonded the audience together and with Marina. The friends' parodies of social rituals are documented in the letters. One letter refers to a series of photographs that capture one of the friends dressed as a bride and the rest of the group as wedding guests (Marina died before receiving her copies). The group of friends saw each other as kin and shared the most troubling events of their daily lives. In one of the letters, the author lamented his forthcoming military service and then tried to cheer Marina up, alluding to their plans to live all together so they could "be and do something great." The group also fought with other youth gangs, treated bars and discotheques as the scenario of these battles, and criticized and gossiped about each other. They mocked parents and authorities and openly discussed abortion and suicide as valid options to be assessed together. Their correspondence serves as a witness to wild sex and queer affects in a period of criminalization. They were not shy about their sexual exploits. The following are fragments from different letters, arranged in polyphonous stanzas, a chorus of unapologetic *viciosos* who share and revel in their erotic delights:

I am such a *vicioso*! I only think about pleasure!
I have grown teeth in my pussy, and I have cravings for biting, better in Torremolinos than in Madrid. I leave on Friday, but first I will hustle [*chapearé*] in our own Sodom.

I will let you know if I sleep (again) with the priest.

I look at myself on the mirror, I find myself horribly ugly, but I still desire myself. I would like to sleep with myself. I stand up to give myself a kiss, but J holds me back.

I got wasted [*me emborrache toda entera*] and dressed like a girl. I stripped with jazz on the background until I was fully nude. It was great. We are preparing a Cock Party [*Poya party*] for these days.

Finally, tomorrow [heading] to Torremolinos. I look forward to being there, I am going to whore so much, not leaving anyone without a kiss in their pretty mouth, and whatever comes after that.

With so much hooking up, Granada has me up to my pussy, which wants to go somewhere else to get some fresh air.

The friends called themselves *vicioso* or *puta* ("whore"); talked about their "pussy" and insatiable sexual appetites; seduced other men, including a Dominican monk who joined their social circle; and cruised in cinemas. There is also the uncanny reappearance of the mirror, which once again metaphorizes the specular qualities of eroticism, the glass that amplifies and makes desire visible for either the purposes of repressive documentation or self-indulgence in the contemplation of one's and others' carnality. Lovers' gazes also create specular desires. In her last letter before committing suicide, Marina wrote of running into a lover: "I saw her and we agreed to meet on Sunday at *La Marquise*, but I knew I would not show up. She looked at me the way you know she looks, full of desire, and I desired her too. I desire her right now, but we won't sleep together ever again." Desire endures while death is on the horizon, the words on the page mark the irreversibility of the decision, Thanatos and Eros touch each other in the letter: "When I look around and picture what I will be doing in a few hours, my heart and my whole body are paralyzed, and my whole being refuses to die, yet it must be. I would like to be writing until the last moment, but it cannot be, because I must send this letter before taking anything." As she finishes the text, Marina says goodbye to her hands that write and to her heart that beats, and she deposits a last kiss to her friends on a medallion she is wearing.

She shares how much she misses her friends; she wishes she could kiss and embrace them—queer affect is not limited to those who sexually desire each other but lives in the space of survival built through shared transgression. Marina asks her friends to invoke her from the afterlife so that she can be with them: "at least that way we will stay together" (*así al menos estaremos unidos*). While the police used this correspondence to prosecute the authors as a group of existentialist *viciosos* corrupted by Marina and set in defying authority, morality, and religion, these letters trace how eroticism and togetherness informed the daily praxis of the marica underground.

Torremolinos, a town on the coast of Málaga, reappears once and over again in the letters, because it was a favorite destination for this group of friends. One of the authors described it as a "marvelous" place where everyone minded their own business. A letter reads: "I had a blast in Torremolinos, I have lost count of the number of men and apartments. I left with 100 pesetas and came back with 10,000." This unabashed celebration of promiscuity and transactional sex in the mundane language of friendly gossip becomes part of the institutional archive through exposure and state violence.[65]

Starting in the late 1950s, Torremolinos became the center of a liberalizing trend in customs facilitated by elite tourism, which would turn into mass tourism by the 1970s. The climate of this region, with mild temperatures throughout the year, and the low cost of living compared to the rest of Europe attracted international visitors despite the political situation in Spain.[66] Moreover, the town had a strategic position—close to the British enclave of Gibraltar, to the U.S. military base of Rota, and to the bohemian expatriate community of Tangier, Morocco.[67] The regime's moral permissiveness in Torremolinos responds to the centrality of foreign currency for the government's developmental policies. Until the 1950s, Torremolinos had been a quiet coastal village where most people worked in farming and fishing. In the 1960s international movie and pop stars, including Brigitte Bardot, John Lennon, and Frank Sinatra, visited the village attracted by its cosmopolitan yet quaint fame. Torremolinos offered a welcoming atmosphere for those who used drugs (marijuana and LSD) and enjoyed sexual experimentation.[68] A 1960 police report captures the official attitude regarding these phenomena:

> The fame Torremolinos has acquired, not just within the country but also abroad, is due not only to its fantastic geographical situation and its benevolent climate but also to the creation of an environment of libertinage, vice, corruption, and immorality. [. . .] On several occasions, foreigners—sexual inverts—have been identified who have chosen as the object of their preference young men whom they have

induced into exotic lubrications [a euphemism for homosexuality].
The recurrence of these events and the contact between the inhabitants and the foreigner have produced a psychological phenomenon,
specifically, the disappearance of the sense of morality.[69]

The term "exotic lubrications," referring to homosexuality, implied
that foreign currency was a powerful social lubricant that made young
men lower their defenses in the face of international visitors' moral depravation, which led to their emasculation. The language in this report—
including the verb "induce" and the adjective "exotic"—implied as well
that homosexuality was alien to Spanish mores. Yet the report also made
it quite clear that police had limited trust in Spanish young men's capacity to resist the temptation of having paid sex with international visitors.
This report shows how authorities' expressions of moral panic informed
the rhetoric of nationalism, which did not prevent police officers from
looking the other way when it was convenient for the national and local
economies.[70] This policy affected the content of judicial archives, insofar as young Spanish men who dedicated themselves to sex work are
overrepresented in comparison with their clients, most of them international visitors. Furthermore, noncitizens were forced to leave Spain
if their homosexuality was judged to be a threat to society, which was a
mild sentence compared to the "security measures" applied to Spanish
citizens found to be homosexual (imprisonment, work camps, exile from
their hometowns, and surveillance). In this legal environment, the first
gay-friendly bar in Franco's Spain was inaugurated in Torremolinos in
the early 1960s, according to Sasha D. Pack.[71] Gay-friendly bars catered
to visitors from Europe and the United Sates as well as to locals.[72] Most
of these bars were in Pasaje Begoña, called the "street of sin" (*la calle del
pecado*).[73] An American Jewish woman owned La Boquilla, one of the
most emblematic bars.[74]

The presence of international visitors of different ethnicities in the
town ignited controversies on how the regime could reconcile its fascist
origins with a project of top-down gradual modernization. Likewise,
racial tensions resurfaced in court cases because of the accelerated expansion of the tourism industry in southern Spain, as men accused of
homosexuality at the Málaga Vagrancy Court referenced race as a significant factor to sentence someone as a threat to society. For instance,
in 1964, a Swedish man who worked as a tour guide in Torremolinos

accused an American man of theft, describing him as a *mulato* to capital-ize on racial prejudices. The American man's version of the events was that the Swedish man had invited him to have sex, and when he refused, he reported him out of revenge. The case was closed given the lack of conclusive evidence.[75]

Similarly, in 1965 in Torremolinos, an American tourist whom I will call Williams (that was his false name in the local press) was charged with public scandal, in a high-profile case that illustrates the tensions between the Francoist authorities' official rhetoric and tourists' daily practices. International visitors' purchasing power allowed them to live outside the strict Catholic norms forced upon the local population. Wil-liams was arrested in possession of marijuana and a bag containing:

> Several boxes containing fifty-six ordinary condoms packaged either as a cigarette case with cigarettes, or in the shape of a booklet with its case; fourteen covers for the virile member, with pieces of rubber or plastic attached to them, possibly to carry out some sexual aberra-tion, ten fingers for anal massage, also with adhered pieces of plastic and rubber, and seven "mustaches" to introduce the tongue in a cover with the same purposes mentioned above, with the same pieces of plastic or rubber attached to this tongue cover; a vaginal syringe and two tubes of the contraceptive fluid of the brand "Emko" to be used with it.

> *Diversas cajas donde figuran cincuenta y seis preservativos corrientes envasados ya en forma de pitillera con cigarrillos, forma de librito y de estuche; catorce fundas para el miembro viril en donde figuran adher-idos trozos de goma o plástico posiblemente para llevar a cabo alguna aberración sexual, diez dediles para masaje anal, también con trozos adheridos de plástico y goma, y siete 'bigoteras' también para revestir la lengua con una funda y los mismos fines anteriores, revestida la funda de la lengua con los mismos trocitos de plástico o goma; una jeringa vaginal y dos tubos de líquido anticoncepcionista de la marca "Emko" para utilizar con aquella.*[76]

This passage showcases a striking diversity of practices and devices for sexual stimulation and the use of plastic/rubber protrusions to maximize friction. Apparently, the confiscated objects had been used by Williams to sexually stimulate an American woman, Marilyn (also a false name). This collection of objects was a counterpoint to the denial of the female libido in the school manuals disseminated by the Women Section of Falange (the Spanish fascist party).[77] While these manuals institutionalized an official rhetoric that deprived women of any right to have sexual desires, the "fingers," "moustaches," and covers confiscated from Williams went beyond the procreative ends that the regime attributed to sexuality. According to a police report issued in January 1966, Williams, a Jewish lawyer from New York City, was "intelligent, cultured and well-versed in law," but his aspect and behavior betrayed that he was "mentally disturbed" and had "morbid inclinations."[78] The investigations on him were initiated on 24 January, when Williams tried to force Marilyn into a taxi. He declared that Marilyn was a divorcée to whom he had every intention of getting married. He further clarified regarding the contraceptives and other obscene objects that he had purchased them "in Barcelona just because he had never seen such things, and he found them to be comical. He has never used them, as can be corroborated by the fact that they remain new. He only used them to have some laughs and preserved them out of mere curiosity."[79] This declaration fits within the predominant mode of self-representation among men accused of possessing pornography, who performed naivete by using terms such as "curiosity" and "comical" to claim that confiscated materials had a recreational purpose other than sexual pleasure, and characterized obscenity as an phenomenon alien to Francoist Spain—or as in this case, originating in Barcelona, a city historically and dangerously prone to embracing foreign cultural trends in Spanish authorities' view. Performing naivete did not work to exculpate Williams, as it did for many other pornographers, because he also claimed that erotic magazines were already a normalized phenomenon in Western democracies, including the United States, in contrast with the fascist, antisemitic attitudes that undergirded the Franco regime.

Someone filtered the case to journalists, probably with the intention of hurting Williams. A local newspaper called *La Hoja del Lunes* published the story using false names for the defendant and his lover. Williams published his response in the same newspaper, to argue that he had been treated unfairly due to a combination of intimate and sociopolitical factors. According to his narrative of events, he and Marilyn had met in New York City some years earlier. He assisted her when she sued for divorce in Mexico and later supported her to confront her psychiatric and addiction issues. Even though there was strife in their relationship, it was always consensual. According to Williams, Marilyn suing him for abuse was just her way of getting rid of him so that she could get back to her addiction to alcohol and barbiturates. Following Marilyn's complaint, the police registered their apartment and found multiple pornographic magazines. As a response, Williams argued in his article in *La Hoja del Lunes* that consuming publications of that sort was a normalized practice in Western democracies, pointing out that *Playboy* was selling over three millions copies a month in the United States, which in Williams's opinion meant that it could not be described as pornographic.[80] In other words, Williams's self-defense was defining pornography through restrictions of access and prohibitions, versus the gradual normalization of soft-core in the United States in the 1960s. In this mode of argumentation, mass consumerism and restricted access were two opposite poles, and pornography was defined by the latter (this is also the premise of Kendrick's work on the origins of porn).[81]

Alberto Peláez, the journalist who covered these events, responded to Williams's note in a way that escalated the dimensions of the debate by representing the case as symbolic of the definition of the Franco regime as either a reactionary relic of interwar fascism and the antisemitic foundations of the Hispanic monarchy or a Western (organic) democracy that guaranteed basic individual rights and freedoms. Peláez argued that the policy of the newspaper and the publication of the note written by Williams proved that there was freedom of expression in Francoist Spain. This would refute—in Peláez's opinion—the rumors that Williams had spread amongst his acquaintances, making them believe that he was being prosecuted and victimized because he was a Jew living under a regime that had collaborated with Nazi Germany, through the Blue Division *(Division Azul)* military unit. The consumption, representation, and treatment of erotic materials thus became emblematic of long-standing debates on Francoist Spain's geopolitical position and racist attitudes in a comparative framework. Peláez contended that Spanish citizens who supported the regime were not racist, especially when compared with the contemporaneous situation in the Deep South in the United States (these notes were published in 1965, the same year that Dr. Martin Luther King Jr. led the protest march from Selma to Montgomery). Following this line of argumentation, Peláez declared himself to be proud that Spain's Blue

Division had supported a "friend nation" (referring to Nazi Germany without explicitly mentioning it) and portrayed American government officials as hypocrites who had employed German scientists to develop their space program. Peláez suggested that Williams's note betrayed his racism, because he had listed the fact of Marilyn's lover being black among his negative features (alongside ugliness, lacking education, and poor health). By referring to Marilyn's black lover as a "gentleman," Peláez communicated that he was less racist than Williams. Peláez concluded his note with an admonition that unintentionally undermined the general tone of his arguments about Spain as a modern and inclusive nation insofar as he recommended Williams to seek that "medicine, old and yet forever new, which is called God's grace."[82] Peláez's note epitomizes the ambivalences and paradoxes that were intrinsic to the geopolitical positioning intended by the Francoist authorities, who never publicly apologized for their collaboration with Nazi Germany, yet aspired to join the community of Western democracies in the 1960s. Furthermore, the vision of sexual privacy as a fundamental right in democratic systems underpinned Williams's arguments. This vindicative position did not play in his favor. In March 1966, the judge ruled that Williams was a threat to society because of his "drug addictions" (*toxicomanía*) and forced him to leave Spain, which proves that ultimately his defense strategy could not resonate with the Francoist institutional apparatus.[83]

Similarly, a police investigation targeted two upper-class sisters, both married and separated from their husbands (I gained access to the sisters' story through the files of some of their acquittances, charged with homosexuality at the Málaga Vagrancy Court). The sisters were suspected of having relationships with young waiters, which was considered scandalous conduct. Police reports highlighted that one of the sisters maintained a "libertine" lifestyle despite being married and having two children. The second sister had apparently taken a nineteen-year-old hotel bellhop as her lover, and police officers assumed that the latter was under the corrupting influence of such a "perverse woman." This was the trope of the seducing Eve, of an innocent young man who fell victim to a female sexuality that—when outside the restraint of marriage—was intrinsically perverse. The police blamed wealthy women and homosexual tourists for sexually corrupting the local youth, but they did not express equivalent concern about straight men's ability to pay for sex. Not all niches of the sex market were equally worrisome to the regime. The truly alarming phenomenon was that women and maricas could subvert power hierarchies and be economically dominant in their relationships with "straight" men. Furthermore, married couples of international tourists did not conform to the strict patriarchal order that the report took to be natural. The police report complained that foreign men "left their wives in absolute freedom, with naturalness, carefreeness, and lacking the slightest feeling." Ultimately, the police sought to solidify gender hierarchies that demanded submissiveness from both maricas and women.

Perhaps the rumor that most hurt the sisters' case—narrated by the protégé of one of them—was that they had organized a "virility contest" a couple of years before. The policeman who wrote the report referred to these events as "lustful aberrations, which disgust this informant's conscience as he transcribes them." He was performing moral panic to distance himself from the document he was producing. The "virility contest" took place when one of the sisters invited a group of men "whom she aroused in their sexual desires and instincts by offering her caresses as a reward to the first one who gave signs of his virility."[84] In other words, the report implied that this sister had organized an orgy with a group of men whom she had incited to show an erection. This narrative—which could either be factual or just a rumor—centers the sexual desires of a particular woman who played the active role in relationships with multiple partners, subverting the ideal of procreative sex within marriage.

The authorities had kept a detailed record of her sexual and intimate life since the 1950s. The official reports communicate that she had an affair and run away with a circus performer; that her husband had a fight with one of her lovers; that in 1950 she was sanctioned for her scandalous dressing style; and that during the same year she was also sanctioned for showing an "offensive" banner to protest in front of the governor's private residence, in an action that she carried out along with an aristocrat who was acquitted on charges of homosexuality by the Vagrancy Court. The tableau of an independent woman and a homosexual aristocrat daring to publicly protest the governor with a banner in front of his private house suggests that the small sector of the elite that maintained a critical perspective on the regime could find ways of expressing it. The homosexual aristocrat came from a family that had a long-established role in cosmopolitan elite networks, in which Hollywood starlets and the old European aristocracy shared the same spaces,

from private parties to summer resorts on the Mediterranean coast. The
judicial file includes a photograph of the sisters at a private party, treated
as evidence of their licentious life. According to the description of the
photograph, there were multiple clues that made it scandalous. On the
left side, a man is passing his arm over the shoulders of one of the sisters, which according to the report undoubtedly demonstrated that they
had an indecent relationship. The man who posed at the center of the
photograph was—according to police—a "sexual invert" who worked as a
barman. The second sister is looking away from the camera. The officer
who wrote the report suggested that, through this gesture, she betrayed
her awareness that something shameful was going on when she was captured with her "little friend" (amiguito, a euphemism that implies the
possibility that they were lovers) passing his arms around her. Police
officers took a photograph that to our eyes today seems quite inoffensive
and read it as evidence of a threatening trend toward women's sexual
liberation, which in their view undermined Spain's moral customs.

The Vagrancy Court of Málaga also judged the case of a citizen of
Cuba (colonized by Spain until 1898) who was racialized by the assumption that he was "naturally" prone to physical contact and lacked the
prejudices that defined "civilized" nations. In other words, legal arguments deployed in cases of racialized subjects significantly differed
from those used for northern European defendants. The Cuban citizen,
Norberto, was arrested in 1965 in Málaga, along with a Spanish citizen
called Carlos, who was apprehended while running in the street wearing
only a shirt. Carlos claimed that he was escaping from indecent advances
by Norberto. According to Carlos's statement, Norberto had invited him
over for dinner, offered him a few alcoholic drinks, and then suggested
that he take a warm bath and lie down on a bed for a massage. Following these activities, Norberto showed him pornographic photographs of
women and men, including himself, and then tried to hug him and climb
into the bed with him, at which point Carlos jumped up and ran out into
the street, semi-naked.[85] Throughout his statement, Carlos repeatedly
made references to Norberto's blackness, suggesting that it made him
feel like potential sexual prey. When Norberto, who was employed by a
touring variety show, was arrested, he clarified that he had indeed mas-
saged Carlos with Vicks VapoRub, but only to cure the latter's coughing,
and that the photographs that he had shown were of the performance
troupe to which he belonged.[86] Norberto's lawyer acknowledged that his

hospitality was excessive when measured by Spanish standards. Yet—he argued—it was common in Cuba's latitudes. He also argued that Carlos, who had just left the seminary, had misinterpreted Norberto's gestures as a threat to his virtue. In other words, the lawyer suggested that Carlos overreacted on account of the sexual puritanism instilled in him by training to be a Catholic priest.[87] Norberto was acquitted; perhaps the evidence was not strong enough to demonstrate that he had used photographs to seduce Carlos, or if the latter had misinterpreted the images and Norberto's hospitality because of his own racial paranoia and sexual prudery. At stake here was the definition of pornography as either absolute or relative to how different cultures define appropriate interpersonal physical boundaries. Based on the second definition, Norberto's lawyer argued (and the judge apparently agreed) that his defendant was just acting on a "natural" tendency to establish closer physical contact, stemming from environmental factors such as "latitude." In this way, othering black defendants became a way of asserting that Spain's European status was evident in local people's respect for interpersonal physical boundaries. As the next chapter narrates, the definition and protection of besieged national essences was also the vantage point from which the Supreme Court and the Cortes approached the issue of pornography.

Conclusion

The Spanish Civil War did not fully vanish popular erotic cultures. First of all—as the next chapters will further explore—Francoist censorship made classical art as titillating as it had been in the early modern era; art came back to clandestine spaces, to be touched by consumers whose access to other forms of erotica had been restricted.[88] In general, the study of authoritarian censorship policies illuminates the relationship among geography, temporality, and consumer taste. The consumer taste of Spaniards in the Franco period was significantly asynchronous from a European perspective. Many of the materials that the authorities confiscated as obscene were no longer considered such in other countries. At the same time, the circuits of amateur production, exchange, and commercialization of erotic materials challenged the chimera of an ideologically and sexually homogeneous society, dedicated in body and soul to the maintenance and reproduction of the traditional Catholic family as the basic unit of imperial Spain. The policing of obscenity revealed the

tensions between socioeconomic modernization and traditional morality, while state authorities tried to legitimate the Franco regime's folly of
believing that it could reconcile both trends. Judicial rulings demonstrate
that the regime created zones of moral exceptionalism for elite tourists
while it did not generally consider the underclasses as worthy of moral
protection. The judicial and archival treatment of erotica also served to
solidify the prerogatives of "real men," core to the Franco regime, as the
next chapters explore in further depth.

THREE

"Plastic Objects of Obscene Configuration"

FROM ORDINARY TO EXTRAORDINARY
LEGAL FRAMINGS (1950–1975)

In 1972, the parish bulletin of a small Catalan town published a poem on sexual intercourse, leading into an investigation for public scandal. That same year, the police found multiple men in the nude sharing beds in a Madrid boarding house. During the raid, they confiscated "pornographic prints and plastic objects of obscene configuration." Both cases made it to the Supreme Court, but the treatment given to the confiscated materials could not have been more different. In the case from Madrid, the magistrates ordered the destruction of all the confiscated materials, while the poem published in Catalonia was transcribed into the Supreme Court's ruling—reverting the court's policy of censoring rulings studied in chapter 1—and therefore remains available for public consultation. This chapter delves into judicial and legislative efforts to control the expansive trend in the production and consumption of erotica between the 1950s and mid-1970s.

The tensions between the "bourgeois sexual-moral order" (a civil society built on married men's authority and autonomy) and liberal egalitarianism intensified in this period but by the 1970s seemed resolved in most of the Western world. The implementation of the "harm principle" to foster citizens' self-regulation led to the decriminalization of abortion, homosexuality, and adultery. Pornography represented a particular challenge to this liberalization trend because adult masturbation (solipsistic, fantasy-oriented, and secret) was a sign of arrested development. Still, from the late 1960s legal hard-core came to dominate the erotic marketplace.[1] The commodification of sex conforms to the logics of postwar consumer capitalism.[2] Sex was no longer a private issue known exclusively through personal experience; a "media revolution" destabilized the boundaries between the private and the public in the late 1960s.[3] In 1969 in the United States, Justice Thurgood Marshall put in words the Supreme Court's unanimous belief that the Constitution protected citizens' private possession and consumption of obscenity, which opened the floodgates to the mediatization of sex.[4]

In Spain, on the contrary, the intention to fixate shifting moral concepts underlies the rulings of the Supreme Court. In technical terms, the magistrates acknowledged that the definition of scandal had "sociological foundations" (namely, it emanates from the social majority's criteria) but judged pornography according to a "metaphysical" view of the nation. In this view, scandal encompassed anything that contradicted Catholic morality. The Supreme Court sought to resolve this tension between the relative and the absolute through its rulings, while betraying magistrates' personal belief systems. The language and reasoning of the Supreme Court's sentences incorporate gender dynamics that are culturally and historically specific. Magistrates were positioned historical actors who were personally involved in maintaining a hierarchy between sexual identities. Through their convictions and acquittals, the magistrates de facto established a gradation between the threat of obscenity depending on the role that eroticism played in the (de)formation of masculinity. They were more lenient toward pornography consumed as a rite of passage and expression of masculinity than toward maricas and countercultural youth circles. Likewise, court proceedings generally revolve around the presence of a female victim who had been offended in her modesty, since in theory women were impervious to lewd desires such as exhibitionism (yet there were some legal debates on whether "fallen" women were an exception).[5]

This chapter focuses on a period of socioeconomic change that undermined the image of moral stability projected by judicial authorities. In the early 1950s, confiscated materials reflected amateur circuits, as many cases focused on the production of erotic images for self-consumption.[6] By contrast, by the beginning of the 1970s, judicial authorities perceived that a normalization of pornography was taking place in the most diverse spheres—from gossip columns to parochial bulletins—threatening to disintegrate the moral compass that had guided Spaniards until then. The Francoist Supreme Court established through its jurisprudence a distinction between art and pornography that stemmed not from objects' aesthetic qualities, but from contexts of consumption in which women and young people were exposed to explicit images (some of which were deemed harmless if exhibited in museums). While official discourses centered the moral protection of the poor as well, in practice the Francoist Supreme Court did not seem particularly invested in protecting this group's morality, probably because the regime's social platform was built on antagonism toward working-class movements.[7]

This chapter focuses on the cases used by the Supreme Court to set the boundaries of permissible sexual behaviors and representations depending on changing perceptions of majority moral values. The first section explores the Supreme Court jurisprudence on morality and crimes of public scandal, situating pornography within this legal framework. The second section deals with cases treated as "pornography" and adjudicated in the 1950s and 1960s. In these decades, the production, distribution, and consumption of erotic materials gradually became an ever more visible (or less hidden) phenomenon. In 1966, Secretary of Information and Tourism Manuel Fraga Iribarne promoted the passing of a new press law that theoretically replaced *a priori* censorship with publishers' "voluntary consultation" to state censors, a mechanism to incentivize self-censorship.[8] While censorship was a constant throughout the Francoist period, from the late 1960s writers, journalists, and publishers had the option of challenging it while assuming that they were going to be penalized.

Magistrates, however, maintained their commitment to preserving traditional norms by regulating people's relationship with visual and material culture based on their gender and sexuality. The 1958 Law on the National Movement's Principles established: "The national community is founded on the man, who bears eternal values, and on the family, which is the foundation of social life" *(La comunidad nacional se funda en el hombre, como portador de valores eternos, y en la familia, como base de la vida social).*[9] According to this straightforward formulation, family men would constitute the core and foundation of the nation. At the same time, entrenched societal paradigms granted men—but not women—multiple sexual opportunities outside of marriage. According to the 1944 Criminal Code, married women committed adultery (punishable by prison) when they had sex with another man, whereas married men were not liable for adultery as such, although they could be charged with cohabitation (*amancebamiento*) if it became public that they were living with another woman.

What is more, if a married man caught his wife committing adultery and killed her or her lover, he would not go to prison (instead, he would just be forced to move elsewhere). If he assaulted them physically, even causing injuries, then there was no penalty at all.[10] The legalization of prostitution from 1941 to 1956 was also geared toward this male privilege. Brothels were homosocial spaces that—in the authorities' view— served the purpose of channeling men's sexual impulses with "fallen" women in order to protect decent women and public morality.[11] In this regime of (in)visibility, extramarital sex was a sanctioned, if unspoken, male prerogative, whereas prostitutes and "effeminate" men had to bear the brunt of stigma.[12] Self-regulation of body boundaries ("the privatization of the body") marks the beginning of the modern era, as "societies cultivate certain forms of intimacy and discourage others."[13] For Spanish males living under the Franco regime, the privilege of self-regulation absolved them from the legal repercussions of extramarital sex with socially degraded partners.

This traditional sexual regulation paradigm gradually lost ground during the Francoist period. The third section delves into the 1970s, tracing how Francoist authorities responded to a liberalization of customs that became evident in every aspect of daily life. In the late Francoist period, mass media and tourism contributed to loosen up moral controls. Young people increasingly embraced countercultural practices, experimenting with artistic creation, erotic freedom, and psychedelic drugs. As a response, as the last section traces, the dictatorship replaced the Vagrancy Law with the Ley de Peligrosidad y Rehabilitación Social, enacted in 1970. This law codified the distribution of pornography among other violations that in the authorities' view represented the incorporation of alien mores into Spaniards' consumption habits, shifting the target of the extraordinary jurisdiction from the "underclass" to the youth counterculture and new consumer habits that undermined traditional mores.[14] The pornography business was typified as antisocial, but consuming porn was not.

The Ley de Peligrosidad was inscribed in an international process of recalibrating sex's visibility in relation with the distinction between public and private. The late 1960s and early 1970s were a "fairly fleeting, but highly volatile, period of destabilization" for that distinction. In fact, the same month that the Ley de Peligrosidad was passed in Spain, in the United States the final report of the presidential Commission on Obscenity and Pornography was leaked. This report went in the opposite direction than the Spanish Law, concluding that pornography "did not cause crime, delinquency, sexual deviancy or emotional disturbances."[15] Although the Senate rejected the commission's recommendations, the political debate remained open, and the anticensorship side seemed to attract plenty of popular support. For this very reason, Francoist legislators looked instead to Communist regimes, such as Cuba—otherwise an ideological foe in the Cold War international context—and found inspiration in their antipornography policies.[16]

Pornography as Public Scandal

Pornography fell under Article 431 of the 1944 Criminal Code, which punished people "who in any way offend modesty or good customs with acts of serious scandal or transcendence."[17] The Supreme Court rulings were the main tool to delimit this vague and relative formulation. Magistrates believed that one of their roles was to disentangle pornography and art. As magistrate José Manuel Martínez-Pereda argued in 1970, the aesthetic value of pornography made it even more threatening: "the artistic value of a manifestly pornographic work with an elegant language, with true aesthetic merit, makes it much more dangerous [. . .] the obscene is never art."[18] Porn's aesthetics led to "erotographomania" and "monumentophilic," which Martínez-Pereda defined as an absorbing passion for the production and consumption, respectively, of obscene objects.[19] Pornography was a public scandal that used the pretext of "literary culture" to facilitate "vice and prostitution."[20] Martínez-Pereda assumed that pornography consisted first and foremost in the literature circulated and consumed in brothels, which by 1970 was already anachronistic.

The Supreme Court magistrates equated their own belief system with nature through their rulings: in 1969, on the "natural" antagonism toward photographs of models in bikini; in 1968, on the "natural contours" of freedom of expression; and, in 1970, on the morality of other countries being different from that prevailing in Spain, which was immune to "sexual deviations, contrary to natural law."[21] These "deviations" undoubtedly included homosexuality, represented as a foreign "vice." In defining Spanish morality, the Supreme Court incorporated two schools of thought—the metaphysical and the sociological. Being incompatible in theory, both schools converged in their practical implications. On the one hand, the metaphysical school foregrounded the official definition of Spain as a Catholic nation in Francoist laws, which entailed that the Supreme Court had as its mission "the spiritual defense of the West" against relativism. As the Supreme Court put it, "the national conscience must be formed according to the principles of Catholic morality," a criterion that was applied regardless of individual citizens' personal beliefs.[22] The sociological school, on the other hand, understood that the "concept of morality is abstract, relative and variable" (as stated in a 1969 ruling by the Supreme Court) and must be concretized according to the customs that predominate in each country at a given moment.[23]

During the Franco regime, the Supreme Court advocated for the protection of the morality of the "average citizen." This was a significant shift with respect to the criteria that prevailed in the late nineteenth and early twentieth centuries (traced in chapter 1), according to which public scandal was defined by the feelings of "cultivated people."[24] Based on the sociological school, there could be flexibility and change with respect to Spanish morality, as illustrated by two 1970 Supreme Court rulings, which concluded, respectively, that photographs of women in bikinis did not violate morality laws and that "bad taste" was not punishable.[25] However, the contradiction between the metaphysical and the sociological schools was resolved in the corpus of rulings through the Supreme Court's premise that the average Spanish citizen was, by definition, a practicing Catholic and therefore had "a principle of sincere modesty, alien to the moral-sexual practices of Anglo-Saxons and Scandinavians."[26] This tautology foreclosed the potential fissures that sociological assessments could open in the judicial consensus on obscenity and legitimated a definition of immorality that encompassed everything "that tends to the triumph of bodily passions over the spirit, to the obfuscation of intelligence by sensuality."[27] The notion that sensuality and bodily passions devoid of metaphysics were intrinsically obscene undergirded the Supreme Court rulings on pornography and the magistrates' expressions of concern regarding visible changes in majority moral customs.

The Repulsive Tradition of Concealing Knowledge (1950s–1960s)

The Supreme Court rulings describe practices that challenge any potential romanticization of popular material cultures. A very common pattern is the use of pornography to seduce underage people (considering that in Francoist Spain men reached the age of majority at twenty-one and women at twenty-three). Compared to other cases, those that followed this pattern provoked less of a debate at the Supreme Court, since there was widespread agreement among the magistrates and other involved actors that the defendants' conduct constituted a public scandal.[28] The first mentions to pornography during the Francoist period in the Supreme Court rulings do not reflect a systematic policy of seizure and destruction of obscene materials. Instead, clandestine pornography was often accidentally confiscated when those who owned it were searched or arrested for other reasons.[29] In 1948, for instance, a defendant assaulted a man on the head with an iron bar, after which he stole money, documentation, and "some pornographic photographs" that the victim carried in the inner pocket of his jacket.[30] The Guardia Civil recovered all the stolen effects and returned them to the owner that same day, with the exception of the pornographic photographs (the ruling is strikingly silent on the Guardia Civil's way of handling them, which means that the officers might have kept them). The rulings also demonstrate that pornography was commercialized since the forties using other businesses or formats as alibis. In 1949, the police found out that the owner and an employee of a secondhand bookstore were buying "publications of pornographic content" to sell them.[31] Similarly, in 1953 the police arrested a young man, from whom they seized "seven photographic reproductions of as many highly pornographic drawings," which he had obtained from another defendant. The latter had been renting a place where he clandestinely traded in international pornography and developed negatives of erotic photographs: "[Police] intervened various photographic negatives corresponding to female nudes of immoral tone, arranged for development; twelve color plates of women in unseemly and immoral attitudes and ten French pornographic magazines."[32]

Importing French publications and taking semiprofessional photographs of local models would remain the two major strategies for marketing pornography under the Franco regime in the following years. In 1961 and 1962, a photographer convinced two young women (aged sixteen and twenty) to come to his studio and pose in the nude for him, promising that he would help them work in the film industry. The mother of one of the models reported the ruse to the police, who registered the studio and found two films and over a hundred photographs. In cases like this, the Supreme Court established jurisprudence on two types of recurrent legal arguments presented by the defense: erotic photographs' "artistic purpose" and the lack of advertising on the business of pornography (lawyers argued that when pornography did not "transcend" to the public, it could not be classified as public scandal). The Supreme Court magistrates established that neither of these arguments was valid. In the case of the photographer, the magistrates concluded that he had committed an "attack against the modesty of many members of the social body" because a professional studio was not a private space and because the mother of the model had expressed her disgust.[33] At the same time, some judges questioned the moral rectitude of women who posed for erotic photographs, even if they had been "tricked." For example, in 1952 a defendant allegedly tricked multiple young women into posing for him in the nude without having to pay them. The Audiencia judges concluded that the models' personality traits had made this plot possible:

[He] established friendly relations with several women, who were easily accessible [. . .] by exploiting their vanity and feminine coquettishness [. . .] He was able to get them to agree to be photographed in various attitudes and lewd postures and more or less devoid of clothes. For those who offered greater resistance he used the fiction that [the photographs would] be published in foreign magazines and not disseminated in Spain. The truth is that once the photographs were taken, he took a copy of them or compositions of them, and separated their sex or genital organs, to isolate, enlarge, and combine them with other openly pornographic and lewd images that he owned.

Entablando relaciones de amistad con varias mujeres, fácilmente accesibles y mediante embaucaciones de toda clase, en la explotación de la vanidad y coquetería femenina [. . .] obtenía de las mismas que accedieran a dejarse fotografiar en diversas formas, actitudes y posturas lascivas y más o menos carentes de ropa, utilizando en las que ofrecían mayor resistencia la ficción de que se trataba de hacerlo para salir o publicarse en Revistas extranjeras y no para ser divulgadas en España, siendo lo cierto que una vez logradas las fotografías, sacaba copia de las mismas o composiciones de ellas, en la separación del sexo u órganos genitales, aisladas y ampliadas, conjuntándolas con otras abiertamente pornográficas y lascivas de su particular posesión.[34]

The transcript, confusing as it is, suggests that the defendant had used different photo montage and composition techniques to foreground the models' "sex" and combine the photographs that he himself had taken with pornographic images (possibly of foreign origin). The Audiencia that first judged the case acquitted the defendant considering that everything he had done was for "his own unhealthy delight, proper to his perversity, to his decadent and depraved manhood, in the same way that [the models] collaborated because of the mere materiality of his particular deception." In other words, the sentence established that there had been no crime of scandal because the photographs were intended for the defendant's private use (in line with the tradition of tolerating straight men's sexual entertainment). Indeed, the police had found the photographs in a safe box while investigating a different crime. The prosecutor appealed the sentence on the grounds that the confiscated photographs had jeopardized the "modesty" of the models themselves and of other people who had a hypothetical role "in the development of copies and in the arrangement of photographic compositions." The female models' morality became the main source of contention between the Audiencia and the prosecution. If the young women who posed for the photos had shown themselves to be excessively flirtatious or "accessible," as the judges asserted, there was no need to convict the defendant to protect their modesty, since they had already lost it before meeting him. On the contrary, the prosecution's strategy was to present these young women as pure and vulnerable to claim them as victims. The Supreme Court convicted the defendant. Different instances of state power considered either male privilege or female purity to have preeminence. For the Supreme Court, the "transcendence" of public scandal referred to "the repulsive effects [. . .] when the hidden became manifest or known."

Knowledge of obscenity caused repulsion in people who possessed "natural principles of morality, as indeclinable bases that sustain civilized societies."[35] The Supreme Court's ruling restored the female models to their role as modest victims—defenseless and lacking any agency—assuming that they had only agreed to pose because the defendant had overcome their initial resistance and seduced them with the prospect of appearing in international magazines. The magistrates purposefully ignored that this perspective attracted the models.

In the early 1960s, the Supreme Court ruled on another case initiated because the police accidentally confiscated pornography. The defendant, Marcial, lived separated from his wife Teresa. He met Carla, also on trial, and according to the ruling they had an "intimate friendship, visiting him frequently at his home [. . .] it has not been proved that such friendship had a sexual nature. Although they occasionally went out together for a walk on the street, he never presented her to anyone as a wife or intended to pass her off as such."[36] However, Teresa reported Marcial and Carla and accused them of *amancebamiento* (cohabitation). On 5 March 1963, the police went to Carla's home, where they found Marcial. The officers also found "thirteen photographs, some of them pornographic [. . .] and a pornographic French book, featuring figures of women."[37] The French book, published in 1961, was *Métaphysique du striptease* by Denys Chevalier. Jean-Jacques Pauvert (1926–2014), who was listed as the editor, is a fundamental figure in the liberalization of the French publishing industry in the twentieth century. In the 1940s, Pauvert became a target of censors after publishing the complete works of the Marquis de Sade. In the 1950s, he edited Pauline Reáge's *Historie d'O*, a cult novel about sadomasochism that generated monumental controversy. Also in the 1950s, the publication of the Bibliothèque Internationale d'Érotologie, which includes the volume seized at Carla's home in 1963, also put Pauvert at odds with the censors.[38] The visual language of the volume, including the black and white photographs and the cover image of a classic statue, gave it a sophisticated, artistic air to appease censors. The French publishing industry gradually won the battle to extend freedom of expression to erotic taboos. This process indirectly impacted Spanish readers interested in themes and images banned under Franco and whose consumer habits were not in sync with those of western Europeans. Significantly, the judges at the Madrid Audiencia ruled that it was not possible to prove that the male garments found in Carla's home belonged to

Marcial, but they took it for granted that the pornography was his, taking women's lack of interest in obscenity for granted. The Audiencia ordered the confiscated pornography to be destroyed and acquitted the defendants of the charges of cohabitation, but Teresa appealed, and the case was brought to the Supreme Court. The magistrates, more dismissive of Teresa than of the allegedly unfaithful husband, confirmed the acquittal based on the lack of evidence of "carnal relations" between Marcial and Carla. In other words, despite the Supreme Court's generally harsh treatment of pornography, they occasionally showed benevolence when the accusation focused on men's infidelity, revealing that they participated in a paradigm that equated manhood with sexual appetites that were hard to contain within marriage.

Throughout the 1960s, dispersed networks for the circulation of pornography consolidated through the importation of foreign publications and the clandestine collaboration between distribution businesses and small-scale sellers. The fact that these publications showcased non-normative sexual preferences and behaviors—homosexuality foremost—was one of the reasons that judges insisted on using the criminal law to punish small-scale sellers. In 1966, the Audiencia of Santa Cruz de Tenerife tried a case involving a businessman who clandestinely imported pornographic magazines from abroad. According to the transcript, these magazines "contained numerous photographs of nude people of both sexes, in provocative and titillating attitudes to entice eroticism, of a pornographic nature, inattentive to feelings of modesty and morality."[39]

Among the confiscated magazines, the report mentions *Playboy*, *Sunbathing* (possibly the Canadian naturalist magazine *Sunbathing for Health*), *3D Girl*, and *Pimienta*. The Audiencia judges read *Pimienta* (which was published in Spanish in Miami) and concluded that "it advocates sexual promiscuity and even homosexual deformations by free agreement."[40] The ruling drew an image of a kind of perfidious conspiracy between booksellers to market pornography and articles on promiscuity and homosexuality. One of the booksellers had a criminal record for being "red" (*rojo*, namely left-leaning); in 1937 he had been sentenced to thirty years in prison for the crime of rebellion (that is, for remaining loyal to the Second Republic during the Civil War). The defenses appealed the conviction, claiming that—while the defendants had acted in a "dirty, dishonest, and shameful" way—their acts had not had publicity nor transcendence, which were the *sine qua non* requirements in the definition of the crime of public scandal. The magazines had never been "exposed to the public eye," and the buyers were individuals who had a previous interest in these publications, so their "modesty" was not jeopardized by the defendants' actions. The Supreme Court dismissed the appeal, considering that selling pornography in a bookstore was in and of itself an advertised crime of scandal, even though the sales were made "in a more or less hidden way." What is more, the magistrates acknowledged that erotic taboos aroused the curiosity of many citizens, as they speculated that concealment could have been a commercial strategy to raise consumers' interest.

Like bookstores, newsstands were key strategic points in the urban mapping of pornography distribution. In 1964 and 1965, Pablo, owner of a newsstand, showed prohibited materials to young people, including explicit photographs, drawings, nude magazines, "a five-page typed booklet entitled *Sueño de Lolita* [Lolita's dreams], another six-page booklet titled *Algunas manifestaciones del Doctor Marañón* [Some statements by Doctor Marañon] and a sheet of typewritten verses entitled *Confesión de una hija* [Confession of a daughter], all of them were writings of pornographic content and therefore [aimed at] sexual arousal."[41]As proof of the repertoire of erotic literature available in Francoist Spain in the mid-1960s, this list raises a series of intriguing questions: How could Gregorio Marañón's medical works be reformulated as "pornography"? Did his "statements" consist of his theory on homosexuality as an endocrine disorder? Who was the author of the typewritten verses and stories? Maybe Pablo himself? Apparently, Pablo's intention was to induce young people to masturbate and to perform reciprocal masturbations with them, "making insinuations leading to moral perversion." In the same city, Ernesto, also a newsstand owner, shared the habit of exhibiting erotic materials to young people, in his case "a German naturist magazine, with nude photographs, of both men and women, and a magazine entitled *Chicas y chistes*, with drawings and jokes more or less racy."[42] However, the Audiencia judges who issued the initial ruling on this case were much more lenient toward Ernesto than toward Pablo because they considered that Ernesto's motivations were related to rituals of homo-sociability and erotic initiation among men that constructed a masculine identity. The young people with whom Ernesto shared the magazines were "all friends of his trust," and the judges concluded that the confiscated materials could not be considered pornographic. The criteria by which judges assessed whether confiscated materials were pornographic were entangled with the personal traits attributed to defendants. Marañón's scientific writings became pornography because Pablo found sexual pleasure in providing young people with material "of sexual arousal," whereas Ernesto and his friends consuming explicit photographs and texts that reinforced their collective masculine identity, as a male ritual of passage, did not constitute a pornographic practice according to the magistrates. The Audiencia convicted Pablo and acquitted Ernesto, in a ruling that was appealed by Pablo but confirmed by the Supreme Court. Erotic consumption without commercial purposes as an egalitarian ritual performed by men undergirded the lenient treatment granted to Ernesto, rather than the concrete characteristics of the confiscated material. Magistrates likewise showed benevolence toward mainstream pornography in a 1973 case in which the Narcotics Brigade searched a defendant's house and found multiple issues of *Playboy* and other erotic publications. The Supreme Court ruled that the defendant's possession of these materials was not a public scandal, considering that he had had no intention of selling them, nor did he have an active role in the police search that led to the exposure of his personal porn.[43] This decision contrasts with the 1972 case (analyzed earlier) in which the Supreme Court established that homosexual people committed a crime of public scandal when they were exposed against their will. In other words, homosexual and trans people were constantly threatened with exposure, while straight men had a recognized partial right to privacy.

The Supreme Court established that art—no matter its aesthetic value—was pornographic and harmful to collective hygiene if it was commercially distributed for immoral purposes. In 1967 a defendant was accused of selling "a dozen pornographic postcards" to minors. The defense appealed on the grounds that the images could hardly be classified as pornographic, since they were reproductions of paintings and artistic works, many of which were exposed to the public in museums.[44] The Supreme Court ruled that the question of whether the paintings and artworks were libidinous or pornographic *per se* was irrelevant—"dispensing by now with the exact and correct assessment that they deserve"—because the transaction with the minors had had an "immoral character." For this reason, the magistrates wanted "to affirm categorically the deviant nature of these prints that were an attack on public modesty [. . .] dissimulated under the pretext of art, which has been done since old times, so that works of high aesthetic value can be profoundly obscene and as such [they are] outrageous for the public decorum and mental hygiene of the collectivity."[45] In other words, pornography could be beautiful and aesthetics a dangerous alibi for obscenity.

The Supreme Court traced in its rulings the cultural references and spaces associated with youth sociability in the late 1960s. In 1969, an Audiencia convicted Manuel, charged with the corruption of minors and public scandal because he had rented apartments to young people whose "customs" had offended the neighbors, triggering a complaint and the corresponding police intervention. Manuel's young tenants reportedly "used [the rented apartments] for '*guateques*' [a slang term for private parties] in which outrageous moral violations took place. [. . .] In some of the rooms there were posters alluding to free love, extravagant 'hippie' paintings, deteriorated divans, a double-size bed, musical magazines, record players, medical books, one book entitled *Érotologie de la Chine* [. . .] and one of the boys was arrested in the possession of sixteen pornographic photographs."[46] Through this amalgam of elements, the ruling offers a tangible description of the aesthetics and material culture through which young people departed from the regime's moral norms and created their own spaces to enjoy music and sex. The ruling cements the idea that youthful excesses were due to modern, exotic, and foreign influences and fashions, from hippie aesthetics to Chinese erotic cultures. Wou-chan Cheng's *Érotologie de la Chine: tradition chinoise de l'érotisme* had been published in 1963 by Jean-Jacques Pauvert. The volume has a luxurious format, a scholarly text (it has been cited in academic works), and the erotic images were not contemporary photographs but historical illustrations, all of which may well have been part of Pauvert's strategy to circumvent French censorship. The Supreme Court established that the young tenants had intended "to escape all sorts of family and social controls." The vivid description of the "reigning environment" (i.e., hippie aesthetics, music, posters and paintings, medical books, and *Érotologie de la Chine*) undoubtedly demonstrated that the apartment was a deeply sexualized space. The ruling reified the notion that there was something inherently corrupting and scandalous in the youth counterculture, when the (implicitly political) craving to escape social and family controls, foreign aesthetics, and sex were given free rein in spaces beyond the authorities' gaze.[47]

Even the Church Publishes Pornography (1970s)

In the early 1970s, the pornography business became professionalized as the volume of imports increased thanks to international collaboration networks. For instance, in 1972 the Sevilla Audiencia judged two defendants, who "through a previous agreement with an Indian subject, who will be judged *in absentia*, introduced in the [Iberian] Peninsula 32 pornographic films . . . [including] eighteen 'always Hood, Quality Fantasy,' three 'Underground Filme' and seven 'Mercur Film.'"[48] The Supreme Court also focused its attention on the border between Catalonia and France as the main point of entrance for international pornography. In July 1972, during a routine search at La Junquera border control, two men were arrested while carrying "51 pornographic magazines with full-color photographs of nude men and women, performing intercourse and acts against nature."[49] Finally, a truck driver who covered the route to Frankfurt set up a whole network of import and distribution of pornography between 1970 and 1973. The ruling specified that "most of [the confiscated magazines] represent acts against nature between people of different and even the same sex, namely onanism, lesbianism, and sadism." Significantly, the defense characterized pornography and sexual liberalization as essential vehicles of integration into the European community: "in the countries of our geopolitical and cultural area, which is none other than Western Europe, towards which we progressively lean [in a process of] integration that, regardless of any subjective will, is irreversible and essential, the act in question is not considered criminal in any way."[50] However, the Supreme Court dismissed the appeal based on a welter of agreements by international organizations signed between the 1910s and 1940s, which is quite indicative of the anachronism of the Francoist legal framework.

Obscenity continued to spread in the early 1970s from areas that *per se* were typified as a threat to society—especially homosexual meeting places—to media platforms hitherto considered central pillars for the construction of a collective National Catholic consciousness, such as parish bulletins. Regarding homosexual networks, the Madrid Audiencia ruled in 1973 on a case that centered on a boarding house run by Fernando, a sixty-two-year-old "sexual invert" who hosted his "acquaintances, morons of homosexualism [sic, *tarados* in the original]" and matched them with "boys from fifteen to twenty years old" who charged

around 500 pesetas for their sexual services. One of the young men who
made a living in this way made the mistake of bragging in a bar of how
lucrative his occupation was, which triggered the police investigation.
On the night of 16 January 1972, the police raided the boarding house
and found three men in the company of eighteen-year-olds, "all of them
nude and with patent signs of their unnatural activity." The police set a
trap for Javier with a decoy, by convincing Fernando to call him on the
phone and invite him to go to the boarding house, where a nineteen-
year-old youth would be waiting for him. Once Javier was in the room
with the youth, the police broke in and surprised them in the nude. They
also found "a carry-on that contained pornographic prints and plastic
objects of obscene configuration."[51] The confiscated materials were destroyed. Reading between the lines, the "obscene configuration" of plastic objects used in a homosexual context could perhaps refer to dildos or
other sexual toys.

Judicial transcripts on homosexual acts were occasionally quite
explicit. At the same time, police officers and court secretaries used
multiple euphemisms. In the report on the raid at the boarding house,
for instance, plastic does not materialize in a recognizable shape but
rather remains in the amorphous terrain of obscenity, its contours insin-
uated but not defined. This writing style contrasts with detailed reports,
included in the same file, that focus on homosexuality as an issue or
disorder. A defendant is described as "sick of sexuality, due to his abnormal cerebral electro-genesis"; another would suffer from "an anomalous
sexual instinct, of complex etiology, that he corrected out of his own
volition during a year when he underwent medical treatment"; and the
report on a third defendant points out that "he has suffered prolonged
crises of acute alcoholism, which put his life at risk, but he voluntarily
subjected himself to medical cures that have managed to restore in part
his health."[52]

These transcripts, and their way of representing homosexual experiences, are biased. Authorities preferred to be more specific about homosexual suffering than about sexual toys. Defendants themselves were
invested in presenting a narrative about their life trajectory that foregrounded trauma and psychiatric diagnoses, being aware that judges
were more likely to be lenient when homosexuals claimed to be victims
of their own "disorder" and other external factors. The defense lawyers
argued as well that "intimate, private and secret acts" could not be judged

as pertaining to the crime of public scandal. This was all in vain. The Supreme Court dismissed the appeals and established that the vague language used in the trial was a legitimate way of approaching these issues ("it does not take away the necessary light from the story, so the latter does not fall into darkness").[53] In other words, in terms of style, expressions such as "obscene configuration" provided enough information for judges to issue a conviction. Finally, Javier's defense appealed on the grounds that police officers themselves propitiated the situation of which he was accused, through an orchestrated call and the complicity of the young man with whom they found Javier nude in the room. The magistrates concluded that such a stratagem was legitimate and pertinent as "means for revealing what was already happening." As Hunt argues, the censorship of obscenity is a battleground "on the border between the zones of darkness and light, the secret and the revealed, the hidden and the accessible."[54] The Supreme Court's ruling legitimated obfuscating and shedding light on different facets of homosexuality, highlighting pain and obliterating dildos.

Not only homosexual material culture posed a challenge to National-Catholic morality; gossip columns also incurred in public scandal. Despite the harmless appearance of the extensive photographic reports on national and international celebrities, their lives did not conform to the dogmas of Catholic canonical marriage. In October 1970, a very popular gossip magazine published a note that was eventually judged by the Supreme Court. According to its ruling, the very cover of the magazine aroused an unhealthy interest, through "a color photograph that occupies almost the entire page, representing a man and a woman wearing scarce sporting and swimming clothes; she sits on his knees, they hug each other and smile."[55] He was a bullfighter married to an actress, and the woman who sat on his knees was his lover, married to another man. The ruling implied that the magazine presented such a relationship in sympathetic terms, with phrases such as "D. and M. live [. . .] a long and warm summer crowned by love." In 1973, the Barcelona Audiencia acquitted the photographer, the editor, and the editorial assistant of the crime of scandal but ordered the burning of all copies of the magazine. The prosecution appealed this sentence on the grounds that it was unduly benign. The defense lawyer argued that extramarital relations between celebrities were no longer de facto a public scandal, considering the profound transformations in majority social attitudes that should be recognized by the court. The Supreme Court disagreed with the lawyer's pragmatism, making it clear that protecting good customs entailed preserving the role of marriage as an "essential cell on which social structures rests." Considering that both the photographs and the accompanying text showed "intimacies" that exceeded "the minimum standards of decorum," the Supreme Court declared that the three defendants should have been convicted of public scandal.[56] In short, the magistrates rejected the argument that the liberalization of customs was irreversible, while the authorities' benevolence toward men who were unfaithful to their wives suggests that in this case the scandal lied in a married woman openly posing with her celebrity lover.

One of the cases that most aroused the Supreme Court implicated a Catholic parish bulletin disseminating obscenity. These sorts of bulletins epitomized a pastoral action that aimed at penetrating parishioners' daily lives. New airs of change and modernization impacted on-the-ground initiatives at Catholic parish churches since the Second Vatican Council in the mid-1960s, also in Francoist Spain. In addition, in Catalonia a significant sector of the Catholic clergy sympathized with Catalonian nationalism, which, as a political movement, was banned by the Franco regime (fixated as it was in keeping the unity of the Spanish nation).[57] The clergy was divided in terms of its political loyalties and positions on social issues, in contrast with the virtually unanimous support that the highest echelons of the Catholic Church gave to the regime in its first decades. This is the context for the deliberations that took place in the Supreme Court in 1974 regarding the publication in 1972 of a "pornographic" poem in a parish bulletin based in a small Catalonian town. The parish board edited this bulletin in Catalan and circulated it among the parishioners. The bulletin included "statistics" as well as "liturgical commentaries and feature articles." To give it a lighter tone by including contents not merely on ecclesiastical matters, the priest who presided over the parish team had the idea of publishing a selection of poems. That was the beginning of the scandal. A draughtsman called Saúl submitted by invitation a selection of his poems to the bulletin, for which he would eventually be prosecuted. Six of his poems were published in the bulletin in the summer of 1972, among which the one entitled *Llit de panxa enlaire* ("lying on my back") was the one that triggered the complaint[58] of the prosecutor's office:

Trembling under me, her body congests
hot and cold at the same time.
She bares the heat of
her soft skin that
provokes in me a strange,
inexplicable happiness.
Open eyes wetter than ever
tight mouth
and a sweet, very sweet pink [sic].
Strange woman.
Thoughts are suddenly forgotten
and complicated at the same time.
Galloping bellies
crush on each other.
Eyes close and sweats mix.
Who will explain
these unsuspected reactions later?
Meanwhile, the twilights
are distant, and flashes
illuminate the great situation, which becomes wet and sticky
on any sheet
well judged
by those who wash it.[59]

It is worth noting once again that materials like this poem—which the Francoist authorities considered obscene, offensive to public morality, and unpublishable—are now publicly accessible precisely because the judicial process involved their preservation. The Supreme Court sentenced Saúl as criminally responsible for delivering the poem to the board even though he had "perfect knowledge" of its "erotic content." However, for the magistrates the most outrageous factor in this case was the format and alleged intention of the bulletin:

CONSIDERING that the more or less literary description of an act of sexual intercourse, without euphemisms, in a parish bulletin, is a fact that, fortunately, cannot be considered frequent or ordinary in our country, even in this era of intense erotic display when disguised— or, to put it more accurately—conspicuously masked pornography besieges and surrounds the individual in a climate of sexuality, through media, movies, theater plays, novels, and even with photographs of women in provocative attitudes and the double-entendre of advertising slogans on the posters in the streets and public places. Therefore, when in spite of this environment, an event like the one narrated in the transcript takes place and gives rise to a surprising scandal that must be described as serious, not only because of the publicity achieved by the insertion in such a bulletin, but also because of the bulletin's special nature, dedicated to promoting and defending ethical-religious values, honesty, modesty, and decency, considered as the basis for the subsistence of Christian civilization, and among which values, the domestication and socialization of instincts and, in particular, of sexual instincts, has a preferential place.[60]

For the magistrates, the pornographization of Spanish society had reached the most unexpected and outrageous levels when even Catholic parish bulletins had to be censored. They were quite fatalistic about the effects that the *destape* was having on media, artistic creation, and advertising, but they insisted that parish bulletins were and should remain the last bastion of "Christian civilization." The magistrates also warned that pornographic content could be "easily and surreptitiously introduced into homes" through this sort of bulletins, given that "family surveillance" did not target religious publications. They were particularly concerned about the possibility that pornography published in liturgical bulletins would reach minors, provoking either disgust or a "dangerous and premature stimulus." In other words, the ruling made it very clear that parish bulletins would not become the Trojan horse through which pornography reached Catholic parishioners and decent families.

The Debate on Pornography as a Threat to Society

The inefficacy of the framework of ordinary criminal law to prevent the spread of obscenity led Francoist legislators to incorporate pornography into the extraordinary legal framework of dangerousness, which encompassed social phenomena that were not a crime per se but whose participants were subjected to policing and "security measures" (imprisonment, work camps, exile, and surveillance). In 1970 the Cortes (the

Francoist nondemocratic legislative body) debated the substitution of the 1933 Vagrancy Law for a new Social Dangerousness and Rehabilitation Law that was meant to respond to widespread changes in social mores, sexual liberalization, and the youth counterculture by expanding the range of typified behaviors. In this context, the debate in the Cortes, and beyond them, also addressed the pertinence of harshening anti-obscenity policies by including pornography as a dangerous typology. Antonio Sabater Tomás was a reactionary jurist who served as judge at the Vagrancy Court of Barcelona and advised hardline legislators on the threats to society that he perceived at the courtroom. The sixth chapter of Sabater Tomás's *Peligrosidad social y delincuencia* (1972) is dedicated to the trafficking and exhibition of pornography. Sabater Tomás points to "pluralism in sexual [and] social ethics, the massive influence of tourism and migration, psychoanalysis, increasing living standards [and] the exploitation of sexuality for commercial purposes" as major issues that had justified the enactment of new legislation on dangerousness. Sabater Tomás's belief that there was a correlation between material welfare and sexual excesses was shared by many participants in the debates that led to a harshening of the policing apparatus. By discussing the dangers of overdevelopment, policymakers simultaneously asserted the success of the regime's economic policies. A profusion of colors and high-quality printing were technical attributes that, according to Sabater Tomás, contributed to the normalization of pornography. Insofar as modernity led to the hypersexualization of society, reactionary thinkers like Sabater Tomás problematized the alignment of Francoist Spain with the Western bloc of the Cold War.

Sabater Tomás believed that the "devastating effects" of a "hyper-eroticized environment" had impacted the Global North ("the north of Western civilization") and not the communist bloc. While Francoist political rhetoric had consistently represented Spain at the vanguard line of Western Christianity in the battle against Bolshevik communism, by the 1970s Soviet regimes had become a model for Francoist policymakers regarding morality. By contrast, the United States was, according to Sabater Tomás, the center from which depravation irradiated, through the normalization of "swingers clubs; advertisements for sexual relationships among married couples or between homosexuals; schools where women are taught to undress with maximum erotic efficacy, etc."[61] Likewise, Nordic avant-garde films were also illustrative of the depravity of modern culture, according to Sabater Tomás. He cited the Swedish film *I Am Curious (Yellow)*, produced and screened in two parts between 1967 and 1968, as an example of the "artificial arousal of the senses" for the sake of profit. The history of this film's distribution in the United States touches on opacity, discontinuity, and tedium as effective alibi to circumvent censorship. The film was well received by the U.S. intelligentsia, as a hybridization of "the general release film, the exploitation film, and the art cinema" at a moment when the legal and market boundaries among these three categories were exceptionally fluid. The director was Vilgot Sjöman, who had initiated his career working with Ingmar Bergman and was well familiar with experimental techniques (cinema vérité, unscripted interviews, and so forth). The script was plagued with narrative discontinuities, which made it difficult for U.S. authorities to classify it, since judicial precedence had established that the work "as a whole" ought to show "a morbid or prurient interest in sex or nudity" for it to be prosecuted as obscenity. While in the first chapter I discussed how the performance of fragmentation allowed Spanish authorities to disqualify aesthetic considerations and treat transgressive literature as pornography, by the 1960s the opposite discourse undermined censorship internationally, insofar as the notion of the artwork as a discreet unity of meaning legitimated sexual explicitness for the sake of art's redemptive faculties. This does not mean that the film entered the United States uncontested. On the contrary, violence accompanied its distribution and escalated along with it: it was seized by U.S. Customs officials in New York in 1968; a district court judge prevented its release; a jury of citizens found it to be obscene; and a theater in Houston was set on fire for showing it. Eventually, as the Supreme Court was unable to set precedence on the obscenity of *I Am Curious (Yellow)*, it fell to local authorities to regulate its viewership.[62]

I Am Curious (Yellow), for all its opacity and pretentiousness, explicitly links sexual freedom (embodied by the protagonist's erotic adventures) with social movements for social justice, including antimilitary conscientious objection and the mobilization of Black citizens in the United States (Dr. Martin Luther King, Jr. was interviewed in the film). The protagonist is a young woman who partakes in a demonstration in front of a Swedish travel agency to denounce the Franco regime. Later, she goes to an airport and interviews actual tourists in their way back from Spain, asking them whether they feel ashamed for having spent their holidays in a country that suffers under a dictatorial regime. In their responses, the interviewees talk about the low cost of living, the sun, and beaches as Spain's main touristic attractions.[63] The politicization of the protagonist of *I Am Curious (Yellow)* contrasts with films produced contemporaneously in Spain, in which local men were fixated on seducing Swedish female tourists, and politics were overlooked (as in the comedy *Amor a la española* (Love the Spanish way), which had more than two million viewers when projected in Spanish cinemas in 1967, the same year that *I Am Curious (Yellow)* was screened abroad).[64] In *I Am Curious (Yellow)* photographs of General Franco and World War II concentration camps became symbols of the atrocious historical legacy that young Europeans had to confront in the 1960s. The protagonist is the daughter of a Swedish volunteer of the International Brigades who had fought for the Second Republic in the Spanish Civil War. The film advocates for sexual liberation and highlights European democratic governments' hypocrisy in allowing Franco to remain in power. Sabater did not analyze the film's anti-fascist underpinnings, instead citing it as an example of the porn industry's large profit margins to dismiss leftist political critique as mere sexual commodification.

In view of the intertwined threats of political radicalism and sexual liberation, Sabater Tomás followed with great interest the debate in the Cortes on the new Dangerousness Law and studied the amendments proposed by *procuradores* (legislators). He argued that overlapping typification of obscenity in censorship laws, criminal laws (as public scandal), and the Dangerousness Law was a minor technical issue in comparison with the expansion of the pornography industry. *Procuradores* in the Cortes most often characterized pornography as the illegal importation of foreign materials into Spain, because problematizing the publication and domestic circulation of pornography entailed an acknowledgment that the regime's censorship policies had failed. Still, the members of the Cortes committee tasked with elaborating a report on the content and admissibility of the amendments were aware that including the term "pornography" in the Dangerousness Law implied recognizing that state policies—police departments and the 1966 Press Law—had failed. According to the committee report, incorporating pornography in the law would create a "technically undesirable" overlap between the Criminal Code and the typification of dangerous conduct (which in theory was policed preemptively, not as a crime).[65] This is why pornography was not included in the first draft of the Dangerousness Law. However, multiple *procuradores* criticized this omission.

The leadership of the Falange Women Section advocated for passing as many repressive laws to prevent the pornographization of Spanish society as necessary. Sabater Tomás also articulated this argument in his works: "pornography is a social morbidity that causes the destruction of man by immorality, contributing to his dumbing down and physical degeneration, especially with regard to youth, by becoming an incentive for rude passions and disordered appetites, being an efficient cause of crime, psychosis, and even suicides."[66] Sabater Tomás argued that pornography reduced humans to their animal condition and had a causal role in self-destructive behavior. Hence, it should be included in the new law, whose goal was to monitor and prevent antisocial tendencies beyond an exclusive concern for legality. To support this view, Sabater Tomás focused on illustrative episodes of immorality that were not criminalized under the existing legislation, such as a homosexual convention that had recently been held on the Costa del Sol to "scientifically defend homosexuality."

For Sabater Tomás, whereas the obscenity of homosexual activism was not contemplated as such in the Criminal Code, the Dangerousness Law could fill this vacuum by expanding the range of threats to society. The pornographer should be treated in much the same way as the drug dealer. In fact, Sabater Tomás's text on pornography was accompanied by photographic scenes of drug trafficking. He drew a parallel between drugs and sex; both were addictive and were related to nonconformism. The role of the state apparatus was the implementation of systematic mechanisms that protected citizens from excessive stimulation. To distinguish pornography from art, judges ought to focus on "the work's ideological purpose [and] the sincere form of aesthetic expression."[67] Sabater Tomás recognized that most societies were permissive with aestheticized nudity, which could not be deemed obscene. In the view of Sabater Tomás and others, antiobscenity reforms were primarily intended to apply the lessons learned from observing neighboring European countries, where the legalization of soft-core opened the floodgates to the normalization of hard-core.

In this context, the Cortes assumed the task of guarding Spain's traditional Catholic mores through the articles of the new Ley de Peligrosidad.

The amendments presented by *procuradores* correlated with their positions regarding reformism. José María del Moral Pérez de Zayas presented an amendment that was strikingly explicit in recognizing the failures of the censorship apparatus: "pornographic media are now a quotidian presence [*al orden del día*], despite repressive legal measures, which are evaded or disrespected."[68] Manuel Escudero Rueda also drew attention to the ineffectiveness of censorship to avoid the sexualization of the public sphere and Spanish citizens' customs.[69] By the early 1970s the regime's "reformist" sectors did not oppose censorship but rather its ineffectiveness.[70] Reactionary sectors, on the other hand, relied on a very broad concept of pornography that expressed their moral panic about youth countercultures and psychodelia. As *procurador* Jose María Zaldivar Aranzana put it: "The proliferation of apparently innocuous establishments dedicated 'to listen to young music' serve as an immoral market or prelude to the use of means for the moral corruption of young people—drunkenness, drugs, printed or recorded pornography, lighting devices, fast-paced sound, dangerous promiscuity, etc" *(La proliferación de aparentes establecimientos inocuos destinados 'a escuchar música joven,' sirven de mercado inmoral o antesala de utilización de medios –embriaguez, drogas, pornografía impresa o grabada, aparato luminotécnico, sonorización trepidante, promiscuidad peligrosa, etc.– de corrupción moral a la juventud).*[71] For Zaldivar Aranzana, pornography was part of a multifarious threat involving the dangerous overstimulation of young people's senses by music, sound, light, drugs, and promiscuity. The law should aim, then, at policing younger generations in their use of their senses, to prevent extreme sensorial experiences that undermined socio-political conformity.

In January 1970, a group of five *procuradores* led by Agustín de la Bárcena y Reus (head of the National Fisheries Union) presented an amendment to include pornography in the new law. They presumed that pornographic materials originated abroad and proposed means to persecute those people who facilitated their importation to Spain. To justify the amendment, they argued that the business of pornography trafficking caused a "decline in the spiritual highest values that any society—even more if it is Catholic—must safeguard." They mentioned that the Spanish press continuously reported on the "damage" that the distribution of pornography was doing. Finally, and most strikingly, this group of *procuradores* referred to communist countries as a source of inspiration for the legislation they proposed, pointing out that despite "their materialism and irreligiosity," these regimes had been able to "preserve the moral health of their inhabitants."[72] These *procuradores* were hardliners of Falange, the Spanish fascist party, yet they admired the moral policies of the communist bloc.[73] In other words, antipornography activism traversed Cold War politics and led to anomalous ideological convergences.

Pilar Primo de Rivera, leader of the Women Section of Falange (and daughter of Miguel Primo de Rivera), also proposed amendments, in which she associated pornography with an excess of civilization. Pilar Primo de Rivera's position epitomizes the paradox of a female party leadership that advocated for women to remain in the domestic sphere.[74] She was a hardliner who had advocated for a stronger alliance with Nazi Germany during World War II.[75] In her amendment, Primo de Rivera used a broad formula that encompassed not only trafficking with pornography but also spreading "propaganda" on it, which could refer to any material that made the public aware of increasing sexual freedom in other societies:

Today, in overdeveloped countries, there are publications of truly amazing technique and color, which flaunt their maximum [level of] civilization. This would be worthy of great respect [*estimable*] if they were applied for purposes other than pornography, but those publications are very lucrative, even more so if they are smuggled into Spain, which causes the consequent moral damage to youth. Consequently, I believe that effective measures must be taken to prevent the easy dissemination [of these publications], since—unfortunately—their total disappearance is very difficult.

Hoy, en países superdesarrollados, existen publicaciones de técnicas y colorido verdaderamente asombrosos, con las que hacen alarde de su máxima civilización y ello sería estimable si se aplicasen con fines distintos a la pornografía pero aquellas publicaciones son muy lucrativas y –tanto más si se introducen de contrabando en España, lo cual ocasiona el consiguiente perjuicio moral para toda la juventud y, en su consecuencia,– considero deben tomarse medidas eficaces que eviten su fácil difusión, ya que –desgraciadamente– la total desaparición es muy difícil.[76]

Pilar Primo de Rivera considered that overdevelopment materialized in the high quality of pornographic magazines, establishing a correlation between technological innovation and the sexualization of society. Her primary concern was arguably that pornography would become inextricable from media development and taken for granted—we invest media with extraordinary agency when we naturalize its presence, technology, and functionalities as an irreversible teleology.[77] Josefina Veglison, who also served as *procuradora* by virtue of her role in Falange, was another leading voice in this debate. She claimed in an alarmist tone that pornography had become available for any child to buy at newsstands. Veglison advocated for a reactivation of the regime's fascist ideals. She argued that "women's legitimate political action should aim at collaboration with men, never competition."[78] In other words, fascist women claimed that their political engagement reinforced family values by reifying notions of gender complementarity and codependence between men and women.[79] The intervention of women politicians in debates on public morality was considered an extension of their domestic roles, which is probably one of the reasons that they led debates on pornography. The Dangerousness Law passed by the Cortes in August 1970 imposed penalties of imprisonment, monetary fines, and surveillance on citizens "who promote or foment the traffic, commercialization or exhibition of pornographic material or make their apology."[80] Consumption by itself was not penalized. What is more—as the next chapter demonstrates—defendants charged with pornography were likely to receive a lenient judicial treatment, indicating that mainstream porn was considered a deviation of normal sexuality and less threatening than politicized porn, homosexuality, and transgenderism.

Conclusion

Starting in the 1950s, judges and policymakers were becoming increasingly frustrated by their apparent failure to prevent Spanish citizens' gradual incorporation into global erotic markets. Since the last phase of the Franco regime coincided with the international "porno chic" era, there were concerted efforts to harshen domestic legal regimes, especially in the early 1970s. While the 1966 Press Law had been part and parcel of the regime's strategy of controlled modernization, the inclusion of pornography in the 1970 Dangerousness Law was a step in the opposite direction, setting additional institutional impediments to the sexualization of consumer culture. The press contributed to building moral consensus around this new law, as journalists warned readers about cultural and sexual experimentation in other countries while being aware that their notes could themselves be considered obscene. These journalists counterposed the pornographic excesses of the cultural avant-garde in Western democracies with Spanish state policies, which aimed at maintaining traditional family and religious values amidst a process of socioeconomic modernization. Both journalists and legislators were concerned that the high technical and aesthetic quality of explicit films and publications was a sort of Trojan horse to normalize obscenity. In response, antipornography activists combined religious fundamentalism as their mobilizing base with the outfacing projection of an apparently modern secular discourse, a strategy shared with other international actors.

Among the legislators (*procuradores*), the leaders of the Falange Women Section proactively lobbied to include pornography as a typology of dangerousness, in contrast with "technocratic" legislators who emphasized that the penal code and the Press Law already regulated censorship and punished the commercialization of obscenity. The argument put forward by figures such as Pilar Primo de Rivera was that no legislative effort could be excessive in the face of the porn industry's technical sophistication in developed countries. Pro-criminalization *procuradores* relied on a vague conceptualization of obscenity, encompassing any liminal experience that fostered social unrest—from countercultural music and gay activism to pornography understood as commercialized representations of explicit sex and nudity—and resorted to the idea that citizens had to be forcefully protected from the corrupting influence of modern mass culture. As the next chapter demonstrates, the law's implementation was a different story: judges seemed persuaded that the normalization of mainstream porn was inevitable and focused their efforts on transgressions (blasphemy, maricas' erotica, or explicitly political pornography) that undermined the status quo.

FOUR

Burning the Normal, Preserving the Queer

Performance and archive are part of a continuum that tenses the relative positions of aesthetics, stigma, and pleasure. Francoist authorities incinerated mainstream pornography while they preserved, curated, and even restored transgressive erotica, involuntarily queering their own archival praxis. Whereas copies of Tintoretto, Michelangelo, and Botticelli's masterworks were incinerated, judicial authorities repeatedly watched an amateur movie of three men having sex. What made visual materials obscene, I argue, is how they touched consumers and audiences. Art historian Kelly Dennis argues that the "breach of the presumed boundary between image and beholder" and "the power of the image to move our own flesh" (to touch us) animates much of the public debate on the dangers of obscenity.[1] Centuries-old debates on the relative artistic and epistemic value of "sight" and "touch" center the question of whether proximity to the object endangers the position of the subject. In Francoist Spain, mainstream pornography was treated as a mild violation and burned, while transgressive erotica irreversibly touched consumers (here, the contraposition between erotica and pornography mirrors contemporary usage).

Both obscenity and visible homosexuality were prosecuted as public scandal before and during the Franco regime, under "ordinary" laws.[2] The Vagrancy Law, enacted in 1933 and encompassing homosexuality since 1954, was an "extraordinary" jurisdiction, meaning that it suspended standard procedural protections and provided the state with the authority to detain and prosecute "antisocial" subjects *before* they committed any crime.[3] Thousands of defendants appeared before the vagrancy courts and were subjected to questionable forensic examinations and sentenced to security measures (prison, labor camps, exile, and surveillance) for being "homosexuals."[4] Their files often include personal letters, photographs, and postcards, a testimony to police surveillance and subjects' intimate lives. Hence, most of the erotica that I have found in state archives was confiscated and catalogued before 1970, when the Vagrancy Law was in force and these materials were considered evidence of antisocial homosexual behavior.

My initial expectation was to find a comparable amount of pornography from the same courts. At the courts of Barcelona, with jurisdiction over the French border—the major entryway for international pornography—there are thirty-two catalogue entries related to charges of pornography, which pales in comparison with the number of "homosexuality" files (approximately 400 files for the period between 1956 and 1970 and more than 800 files for the period between 1971 and 1980).[5] What is more, authorities systematically destroyed any confiscated mainstream pornography, in contrast with their detailed documentation and preservation of erotica confiscated from maricas. By the same token, novelist Terenci Moix describes how, when he was a kid in the postwar period, censors forbade the exposure of female cinema stars' bodies, while the torsos of male gladiators and Christian martyrs passed censorship regimes and became homoerotic icons. Moix recalls his sexual awakening to the muscles of Saint Sebastian crossed by arrows in the 1949 film *Fabiola*. For him, this experience was "more exhilarating than laughing. [It] replaced the direct feeling of the flesh and can only be explained by looking at the strangest regions of the mind."[6] Thus, censors favored a homoerotic reading of Hollywood films.

This chapter tracks the regime's inconsistent handling of erotica and porn. Judicial files produced from the 1950s to the 1970s in Vagrancy and Dangerousness courts—and confiscated materials included in these files—are the core archival sources. The first half delves into the treatment of transgressive erotica and argues that state authorities had two priorities that were occasionally incompatible: the full exposure of creators/consumers to the gaze of the state in the courtroom and the protection of affluent and well-connected defendants. As I demonstrate through two case studies, contemporary media spread the notion that same-sex desires were entangled with a frenzy to dismantle the political, social, and religious status quo. Photographs of gay sex and the desecration of Catholic churches went hand in hand in mediatic stories. Related to the trope of deviance-as-obscenity in contemporary media, authorities aimed at collecting and archiving "evidence" of this trope, while defendants often made strategic decisions and destroyed their personal erotica for self-protection. If they were confiscated, homoerotic images were displayed during the trials to engineer "a spectacle of humiliation for which the judge himself is the prime audience."[7] I contrapose this degradation of defendants with their use of visual language and embodied aesthetic ideals. For media scholar Kyle Frackman, homemade queer images "have been creative expression, memento, social tool, and pornography, while also standing as a critique and, importantly, a record of existence."[8] These images "make desire itself the subject."[9] In other words, the perpetuation of desire, rather than its fulfillment, made them appealing.[10] Under authoritarian regimes, these images circulated among, and were preserved by, networks of connoisseurs.[11] The visual language in the judicially confiscated homemade photographs that I analyze was deeply informed by models and artists' choices to balance self-exhibition and anonymity, explicitness and veiled nudity, and classicism and the allure of penetrative sex.

The second half of the chapter focuses on the destruction of mainstream pornography, suggesting that desecration and politicized porn were excluded from the overall policy of implicit benevolence. My take on pornography-related judicial files is that they show a regime apparatus in the defensive rather than in the offensive: violent as they were, the few exemplary punishments mandated by judges within a framework of leniency read like an ineffective policy to deter society from the course it had taken: Spanish citizens (as they appear represented in the media and judicial files) seemed quasi-universally curious about the international Sexual Revolution. Furthermore, the incorporation of Spain in global logistical circuits and trade networks meant that there were numerous imperceptible ways for porn to enter the country (from recycling to sailors), while local entrepreneurs and collectors were highly creative in commercializing and showing obscenity. Even in scenarios when the regime's policies seemed to work—in the sense of arresting time and keeping media and sexual revolutions at bay—this translated into the pornification of cultural objects that otherwise had been sanitized by centuries of art history. I argue that, in response to the widespread perception that pornification was inevitable, judicial authorities and conservative media aligned in constructing a nationalist rhetoric that portrayed Spaniards as the victims of foreign nationals who embodied the excessive liberalism of European democracies and the perversion of racialized Others (a trope that connects with previous chapters). The performative belief in Spaniards' naivete was wishful thinking, a projection of reactionary politics into a reality that refused to conform to them.

These politics materialized through the regime's archiving practices, which construed a distinction—that partially overlapped but did not fully coincide with the hetero/homo binary—between disruptive (marica, trans, sacrilegious, anti-fascist, etc.) and aligned with the status quo (private peccadilloes, male bonding, depoliticized citizens). In the latter case, consumers of obscenity were not classified as inherently deviant. They performed naivete during their trials as the most effective strategy to stage their innocence. While national laws established that men ought to perform the roles of breadwinners, soldiers, and legal tutors of women and minors, I examine how men who consumed mainstream porn intentionally infantilized themselves in the courtroom through their use of a terminology that centered playfulness, curiosity, experimentation, and vulnerability. This rhetoric resonated with judges, who opted for forgiveness if defendants asserted that they had learned their lesson. Francoist courtrooms as theaters of authority display the irony of male citizenship, the constant demand imposed on subjects to perform (im)maturity.[12] Defendants' right to be forgotten was upheld when mainstream pornography was erased, while transgressive erotica was saved from the flames and put on the archive/stage to perform the shame of those who had touched and had been touched by it. Touching it again with care, we may transgress the Francoist courtrooms' instructions and reenact desire.

Surviving through Erasure

In the 1960s and 1970s, Spanish media played a significant role, complementary to state policies, in disseminating the trope of deviance-as-obscenity, which implied causal links between homoeroticism and subjects' craving to desecrate national-Catholic icons. The media coverage of the "Madrid arsonist" was paradigmatic of this trend. The arsonist was the target of much media attention in 1968 after he entered the Prado Museum and slashed several masterpieces with a knife and "profaned" a sacred image in the Church of Jesús de Medinaceli.[13] Newspapers did not clarify what happened at the church, but this defilement inserts the case in the anticlerical genealogy of obscenity that I have been tracing throughout this book. The police finally identified the suspect as Antonio U. T., twenty-two years old, born in Badajoz. He was living in a boarding house, where the police found "packages prepared to ignite fire in mailboxes, a great quantity of magazines about homosexuality, and pornographic photographs."[14] After his attack at the Prado Museum, the police interrogated the Museum staff, drew a portrait of Antonio (eventually published in the press along with an actual photograph of him), and tracked the phone number of a newspaper to which he had made phone calls in the past, which led to his arrest.[15] He declared that he was not "resentful" but "nonconformist." He had been in a Catholic seminary and served in the air force (as state archives attest)[16] until they committed him to a psychiatric hospital in Palencia. After his release, his thirst for notoriety supposedly led him to undertake the destructive actions for which he had been arrested. The media coverage suggested that Antonio had a penchant for pornography and homosexuality, without clarifying which role these factors played in the overall story. Indeed, the coverage promoted the impression that he was "deviant" in every possible way: expelled from the Church and the military, psychologically disturbed, sexually depraved, and determined to generate fame for himself through the destruction of masterworks and sacred objects alike. In doing so, the coverage highlighted how the trope of deviance-as-obscenity operated to frame the arsonist as a threat to the nation and its founding narratives.

Yet, at the same time, Antonio is not a trope but an actual person who left archival traces of his own perspective after these events. In 1985, he wrote and published an op-ed denouncing the deficient treatment of psychiatric patients like himself. In his opinion, police repression and psychopharmaceuticals were too often used in place of "actual planification to foster the patient's social integration."[17] Indeed, the media's sensationalistic accounts of the experiences of people like Antonio fomented the idea that homosexuality and pornography were part of an amalgam of antisocial behaviors (psychosis, arsonism, narcissism, nonconformism, inability to adapt to disciplinary institutions, among others) that were entangled with each other.

The links made among homosexuality, pornography, and antisocial behaviors (deviance-as-obscenity) are also visible in the media coverage of a series of art thefts that took place in the Canary Islands in 1972.[18] A group of eight college students had stolen art—including chalices, paintings, goblets, candlesticks, a statue of the Virgin—worth over two million pesetas from Catholic churches, and when arrested some of them "confessed to being practicing homosexuals and drug consumers." Among the defendants, one student had a degree in philosophy; a second had graduated with a degree in art criticism and history; two twins with unspecified majors also participated in the heists; meanwhile, an art broker placed the stolen pieces on the market. When the police searched the house where the group had stored the pieces, they allegedly found "pornographic photographs, of men only, for which some of the arrested individuals (whose ages oscillated between 18 and 25 years old) had posed. Initially, [police officers] thought that the [students] would also have subversive propaganda, but once they searched the house, they did not find anything of this respect."[19] The police's assumption that college students who posed for lewd photographs, stole art from churches, and had gay sex had to be involved in anti-regime activities speaks volumes about a state ideology that fused all "antisocial" behaviors into the paradigm of deviance-as-obscenity.[20]

In contrast to media narratives, judicial sources on personal erotica demonstrate that it was used for mutual enticement and to build relations, even when the visual content did not focus on same-sex desires.[21] In 1975, in the Barcelona province, a fifty-six-year-old gardener was accused of seducing adolescents by showing them porn, so that they would let the gardener perform fellatio on them. The adolescents mentioned titillating images of nuns. Nun porn is a tradition that dates to at least the nineteenth century. Dennis emphasizes that the appeal of sexualized images of nuns lies in "their blasphemous or parodic aspects at the expense of religion; they also represent the erotic fulfillment of forbidden desire to see what lies hidden beneath the formal and deliberately asexual attire."[22] To counteract the accusation of using blasphemous porn to have gay sex, the defendant mobilized traditional power brokers' support: the Guardia Civil, the parish priest, and the florist tasked with decorating the church, among others, who submitted positive character reports to the court. The judge sentenced the defendant as a threat to society, but the "security measures" applied to him were eventually suspended (likely because the defendant was the sole caregiver for his mother).[23] Erotica in rituals of seduction between males, as with "homosexuality" more broadly, was judicialized on the premise that the subject's multiple social roles held weight in evaluating the supposed threat he posed to society.[24]

The stereotyping of gay sex as predatory is inextricable from courts' role in documenting defendants' performances, aimed at denying their liability in front of judges and forensic doctors. A forensic doctor's framework, for example, mediates the one case I have found of archived photographs of BDSM scenarios, to the point that the defendant's experiences become inseparable from medical notions of trauma and abuse. A twenty-two-year-old male was medically examined in May 1970 by forensic doctor Antonio Sábater Sanz, who would later discuss the "case" in a textbook on psychological testing. However, the case study does not include any information on the location, charges, and resolution of the trial—hence the physical photographs become untraceable and only figure as props in the defendant's psychodrama. In his report, Sábater Sanz noted the defendant's "great desire to collaborate" and his spontaneous sharing of abundant details on his sexual life. This verbal incontinence could be due in part to a defense strategy to win the examiner's favor or to the defendant's desire to own his self-narrative, inserting his voice and perspective in the judicial records.

According to Sábater Sanz's report, the defendant alleged that different men had tried to seduce him years prior, but he opted for a formal relationship with a girlfriend. Since he did not want to be disrespectful to her, he channeled his sexual needs with male adolescents, thirteen to sixteen years old, that he photographed in his studio while he masturbated. On the one hand, the defendant's narration of sordid encounters in a suffocating moral environment of sexual prejudices and sleazy seducers amounts to a self-indulgent tale of his involuntary perversion by other "predatory" men. On the other hand, the police had confiscated his personal photographs, which showed "a *partenaire* with *facies* of pain, handcuffed hanging from the ceiling, sometimes his penis is erect and other times flaccid."[25] The forensic doctor instructed the defendant to write "in an intimate tone" about his experiences, which resulted in an "extremely eloquent" first-person account of sadism and masochism. The high level of forensic interest correlates with the incorporation of images and texts into an institutional archive that reduces BDSM culture to non-consent; the doctor led his interaction with the defendant to extract evidence that sadism is the corollary of improper masculine socialization (homosexual seduction and lack of straight sex).

Moreover, it was in the defendants' best interest to destroy compromising photographs and erotica that documented their intimate life.[26] In 1965, a Madrid woman reported her husband as a homosexual. They had been married for fifteen years and had three children. According to her complaint, "during Easter, one of their little sons looked in the pocket of her husband's pants and found a photograph, the size of a postcard, in which her husband appeared with two other men, all of them nude. She does not know what her husband did with the photograph."[27] The defendant denied being an "invert"—common medical and criminological terminology of the time—and attributed the accusation to marital strife. Yet he did not have much to say about the compromising photograph, beyond the fact that he had torn it into pieces (whether this was true, we cannot know).[28] Photographs were often destroyed by participants in same-sex relationships to protect themselves, leaving dispersed testimonies in lieu of material evidence. The defendant was acquitted a few months later.[29] State power structures fostered the erasure of marica culture by turning erotica into incriminatory evidence and leading subjects who lived a "double life" to disown their same-sex affects and intimacies.[30]

Paradoxical when juxtaposed with the pressures they indirectly put on defendants to destroy their own erotica, judicial authorities made every effort to trace maricas' exposure. On 23 March 1962, the judge of the Madrid Vagrancy Court, along with the court's secretary and bailiff, went to a boarding house, entered one of its rooms, and climbed onto a table to ascertain what they could see through the door slit separating the room from that of a defendant. Their report established that there was "enough visibility to see the top half of a person's body, as well as one of the [two] beds."[31] State agents' intruding gaze materialized in concrete acts aimed at measuring the visibility of homoerotic desires in order to punish them. The original complainant was a resident of the boarding house who claimed to have heard strange noises coming from a neighboring room. She climbed on top of a chair and a table, looked through the door slit, and saw two men undressing, hugging, and kissing one another. She reported this episode to the authorities. Eventually, the Court of Appeals revoked the condemnatory sentence on the grounds that the judicial authorities had only a partial view of the defendants' room through the slit.[32] This judicial decision illustrates the logic that guided the collection and archiving of evidence: it was not enough to look at "perversion" through a slit, drawing its contours in the darkness or under a soft light; rather, the material evidence of homoerotic desires had to be present, catalogued, and displayed in full view of the authorities in the courtroom for them to render a decision confirming or denying the defendant's guilt.

The obsession with documenting transgression entailed setting traps to inculpate those who traded with gay pornography. In 1975 in Cartagena, a group of young men were arrested, and they admitted to having sex for money with local "inverts." Following the clues provided by a seventeen-year-old adolescent, an undercover police detective accompanied him to a bar, where the owner offered them a "homosexual magazine." After that, the police arrested the bar owner. He presented himself as quite homophobic, disparagingly referring to the adolescent as a *marica* and to his own clients as "inverts, judging by the way they talk and their effeminate customs."[33] The judicial distinction between marica and straight transgressors was clear: while the bar owner was not charged, the young man involved in sex work was sent to the Badajoz Prison (allegedly specialized in *homosexuales pasivos*, or males who bottom).[34] Homoeroticism inverted the legal apparatus put in place to assess dangerousness. While the law established that those who profited from selling pornography were a threat (and not consumers), in the case of homoerotic materials authorities focused on defendants' sexual practices to ascertain whether they had circulated these materials out of desire or interest, with the former motivation treated as the primary threat (contrary to what the law stipulated). Hence, the bar owner's performance of homophobic disgust rendered him nonthreatening.

The compulsion to document transgression also entailed recording defendants' private conversations in a way that allowed authorities to link homoerotic materials with underground networks that they targeted to make them visible. In 1972, three men charged with selling gay pornography were put in the same prison cell. Previously, the court authorities had hidden a tape recorder in the cell so that they could use the inmates' private conversations against them. Unaware of this ruse, the three inmates talked about contacting a fourth individual who kept the "material" in his house so that he could destroy it before being caught by the police.[35] The man who kept the pornography in his home was consequently arrested. He was strikingly vocal in questioning the authorities' legitimacy to raid his residence and intimate life, trying to place boundaries on state surveillance through the language of friendship, intimacy, privacy, and sentimentality. He explained to the police officers that "his sentimental life was perfectly channeled with a friend" and criticized how the police's illegal recording practices had "uncovered the intimacies of his private life, which would not have been exposed had the [police officers] obtained a warrant, since in that case he would have had the time to destroy the pornography, as he was planning to do."[36] In this way, the defendant highlighted that police officers had taken on the roles of voyeurs by "uncovering" people's "intimacies" and violating legal protections of citizens' privacy.

Finally, when questioned about the origins of the materials, the defendant referred to a "German gentleman" who was homosexual as well. Since they were very close friends, when the "gentleman" passed away his butler contacted the defendant and asked him to pick up and burn the photographs. In the defendant's narrative, the German gentleman was the missing link demonstrating that the photos that he possessed had only circulated within international elite circles and thereby were not a threat to the morality of the Spanish population. For this narrative to cohere, the defendant emphasized first that he was well off and had no need to sell the photographic materials and second that the models were German citizens who attended the private parties his friend used to organize in his villa. In other words, he characterized gay erotica (disputing the characterization of the photographs as porn in the sense of commercialized) as a byproduct of the international tourism that the regime so vigorously promoted. His defense strategy made sense in a class-biased legal regime that for the most part targeted the sexual practices of unprivileged sectors and spared the elite from prosecution.[37]

In 1960 in Barcelona, another wealthy defendant saw, along with the court authorities, a movie that allegedly captured him seated on a chair and looking at two young men who were making out, the three of them nude. The voyeurism of this scene was mirrored by that of the judicial authorities who organized a screening of this same film to establish the "truth" of the accusations of homosexuality and the defendant's version of the events. The case had been initiated when the defendant's former business partner accused him of maintaining homosexual relationships in their office. As evidence, he submitted the movie described above. Allegedly the business partner had recorded it by hiding in the defendant's office until the latter arrived with two young men. The partner captured the scene until they saw him, at which moment the defendant tried to cover himself with his underwear. The business partner also handed the police other objects that the defendant had kept in his office: a handkerchief that covered a photograph of two men and a lock of hair alongside three bottles containing vanilla, starch, and yohimbine, a veterinary drug used in cases of erectile disfunction. According to the business partner, the defendant received narcotics from a female relative, an abstract painter who lived in France. Thus, he further portrayed the defendant as deviant by associating him with drug use and abstract art in France, in line with Francoist discourses that characterized European democratic societies as prone to *vicio*.[38]

The intriguing collection of hair, aphrodisiacs, and homoerotic images drew the police's attention. The amateur movie was projected at least three times by the authorities. During one of these semipublic screenings, a police inspector supposedly kept pressuring the defendant to confess. The defendant was also forced to confront his business partner in front of court authorities, and the two ended up having a physical altercation. The defense lawyer argued that the whole case was built on a masterful photo montage by the complainant. First, he would record the defendant alone leaving a bathroom (hence his nudity) and then superimpose that image with those of two young nude men. He emphasized the low quality of the images and concluded that it was all a trap orchestrated by the complainant, himself a porn aficionado.[39] The defendant mobilized his network made up of powerful men and then focused his efforts on acquiring the film (betraying that he considered it a threat to his reputation). The city mayor and a consul were among the many reputed people who testified in his favor, moving Judge Antonio Sabater Tomás to acquit him. Sabater Tomás even stated that the fact that a taxi driver had once seen two naked men in the defendant's office was not sufficient evidence of the latter's homosexuality.[40] As the film itself is nowhere to be found in the file, we can infer that the defendant was also able to remove it thanks to his powerful connections. The files document two sides of the same coin: authorities' uncanny fixation with documenting transgression—by taking the position of voyeurs—and defendants' efforts at protecting their intimacy, which entailed destroying photos and other evidence of their sexual life. Despite these efforts, homoerotic images were confiscated and preserved at state archives.

Creating a Homoerotic Imaginary

According to art historian Thomas Waugh, postwar physique culture was a massive phenomenon engaging thousands of gay men in the consumption of bodybuilding magazines that provided the most popular and effective "alibis" for homoeroticism.[41] Spanish novelist Terenci Moix relates how, as an adolescent, he bought this sort of magazine with money he obtained with the ruse of collecting funds for Catholic missions. In contrast, in the office where he worked, male employees enjoyed mainstream porn together, as a bonding ritual, with no need to be as creative as Terenci was in his pursuit of erotica (these were nominally sports magazines that became "erotica" when consumed by gay men).[42]

Physique culture as the dominant vehicle for gay erotica had evident effects on subjects' visual and bodily languages. A defendant from Barcelona, for instance, posed for several photographs on a beach, wearing only a G-string (an icon of sexual liberalization in touristic areas) and a crucifix on his bare chest. These photos capture casual moments of hedonism. His hair is disheveled and wet after swimming, and he smiles to the camera while exhibiting his musculature in a pose that testifies to physique culture's effects on gender performance and visual culture. The defendant also kept a drawing of a brunet sailor penetrating a muscular blond male who only wears a T-shirt, has an erection, and is leaning on a tree and a foreground photograph of anal sex where the man playing the receptive role grabs the penis of the inserter as if to guide it into himself. The faces of the models are out of frame, likely a strategic decision to protect their anonymity.[43] Robert L. Caserio suggests that when pornography and art embrace each other they present "Eros as an opening to positions, rather than any taking of them. Male openings [. . .] are, as it were, culturally most off-base."[44] Amateur photographs associate "male openings" with a visually assertive body language, reframing the relationship among desire, power, and gender by eroticizing men who took a leading role in intercourse while exhibiting their receptiveness to penetration.

The last photograph from this file was taken from behind the model, who elevates his arms and grasps his hands behind his head to form a triangle between his elbows. In doing so, he flexes the upper part of his body, so the chiaroscuro highlights his musculature and curves against a light background. As the photographer used background, lighting, and posture to emphasize the geometrical symmetry of the model's body, he invested homoeroticism with a timeless classicism. The techniques used to invest the male physique with artistic qualities counteracted the authorities' view that homosexuality was inherently a "low art," so to speak. The defendant/model was accused of having a long-term affair with a well-off man who maintained him. The court's forensic doctor reported that he suffered from depression and should be transferred to a medical facility. Instead, Antonio Sabater Tomás sentenced him to a year of "internment" (which he served in the labor camp of Nanclares de la Oca), two years of exile, and two years of parole.[45] The joy, intimacy, and eroticism in defendants' personal photographs contrast with the harshness of the penalties imposed on them once they were exposed as homosexuals.

Classicism transpires in erotic photographs taken for self-consumption and circulation among men who built social networks around tolerant lodgings. As Ann Cvetkovich emphasizes, emotions are "encoded not only in the content of the texts themselves but in the practices that surround their production and reception."[46] One of the first pieces of evidence in a different file from Barcelona is a chest-up portrait of a handsome young man, confiscated during a raid of a boarding house. Ten male guests and the owner were arrested when the police found out that some of them were sleeping together. The police reported that in one of the rooms there was a "large taint, apparently of semen," sustaining the impression that the boarding house was a sexually charged, erotic space.[47] One of the arrested men claimed that he had known the man in the photograph for four years, and on the night of his arrest he had handed the photograph to another guest. The photographer skillfully framed and highlighted the contours of the model's athletic body, who posed sideways and looking up. The bottom half of his body is out of frame, leaving it to the viewer's imagination as to whether he is fully naked (this could be a preemptive strategy in case the photographs were confiscated). That the model and the man who kept the photograph had known each other for a long time and the conventionalisms of the erotic portrait together indicate that this image was produced within "a subcultural community [that] is participating in the representation of its own desire."[48]

FIGURE 7. A photograph of a male model, probably the defendant, taken from the rear. Photograph included in File 155/1965 of the Barcelona Vagrancy Court. Printed with permission by Arxiu Central dels Jutjats de la Ciutat de la Justícia, Hospitalet de Llobregat, Spain.

The model's relationship with the recipient of the photograph suggests that he was in fact an "erotic subject" as much as an object. He is not looking into the camera but slightly up, gesturing toward the sublime.

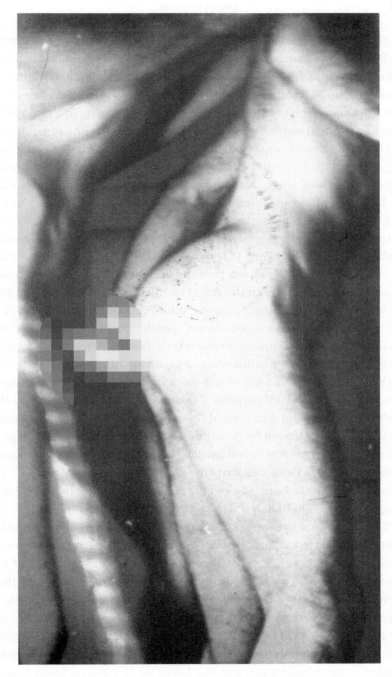

FIGURE 8. A photograph of two men having anal sex. The image has been slightly edited. Photograph included in File 155/1965 of the Barcelona Vagrancy Court. Printed with permission by Arxiu Central dels Jutjats de la Ciutat de la Justícia, Hospitalet de Llobregat, Spain.

The circulation, exhibition, and touch of erotica was entangled with the formation of an urban subculture of men who met semi-clandestinely to form bonds of friendship and sex. A different file includes a photograph of a nude body in its entirety captured from behind. The artist took the photograph of the back of a young model posing in a grain field. This angle preserved his anonymity while foregrounding his buttocks and back muscles. He separated his legs and extended his arms, in a posture that provided a partial glimpse of his penis, and tensed his muscles, highlighting them. He surrendered to the photographer's gaze, inclining his head.[49] While everything in this photo hints at the model submitting to the photographer, the same defendant who kept the photo also owned a foreground image of an erect penis. In this one, the model (who might even be the same one in the previous photo) has his shirt pushed up and his pants pulled down, revealing his hairy body, and delicately holds his erect phallus with two fingers while keeping his other hand on his hips in a self-exhibiting posture. While this posturing may, at first sight, seem to sexualize a "dominant" phallic position, Caserio points out that "penile stands are not prima facie assertive."[50] The way in which the model exhibits his phallus without gesturing to any sexual initiative might also be read as a form of self-eroticization to entice the photographer, who might as well perform a sexual act (such as oral sex) on the model. The defendant who owned these photographs, a forty-nine-year-old sailor, was sentenced by Antonio Sabater Tomás to a maximum penalty of two years of internment (which he also served in the labor camp of Nanclares de la Oca), two years of exile, and two years of parole.[51] He apparently confessed that he used the confiscated photos (which he had bought in the red-light district) to seduce young "inverts."

The distinction between possessing and seeing porn—articulated by Dennis—applies to the logic by which homoerotic materials were prosecuted more harshly than mainstream porn. Defendants accused of homosexuality were in close proximity to the object of representation: they possessed, handled, and curated their photographic and tactile "fetish."[52] In contrast, consumers of mainstream pornography kept their distance from the "fetishism" of sexual representations, which they did not author. The authorities' operational definition of mainstream pornography (implicitly permissible) was not just based on the hetero/homo binary but rather foregrounds political transgression in underground staging techniques that problematize male domination. Analyzing court cases

FIGURE 9. A photograph of a male model taken from the rear. Photograph included in File 800/1965 of the Barcelona Vagrancy Court. Printed with permission by Arxiu Central dels Jutjats de la Ciutat de la Justícia, Hospitalet de Llobregat, Spain.

from València and Barcelona, I highlight the general pattern of judicial leniency toward male peccadillos—namely, small-scale consumption of pornography with a script that does not challenge heteropatriarchy— versus the singling out and persecution of what authorities judged to be subversive pornography.

Mainstream and Transgressive Porn across Borders

Rabies dies with the dog (*Muerto el perro se acaba la rabia*) is a Spanish saying that conveys that the threat of contagion disappears along with the bodies that contain it. This was, in a nutshell, the Francoist authorities' view of mainstream pornography: after being destroyed, it did not leave the marks of deviance in consumers as homoerotic and transgressive materials did. For instance, the Dangerousness Court of València adjudicated 181 cases of homosexuality and 8 cases of pornography during its existence. These statistics, in and of themselves, demonstrate that authorities were disproportionally more focused on curtailing marica culture than on undermining the porn industry. Medical doctor Rafael Borrás Pastor conducted his PhD dissertation research in València in the 1970s, while the court was still operative. Granted access to the court's files for his study, he concluded: "Authorities, given permissiveness in the publication of magazines and the screening of pornographic movies, have considered it absurd to prosecute anyone."[53] Even while the dangerousness jurisdiction was very much in force, it did not take much to realize that, on the ground, the agencies tasked with preventing the pornification of Spanish society recognized the law's absurdity. The court only saw porn-related cases in 1975, the year Franco died, which indicates that the dictator's death symbolically and pragmatically signaled the inexorability of the *destape*. Moreover, Borrás Pastor participated in the reactionary trend that advocated for Spain's moral alignment with the Soviet bloc: "in contrast with socialist countries, western civilization is subjected to the devastating effects of this hypereroticized environment."[54] Not in vain, Borrás Pastor accessed the court files; his argument that Western Europe irradiated sexual excess might have been based on the stories he read.

Denmark pioneered the legalization of obscenity in the late 1960s, and Spanish police records represent the country as the epicenter of the European porn wave. Paradoxically, the same state structure that the Franco regime created to promote the internationalization of the Spanish economy as the primary means to ensure its own survival was porous to the allure of the verboten. In 1975 in Alcoi (pop. 58,977) the Guardia Civil received confidential reports that three individuals were trafficking with imported pornography. One of them was a salesman who represented an Alcoi-based textile company in the Danish market. He admitted to importing "the movies because they are not forbidden in the country of origin, and being aware that here they would be sold to people of high culture and unquestionable morality."[55] His self-defense strategy was not fully misleading; he insisted on the notion, structural to state policies on obscenity, that elite men were able to consume pornography without endangering their own morals and social roles.

At least eighteen men had obtained porn movies from the defendants, in numbers ranging from a single movie to dozens, and totaling more than sixty.[56] Another defendant, a *funcionario* (tenured civil servant) who worked at the tourism and initiatives public office, alleged that he had merely acted as "intermediary for his friends who wanted movies" as a "personal favor" and without obtaining any profit.[57] This defendant went to prison—an exception in the overall paradigm of judicial leniency toward heterosexual porn, which might be related to the subversiveness that judges read in the movies that he distributed.[58] On 5 June 1973, the judge of Alcoi and the court secretary held a "private hearing" to watch two of the confiscated movies and narrativize their content. The judicial transcript is a gem, starting with the description of *Madame Rose*:

> There are two parts in this color movie. In the first part, a Black woman appears performing contortions and violent movements with the intention of sexually arousing herself, which she finally achieves based on her own manipulations of her genitals and breasts; all with close-ups of crude realism. The second part presents a gathering of White and Colored men and women who, after a kind of dance completely naked, perform sexual acts of great violence and in their most degenerate forms, without excluding those carried out by people of the same sex, nor and repeatedly carnal intercourse in various forms. Once these operations are over, the group returns to normality.
>
> *Se aprecia en esta película rodada en color dos partes; En la primera aparece una mujer de color realizando contorsiones y movimientos*

violentos con ánimo de excitarse sexualmente, lo que finalmente
consigue a base de sus propias manipulaciones en sexo y mamas;
todo ello con tomas y primeros planos de crudo realismo. La segunda
parte presenta una reunión de hombres y mujeres blancos y de color
que, tras una especie de baile y completamente desnudos, realizan
actos sexuales de gran violencia y en sus formas más degeneradas, sin
excluirse los realizados por personas del mismo sexo, ni tampoco y
repetidamente la cópula carnal en variadas formas. Terminadas estas
operaciones el grupo vuelve a la normalidad.

The description of Lasse Braun's *Perversion—Cerimony* (1971) follows:

The scene represents a completely naked and crucified young man; a
group of about 5 women dance in front of him, dressed and painted
in strange ways, apparently performing a ritual. Based on exhibitionism and contortions, they excite the crucified man, with whom they
perform violent sexual acts until they exhaust him. The film is shot
in color and, like the previous one, with an abundance of close-ups
of the actors' genital and sexual organs, particularly in the moments
of greatest orgasm, without deleting the most perverse forms and
manners.

La escena representa a un hombre joven completamente desnudo
y crucificado; Ante él baila un grupo de unas 5 mujeres vestidas y
pintadas de extrañas formas, las que danzan al parecer llevando a
cabo un ritual. A base de exhibicionismo y contorsiones excitan al
crucificado, con el que realizan actos sexuales de gran violencia hasta
conseguir dejarlo extenuado. La película aparece rodada en color y al
igual que la anterior con abundancia de primeros planos de los órga-
nos genitales y sexuales de los actores, en particular en los momentos
de mayor orgasmo, sin excluir las formas y maneras más perversas.[59]

Let us imagine the judge and the secretary watching these movies privately, and the kind of erotic and emotional atmosphere that they would
have shared. Did they awkwardly look at each other, trying to assess
whether they were reacting in the same way? Did they find disgust or
arousal in the gaze and body of each other? The ludicrousness of judge
and secretary policing each other's bodies mirrors the law's farcical

pretense in the mechanisms that it created to regulate subjects' libido. It is plausible that the judge, as the higher-ranking official, set the tone of the room, while the secretary would have perhaps tried to mimic his verbal and nonverbal responses to the scenes on screen. The range of the imaginable runs wild: from the judge and the secretary indulging in the shared experience of pornographic consumption (and agreeing on how to obviate this pleasure in the official records); to one of them ashamedly trying to hide his physical excitement in front of the other; to both working together to come up with the right terms to convey their revulsion. Whatever the actual scene, the transcript testifies to the bizarre intimacies that the implementation of the law set in motion, as authorities enjoyed spaces of private consumption of porn to transfigure subversive explicit images into dour condemnatory texts.

The judicial transcript constantly returns to movement as violence; every racialized or ritualized body that contorts in pleasure simultaneously disrupts the artificial "peace" of the established order. The judge's use of the term "violence" unknowingly refers to Georges Bataille's theories on erotism. For Bataille, "the domain of eroticism is the domain of violence, of violation," where he locates "the abrupt wrench out of discontinuity."[60] Bataille's insights on the "violence of desire" account for the Franco regime's use of a punitive framework to enhance citizens' work ethic and bring "antisocial" sexual tendencies under control: "Nature herself is violent, and however reasonable we may grow we may be mastered anew by a violence no longer that of nature but that of a rational being who tries to obey but who succumbs to stirrings within himself."[61] Bataille conceived violence as the (erotic) disruption of the disciplining of bodies required to accommodate the uneventful and alienating flow of a daily life focused on work. Based on this framework, the judge's way of locating violence in the excess of bodies intertwined in dance and orgasm would make sense.

Female onanism, interracial sex, the blasphemy of recasting the Catholic iconography of crucifixion within a storyline in which a group of witches ritually and sexually subjugate manhood; everything is part of the same dance, a satanic choreography in which the gaze's proximity to the body, the visual excess of orgasm, and the dissolution of propriety signal the antithesis of sociopolitical homeostasis. If anyone could acutely trace these movies' potential revulsive effects, it was precisely those who intended to curb them. They might have overvalued porn's

subversive potential, yet it is undeniable that some directors took a political stance through their work. The director of *Perversion—Cerimony* was
the Italian Alberto Ferro (1936–2015, alias Lasse Braun), one of the most
recognized 8mm pornographers, whose biography is hardly distinguishable from the legends he purposefully spread. Braun's father was a dip-
lomat, and Braun allegedly used his own diplomatic passport to smuggle
soft-core magazines from Monaco to Italy.[62] Later in life he directed
narrativized pornography in series of three 8mm films often unified by
a theme or national landscape. In fact, in 1970 (the same year that the
Dangerousness Law was enacted), Lasse Braun was shooting the series
Top Secret in Málaga, exploiting international stereotypes about Spain
(bullfighting, beaches, etc.). This was his signature style, mapping "brief
and condensed narratives" onto "the landscape of sexual imagination."[63]
While the Francoist legislation assumed that all porn was foreign, Braun
was able to shoot in Spain, ridiculing the regime's reactionary policies
and exposing the fiction of unbreachable national/moral borders. In
between the late 1960s and early 1970s, the international distribution
of pornographic 8mm films took place informally, by private mail order
and independent travelers (as in the case from Alcoi, Spain), and Braun
personally assumed the task of bringing negatives of his movies into the
United States. He personifies the maverick or opportunistic transna-
tionalism of a porn industry that was, as media scholar Mariah Larsson
notes, "a vital, creative, and shamelessly commercial activity exploring
the potential of the new explicitness. [. . .] Exploring society's limits of
decorum, this early pornography employed racial and ethnic stereotypes
juxtaposed in blatantly racist but also taboo-breaking and highly political constellations."[64] Arguably one of Braun's most incendiary pieces
was *Perversion—Cerimony* (precisely the one that found its way to Alcoi),
which was contemporaneously censored in Sweden.

That government authorities in Spain and Sweden, who showed completely different attitudes toward obscenity in the early 1970s, concurred
in banning *Perversion—Cerimony* bespeaks the limits of permissiveness
in liberal democracies. In 1973, the Swedish National Board of Film
Censors characterized the film's narrative as "six girls rape a crucified
man" and objected to its public screening "due to being brutalizing."[65]
According to Larsson, "the film's depiction of a man in a helpless position, its associations with witchcraft, black mass, the dungeon-like
setting, exaggerated make-up, and the inclusion of a skeleton could be

considered disturbing. Yet there is very little actual physical violence in the film."[66] The restrained man's penis is flaccid at first but instantly gets erect and becomes a "tool for pleasure" that women use in penetration; he is "obliterated by the women's desire" only insofar as his penis remains within the scope of the camera. Finally, Larsson speculates that, in carrying the anticlerical and blasphemous tradition into avant-garde porn and underground aesthetics, Braun demonstrated his awareness of the contemporary politics of fantasy.[67] This is why in Spain the circulation of Braun's productions by common citizens was met with extraordinary judicial harshness, in contrast with most other scenes of heterosexual sex: Braun's films were self-consciously transgressive and complicated the visual codes of male domination, which law-enforcement agencies implicitly endorsed. Authorities' insistence in avant-garde porn's internationalism maintained the fiction that gender transgression was inherently foreign to Spain.

Likewise, press coverage on the pornography business put the emphasis on the otherness of this phenomenon and the criminal role of foreign-born people. Headlines best illustrate this framing tactic. On 18 November 1969, *El Eco de Canarias* published an article titled "Negocio pornográfico: Un matrimonio iraní, distribuidores de folletos y películas" (Pornographic bussiness: An Iranian married couple distributed brochures and films). According to the note, the Iranian couple and three other foreign-born subjects trafficked porn and drugs that they sold to young people in Madrid clubs. An undercover police officer had approached one of them in a club pretending to be interested in doing business. Through this ruse, they gathered incriminating information: the Iranian couple led the criminal organization; they imported pornography from Denmark, where they lived; they had traveled to Spain in a Mercedes, with a driver who was also implicated in selling porn; they were keeping 250 porn magazines in their accommodations in Madrid when they were arrested; they had already sold porn movies to a musician and 50 magazines to a waiter; the criminal network also included a Jamaican couple; and the latter had organized a screening of "pornographic documentaries" attended by young people of both sexes.[68]

This narrative communicated to the readers that the pornography business was an organized threat by which foreign-born people were able to profit from Spanish youths and maintain a luxurious lifestyle by importing publications that were legal in northern Europe. As I argued in chapter 2, the excessive liberalism of European democracies and the sexuality of racialized Others were two apparently different yet entangled threats in the view of Spanish right-wingers, who understood Spain's ideal position as equidistant from both poles. In 1972, a defendant mobilized this rhetoric of White innocence when he was brought to court for carrying pornographic magazines, marijuana, and a pamphlet titled *Class Struggle* (*Lucha de clases*). He attributed ownership of these materials to an anonymous Black man from Guinea, distancing himself from "social dangers" (porn, socialism, and recreational drugs) by blaming their dissemination on a racialized person.[69] The defendant was exculpated, his case fitting into the pattern of permissiveness toward mainstream porn.

Building on the trope that *vicio* had foreign roots, newspapers throughout Spain represented Barcelona as the hub for the illegal importation of porn. In contrast to the norms for consulting judicial files today, press articles fully disclosed the names of arrested individuals.[70] *La Nueva España*, a newspaper based in Asturias, related in March 1969 that four men had been arrested for screening short pornographic films (15–20 minutes long) for small audiences in two Barcelona bookstores (tickets were very costly, 100–200 pesetas, at a time when the minimum wage was 3,000 pesetas per month). The two bookstores' owners had obtained movies from Denmark and the Netherlands imported by sailors.[71] The fact that bookstores also operated as porn cinema theaters speaks to the long-established connection between literature and obscenity, both in terms of their disturbing effects on a reactionary regime and their shared spaces of clandestine distribution. The Canary Islands—a major trade post between Europe, Africa, and the Americas as well as an international touristic destination—also centered much media attention on illegal porn trafficking. Defendants' testimonies evidence the connection between international commercial routes and the importation of high-value pornography, which sailors brought with them in container ships.[72]

Port cities were connected to the international circuits of porn distribution through individuals whose mobility and anonymity were a byproduct of their role in the logistics and transportation industry. Two files from València's Dangerousness Court revolve around massive amounts of porn introduced in the port of Sagunto through the collaboration between a foreign sailor and a local newsstand owner.

They were exposed by a client, after the Guardia Civil confiscated 49 international 8mm films, 43 magazines, and a projector from him.[73] The client was a thirty-nine-year-old married man with two children who sold household appliances for a living. The judge closed his case.[74] By contrast, the file on the newsstand owner documents the gap between the moral panic that the law theoretically embodied and a pragmatic implementation with specific goals: the judicial apparatus's privacy and economic self-sufficiency, convicts' exposure and erotic and work discipline, and the fantasy of Spain's timeless virtue. The Guardia Civil found 165 magazines and 4 movies at the newsstand, and the owner, a disabled forty-four-year-old widow, confessed that he had sold hundreds of these items, supplied by the unknown sailor. The local police informed that the owner, now defendant, had a "noticeable propensity to eroticism" that was well known to neighbors who had seen how he masturbated in his apartment.[75] The public's gaze was not easily deterred; the continuity between the neighborhood's informal watch and the police's reporting duties communicates the oppressive atmosphere of moral control imposed over those whose sexuality was too conspicuous. On the opposite pole, we find the privacy that judicial authorities maintained for themselves when they watched porn to "examine the evidence," so to speak. On 29 January 1976, Judge Fernando Tintoré and the court's secretary went into an office with a projector and the movies to "explore" them until they were able to determine their pornographic nature.[76] The juxtaposition between the invasive reports about the defendant masturbating in his home and the judge's secretive screening of porn in court returns to the issue of privacy as a privilege that the agents of the authoritarian state retained for themselves.

The ruling, as the most public-facing element of the file, sets the record straight regarding state policies. Judge Tintoré defined porn as "a social scourge that causes the destruction of man due to immorality [. . .] regarding the youth, it incentivizes gross passions and disordered appetites, being an effectual cause of delinquency and psychosis."[77] Whereas the sentence used a hyperbolic language regarding porn's threat to society (destroying manhood, inducing collective psychosis), the penalties were quite pragmatic: twenty-six days in prison, already served during the trial, and a monetary fine, which is the focus of most of the documents in the file. The defendant's car was seized as a guarantor for the fine, and the authorities estimated with excruciating detail the cost of the trial (from internal communication to employees' insurance fees), since these costs fell to the convict.[78] The law set as its symbolic goal the purity of Spain's morals, but the reality of its implementation focused on a series of economic transactions that rendered the repressive apparatus self-sufficient. Files like this one were meant to convey the narrative of authorities taking control and constricting both the international circulation of porn's material culture and citizens' daily experiences, but economic globalization undermined national borders.

The porousness of borders was the result of international corporate activities that did not have a direct relationship to the porn industry. French erotic magazines were imported to València in 1975 to be recycled in a paper factory. An employee smuggled the magazines out of the factory and distributed them through a mechanic's garage. Eventually this ruse was uncovered, and he was arrested and tried. The factory manager testified that he had forbidden employees to "entertain themselves" with the magazines imported from abroad. This prohibition was difficult to enforce since nude photographs would easily get the attention of the employees. The employee accused of smuggling porn used the most common defense strategy in these cases, presenting himself as a curious but otherwise functional and normative citizen. He declared that "he found the magazine and some photographs with some nude pics and jokes in French and out of mere curiosity he cut them [. . .] without exhibiting them to anyone else nor, certainly, selling them. [. . .] He is married with two babies and lives in good harmony with his family" *(se encontró con la revista y unas fotografías de algunos desnudos y chistes en francés y por pura curiosidad las recortó [. . .] sin haberlas exhibido a nadie más ni mucho menos vendido [. . .] está casado y tiene dos nenes y vive en buena armonía con su familia).*[79] The judge filed the case, following the pattern by which the consumption and even trade of pornography by male breadwinners were treated leniently.[80]

Also centered in the region of València, a creative ruse consisted in using the network of a continuing education school to import international porn and distribute it nationwide. In 1971, the police received an anonymous letter that reads: "Dear friend: First, I apologize for not using your first name [. . .] in the Academy we all knew each other by our last names [. . .]. I can offer you all sorts of pornography [. . .] girls in the nude, or getting nude, in hot positions, and having sexual relationships."[81] Apparently, the letter had been sent by Andrés, who was trying to sell porn by using the network of CCC (Centro de Cursos por Correspondencia, or Center for Courses by Correspondence, a large company dedicated to remote continuing education). The police arrested Andrés and searched his apartment in Castellón. Andrés admitted that he had been reaching out to CCC students using their contact information, published in the CCC monthly bulletins. Despite being a private company, CCC referred to clients/students as members of their "learning club" and encouraged "triangular" relationships between them through its publications, as a way of creating a sense of community that fostered both learning goals and the company's loyalty programs. Andrés first came up with the idea of this business when he read an ad published in the CCC magazine by Roberto, a Spanish immigrant living in Leicester, England, who sold magazines and movies. Roberto delivered porn and medication for erectile disfunction to Andrés, who also enlisted a postal service employee affiliated with CCC to distribute the magazines. Among the titles that Andrés sold to CCC members, the police reports mention Holgar Bensons's *100 positions de l'amour,* a book titled *Lesbian caners* (1971), and a magazine called *Sun Health,* which was a recurrent title for naturalist magazines in different countries. Andrés had clients in Catalonia, the Canary Islands, and Castilla la Mancha, among other regions. Yet he pretended to be naive and disconcerted by his own motivation to profit from selling porn: "He does not understand why he dedicated himself to this activity with so much insistence."[82] However, this strategy was counterproductive for Andrés because, as a legal minor himself (he was twenty years old, when the age of majority for males was twenty-one), he also had to respond to leading questions about whether he had been corrupted by his own entrepreneurial activities: "He was not morally affected by the movie. [. . .] He is used to watching or reading things like that, since he has read several legal books about this theme, including *Vida íntima de la mujer* [Women's intimate life], *La vida sexual sana* [Healthy sexual life], etc."[83] Through this statement, Andrés argued that there was a continuum between pedagogical works on the normative aspects of sex and the pornography which he imported and sold insofar as both sorts of materials addressed straight men's natural curiosity. In October 1972, Andrés was sentenced to prison for between six months and a year.[84] Andrés had realized that every list of adult contacts could be used to commercialize porn.

The seamless match between consumers' quasi-universal interest in obscenity and international media markets that surreptitiously

incorporated Spain was the underlying reason why judges' sentences felt
like a perfunctory intervention, a display of the regime's official stance
toward pornification rather than an effective policy to prevent it. Porn
magazines and movies often entered Spain through the region of Catalonia, which shares a mountainous and coastal border with France.
Most of the defendants who were brought to the Barcelona Social Dangerousness Court in the early 1970s under charges of pornography had
acquired it in France—particularly in Perpignan, the closest city to the
border and an icon of sexual freedom for the Spaniards of the late Francoist era—or from international visitors and sailors.[85] Pornography cases
from Catalonia follow similar patterns to those in València: mainstream
pornography was treated leniently, and most of the confiscated materials
were imported from other European countries. At the Junquera border
crossing, one of the main routes between France and Spain, Spanish
police agents meticulously searched cars and found thousands of porn
movies hidden in compartments, under the seats, and even "in lieu of
the radio device."[86] The authorities took note of the provenance of these
movies, documenting the globalization of distribution networks. For example, in a case from 1972, the police confiscated materials produced
in Puerto Rico, Mexico, the United States, the Netherlands, and France.
Police officers later reported that they had not handed these materials
to the court due to an "unintentional mistake," which suggests that they
had tried to keep them.[87] In fact, court authorities focused much of their
efforts on tracing the origins of confiscated pornography and making
sure that it did not get "lost" at some point along the chain of custody,
which indicates that judges were aware that state agents themselves
might desire these materials for personal or private consumption, viewing, or circulation.

The concern for the potential of mainstream pornography to entice
those in charge of policing social dangers was one of the reasons that the
court authorities were so vigilant in destroying it. However, the same
concern was not recorded in cases of homosexuality, because judiciary
acknowledgment that state agents might desire to keep the confiscated
materials would have entailed reckoning with same-sex desires within
the regime's apparatus. In other words, the ineffability of officers' same-
sex desires meant that provenance was taken for granted in the process
of unintentionally building a homoerotic archive. Treating queer visual
culture as evidence worthy of preservation (rather than as natural

detritus to be destroyed or lost, as with mainstream pornography), the judicial system inverted the underlying hierarchies of traditional archival paradigms: the abject and degraded became worth memorializing (shaping memory and identity in the process), and the privileges of male power materialized through destruction and neglect.[88]

Moreover, court authorities developed the criteria that confiscated materials were to be incinerated when they had been exhibited in an obscene way, no matter their artistic value. This was the case when the police confiscated personal materials from an elderly defendant who used to organize slide presentations at his house. The defendant first came to the police to report that two men had assaulted him at his home. Pretending to be secret police, they stole the valuables that he kept in a safe, drove him to the outskirts of town, and threatened to shoot him. Further investigation into the two assailants' motivations revealed that they knew that the defendant was fond of projecting erotic images and films for men and women whom he had invited to spend the night at his house. The defendant explained to the authorities that he occasionally hosted young people in need of lodging and entertained them as a "humanitarian act." Among other movies, he projected the "short documentary" *Mademoiselle Striptease*, a 1957 French comedy directed by Pierre Foucaud. Set in Parisian cabarets, the film features a striptease by Dora Doll.[89] Pathé produced an adult version of *Mademoiselle Striptease,* which includes scenes of nude women and lasts around twelve minutes. This was, most likely, the version that the defendant screened, calling it a short documentary to make it sound inoffensive. He also screened *Rendez-vous avec Paris* (translated in Spanish as *Cita con Paris*), another adult short film produced by Pathé. The defendant declared that he did not have any information on the man who had sold and personally delivered these and other films to his home every three months.

While the movies were treated as pornography in mid-1970s Spain, in France they had already become a historical artifact. Despite the increasing globalization of pornography, there were asynchronies in consumer taste that reflected the policies put in place by the Franco regime to insulate Spain from sexual liberalization. For media historian Eric Schaefer, "voyeurism from a privileged vantage point" was one of the modes that defined "the French films" (films produced in France as well as American movies set in France), which dominated international porn markets in the 1950s: "The observational mode was rooted in a touristic gaze

[. . .] the authentically erotic in France is generally found in performative acts, which are watched by a character within the film but at a step removed by the audience viewing."[90] The other mode was retrospective; these movies reified France as an emblem of toleration for men's erotic "adventures," which reinforced gender hierarchies and the association between sex and shame. The "observational/retrospective" mode served as commentary for the social milieu of the audience at the defendant's showings; sexual shame, traditional gender roles, and male prerogatives were codified by the Spanish law, and sexual liberation was something witnessed from afar. Hence, the old French movies remained relevant. Media scholar Lisa Gitelman argues that media outlets complicated the conceptual mapping of the distinction between art and science: "Like old art, old media remain meaningful. [. . .] Yet like old science, old media also seem unacceptably unreal. Neither silent film nor black-and-white television seems right anymore, except as a throwback. Like acoustic (nonelectronic) analog recordings, they just don't do the job."[91] Extrapolated to porn as media, this analysis captures the qualities of decades-old movies, which are recognizable in their function yet lose their power to sway the viewers' imagination when the latter no longer experience voyeurism as fantasy. For consumers who had first-person knowledge of the Sexual Revolution, the 1950s French movies became antiquarian objects because national disciplinary structures and the fantasy of voyeurism no longer aligned. Since the 1960s, U.S. Americans did not perceive France as the capital of naughty sex; Scandinavian countries came to occupy that role. French filmic plots about watching or voyeurism had become unappealing, as audiences demanded the full participation of the characters.[92] The French films, as media capturing the sexual frontiers of the 1950s, worked in 1970s Spain because watching sex was still a target of authoritarian scrutiny and framed as antisocial behavior. In other words, the lifespan of media has multiple temporalities related to national governments' representational policies.

Similarly, the Franco regime's policies contributed indirectly to eroticizing classical art. On the one hand, since the emergence of "democratized spaces for viewing art" in the nineteenth century, nudity was displayed in accordance with the values of public civility and norms regulating physical distance and touch. Private collectors, on the other hand, could consume artistic renderings of nudity as closely and physically as they desired. The differentiation between regulated distance (sight) and haptic pleasures (touch) informs the distinction between pornography and erotica.[93] When citizens in Francoist Spain created spaces for the clandestine consumption of classical depictions of nudity—in response to moral policing and censorship—they reverted the democratization of access in public museums, which had been the core development leading to a reconsideration of those pieces' erotic intentionality. One of the slides the defendant owned was a reproduction of Titian's canonical *Venus of Urbino*, which for centuries was read as obscene. Mark Twain considered it "the obscenest picture the world possesses" because he inferred that Venus was masturbating instead of showing modesty in concealing her pubis.[94] Sixteenth-century commentators also described Titian's *Venus* as lascivious. For art historian Kelly Dennis, what made this painting so disruptive was that Venus was "clearly and coyly aware of the viewer's gaze" and expressed a sexual demand as she touched herself. Titian's "fleshly eroticism" invited viewers to experience his paintings sensorially and tactically through color and sculptural qualities.[95] In a museum, the *Venus of Urbino* seemed inoffensive, but when displayed privately to an audience of young men and women who sat

FIGURE 10. Titian's *Venus of Urbino*. The painting is in the Uffizi Gallery, Florence, Italy.

COLECCION DE DIAPOSITIVAS DE "CUADROS DE ARTE" FAMOSOS

NOMBRE DEL CUADRO	CLASE o AUTOR	MUSEO o GALERIA	LOCALIDAD
Venus de Badalona	Escultura	Arqueológico	Barcelona
Venus de Medicis	Escultura	Galeria Oficios	Florencia
Tapiz de la Creación	Tapiz	Catedral	Gerona
Tapiz de la Creación	Tapiz	Catedral	Gerona
Tapiz de la Creación	Tapiz	Catedral	Gerona
Nacimiento de Venus	Pintura Mural	Sala Arte Tivoli	Roma
Virgen de Canapost	Retablo	Museo Diocesano	Gerona
Adan y Eva	Pintura Mural	Basilica Carmen	Florencia
Pecado Original	Pintura Mural	Basilica Carmen	Florencia
Adan y Eva	Retablo Mural	Museo Episcopal	Vich
Nacimiento de Venus	Botticheli	Galeria Oficios	Florencia
Nacimiento de Venus	Botticheli	Galeria Oficios	Florencia
Alegoria Primavera	Botticheli	Galeria Oficios	Florencia
Alegoria Primavera	Botticheli	Galeria Oficios	Florencia
Venus y Marte	Botticheli	Galeria Nacional	Londres
La Calumnia	Botticheli	Galeria Oficios	Florencia
Jardín de las Delicias	El Bosco	Museo del Prado	Madrid
Jardín de las Delicias	El Bosco	Museo del Prado	Madrid
Jardín de las Delicias	El Bosco	Museo del Prado	Madrid
Jardín de las Delicias	El Bosco	Museo del Prado	Madrid
Jardín de las Delicias	El Bosco	Museo del Prado	Madrid
Jardín de las Delicias	El Bosco	Museo del Prado	Madrid
Jardín de las Delicias	El Bosco	Museo del Prado	Madrid
Jardín de las Delicias	El Bosco	Museo del Prado	Madrid
Jardín de las Delicias	El Bosco	Museo del Prado	Madrid
Jardín de las Delicias	El Bosco	Museo del Prado	Madrid
Figura	Miguel Angel	Capilla Sixtina	Vaticano
Creación	Miguel Angel	Capilla Sixtina	Vaticano
detalle	Miguel Angel	Capilla Sixtina	Vaticano
de Eva	Miguel Angel	Capilla Sixtina	Vaticano
Pecado Original	Miguel Angel	Capilla Sixtina	Vaticano
Figura	Miguel Angel	Capilla Sixtina	Vaticano
Juicio Final	Miguel Angel	Capilla Sixtina	Vaticano
detalle	Miguel Angel	Capilla Sixtina	Vaticano
Eva	A. Durero	Galeria Oficios	Florencia
Eva	A. Durero	Museo del Prado	Madrid
Castidad de Susana	Pagani	Galeria Oficios	Florencia
Lucrecia	L. Cranac	Galeria Dahlem	Berlín
Adan	L. Cranac	Galeria Oficios	Florencia
Venus y Cupido	L. Cranac	Galeria Borghese	Roma
Eva	L. Cranac	Galeria Oficios	Florencia
Eva	L. Cranac	Galeria Oficios	Florencia
La Muerte y la Doncella	Waldung	Desconocido	Alemania?
Leda y el Cisne	Pontormo	Galeria Oficios	Florencia
Danae	Correggio	Galeria Borghese	Roma
Flora	Tizziano	Galeria Oficios	Florencia
Santa Magdalena	Tizziano	Galeria Pitti	Florencia
Amor Sagrado y Profano	Tizziano	Galeria Borghese	Roma
Venus del Pardo	Tizziano	Museo del Louvre	París
Danae	Tizziano	Museo del Prado	Madrid
Danae	Tizziano	Museo del Prado	Madrid
Venus	Tizziano	Galeria Oficios	Florencia
El Pecado Original	Tizziano	Museo del Prado	Madrid
Una Baccante	Caracci	Galeria Oficios	Florencia
Muerte de Adonis	Del Piombo	Galeria Oficios	Florencia
Lacconte	Greco	Galeria Nacional	Washington
Baño de Diana	Boucher	Museo del Louvre	París
Joven Veneciana	Tintoretto	Museo del Prado	Madrid
Judit y Holofernes	Tintoretto	Museo del Prado	Madrid

sigue ...

FIGURE 11. "Colección de diapositivas de 'cuadros de arte' famosos" (collection of slides of famous art paintings). List of confiscated slides included in File 385/1975 of the Juzgado de Peligrosidad y Rehabilitación Social de Barcelona. Printed with permission by Arxiu Central dels Jutjats de la Ciutat de la Justícia, Hospitalet de Llobregat, Spain.

in close proximity to each other in the dark, it might have been as tit-illating as it was in the sixteenth century.[96] Shifts in viewing contexts conditioned the sexual charge (and consequent judicial condemnation) of image reception and interpretation, rendering fine art pornographic and an object of censorship.

Still, the defendant resisted the notion that Tintoretto's *Judith and Holofernes*, Velázquez's *La Venus del Espejo,* or Rubens's *The Three Graces* could be classified as obscenity to be incinerated. According to the judicial transcript: "He wants to say for the record that–in his humble opinion–objects such as the different slides of artworks [confiscated from him] absolutely do not undermine the principles of morality and good customs, so there should be no legal obstacle to them being returned to their owner."[97] Slides contributed to impose the conventions of positiv-ism in art history, representing artworks as facts.[98] This is the tradition that the elderly citizen mobilized in his defense, collapsing the distinc-tion between art and slide to elevate the latter to the status of canonical object. The judge ruled in response: "The slides are not pornographic material by themselves, but they have been used, by exhibiting them to minors and jointly with the movies, as elements that entice acts that by themselves corrupt good customs. Thus, I rule that they must also be con-fiscated and destroyed."[99] The defendant was declared a threat to society and sentenced to jail time, but his daughter-in-law reported that he died before serving his full sentence. The main reason that this defendant was condemned was that he exhibited what was framed by the judiciary as obscenity (art history slides and antiquated French soft-core) to an audience of "vulnerable" young men and women.

By contrast, male defendants who purchased mainstream porn for their own consumption were able to appeal to the authorities' sympathy for masculine yet naive men. "Playing naive" was probably the advice that many defense lawyers gave to their clients when the latter had been arrested carrying hard-core movies purchased in France. This would explain why curiosity, playfulness, and humor were among the most common terms used by these defendants to excuse their actions. In 1974 in Barcelona, one defendant explained to the judge that, in Perpignan, hard-core was showcased everywhere. He and his friends had bought some of these movies out of curiosity, to watch them together in private as a "joke," a "silly act that nonetheless has caused a true family trauma for both the defendant and his parents."[100] This defendant attributed his acts to sexual naivete that rendered him vulnerable to the normalization of porn in France. According to this defense strategy, Spaniards, as a viewing audience, were unprepared to confront porn precisely because the regime had kept them oblivious (within Spain's borders) to the most perverse manifestations of global consumer culture. This argument worked by appealing to the authorities' unstated sympathy for naive masculine men; both the prosecution and the judge agreed that the case could be filed with no further action taken.[101]

The defendant's performance of naiveté evokes the contemporary filmic trope of the rural and working-class macho, which reflected the imbrication between developmentalist policies and the reification of moral exceptionalism. The stereotypical narrative of Spanish films produced in the late Francoist period centered on an Iberian macho, sexually naive and overly excitable, seducing attractive blond women from Northern Europe.[102] These films exposed the government's flexible application of morality legislation when it came to international visitors.[103] Women's liberation was portrayed as a foreign phenomenon, whereas Spanish machos, no matter their comical naivete, still demonstrated their masculinity through aggressive sexual urges. By the same token, insofar as defendants attributed their pornography consumption to an innocent yet masculine curiosity, as Spaniards' common reaction to foreign mores, their performance could strike a chord with judicial authorities.

Similarly, in 1975, another defendant claimed that he had bought pornographic movies just for curiosity, as a joke, and hadn't even been able to watch them before he was arrested while carrying them.[104] The defense lawyer, aware of the law's intricacies, highlighted that trafficking with pornography was codified as a threat to society, but its consumption was not, no matter the ethics of this taste. The lawyer was challenging the court to acknowledge that, in the last instance, eroticism (sexual satisfaction and taste) belonged to private ethics and thereby did not fall under the court's purview—an argument that did not appeal to the judge. The lawyer went on to suggest that if every Spaniard who went to France on the weekends to consume erotic materials was to be classified as a threat, the Spanish prison system would be well beyond its capacity. The law was not aimed at moralizing the individual, he continued, and public morality was certainly not at risk just because a group of (implicitly straight) male friends occasionally gathered to watch some titillating movies.[105] It was one thing to argue that a defendant had naively acquired porn in a way that demonstrated Spaniards' unpreparedness to confront this foreign phenomenon and a much different thing to argue—as this lawyer did—that citizens were entitled to privacy in matters of ethics and sexuality. The defendant was declared a threat to society.[106] In my reading, the courtrooms' *mise-en-scène* was meant to dramatize moral exceptionalism. When the lawyer shifted the focus to individual citizen rights he deviated from the script, while the defendant stayed in his role of subject of the law, performing arrested (sexual) development as a national condition.

Conclusion

In this chapter, I have traced in judicial records the regime's differing interpretations of innocence and guilt (or *vicio*) based on how agents of the court (forensic experts, judges, and police officers) read defendants' performance of masculinity and sexuality to align with dominant codes of "proper" masculinity and (hetero)sexuality more broadly. Ideas and claims about global consumerism, tourism, liberal democracy, and Spain's role in relation to other European countries (France, Scandinavia, and the United States above all) circulated between courtrooms and media transforming subjects' erotic intimacy into a matter of national identity based on Catholic exceptionalism. I argue that the authorities' overall policy of leniency toward "straight" consumers of mainstream porn betrayed their unspoken belief that the effects of the global sexual/ media revolution overpowered their own capacities for surveillance. However, they dramatized Spain's moral exceptionalism through their perfunctory implementation of the law and singled out transgressive porn (blasphemous, centering women's sexual agency, or critical of reactionary sectors) and homoeroticism as targets of selective punishments. The authorities screened explicit movies and preserved homoerotic photographs and personal letters to degrade defendants. Paradoxically, state agents were the voyeurs—contemporaneously denounced as such by some defendants and lawyers—fixated with creating a visual and textual archive of transgressions that became such through the very visibility mandated by the state in courtrooms, clinical examination rooms, and police stations. These roles and scripts made up the theatrical production of public scandal that threads together every story in this book: the self-appointed guardians of morality staging a spectacle of obscenity,

occupying simultaneously the roles of directors and audience, in order
to increase the culpability of the transgressors.

I analyze defendants' performance in court based on written records
of their verbal statements and emphasize the tensions between this
textual archive and the visual codes of their confiscated photographs,
moving between different senses to problematize the relation between
the scripts of repentance and homoerotic aesthetics in scenarios that
precede and exist independent of criminal prosecution. Prior to being
confiscated, erotica, porn, and photographs played a central role in
defendants' intimate practices. Visual and material culture was a core
component of social networks built on homoerotic sex and aesthetics.
In archiving these materials as judicial evidence, authorities kept them
away from the touch of those who cared for or desired the models. Court
files become discontinuous fragments of erotic cultures, as the next
chapter shows, centering trans women's experiences with photography
prior to and during their trials.

FIVE

Running Mascara

TRANS VISUAL ARCHIVES IN THE 1970S

In 1972, the Madrid police department took two photographs of Daniela. In the first one, she is wearing a long black wig, but in the second one the police has forced her to remove it, revealing her short-cropped blond hair. She wears a dark jacket, and her eyes are set among long eyelashes. Her mascara is smudged. Even though she is at the mercy of the police, she stares out and closes her mouth tightly.[1] As a trans woman, Daniela had to confront police violence daily, but she persisted in expressing her gender self-determination through her body and aesthetics. This chapter traces the capturing and preservation of visual archives of trans subjectivity in the late Franco era in Spain and the early period of democratic transition, arguing that the definition of photographs as "material performances" leads us to reconsider recent debates about "the ethics of turning away" from police and forensic documents on trans experiences. Scholars such as Emmet H. Drager, Zeb Tortorici, and I have called attention to certain historical actors' stated refusal to be observed and classified by the clinical gaze of inquisition, police, and medical authorities. In these cases, silence, absence, and omission ought to be incorporated into historical writing *not* as impediments to be overcome but rather as fundamental strategies for forming and maintaining an autonomous self in the face of authorities' denial of one's very existence.[2] This perspective undoubtedly applies to the judicial cases against trans women arrested and prosecuted in Spain in the 1970s on account of their gender being legally classified as a "danger to society."

However, while the plethora of legal transcripts of depositions, forensic exams, and affidavits was clearly produced and archived against the will of these defendants, the personal photographs confiscated from them call for a slightly different approach. This chapter focuses on the stories of Daniela, Carla, Romina, and Tania. The first three are pseudonyms for defendants charged with "homosexuality" at the Dangerousness Courts, while Tania Navarro Amo is the real name of the author of the memoir *La infancia de una transexual en la dictadura* (The childhood of a transgender woman living under a dictatorship), with whom I have been collaborating to locate and access archival documents that reflect her experiences with state violence. The personal experiences of these four women showcase the centrality of photographic performances and visual culture for trans communities living under the Franco regime.

In the first section, I will thread together recent scholarship addressing the inseparability of visibility from trans materiality with a discussion on the historical particularities of the inscription of transphobic state violence in Spanish archives. In the second section, I relate the experiences of Daniela, who tried to marry her fiancé in 1968 by adopting her sister's legal identity. The transcripts of her arrests indicate state agents' uncertainties about Daniela's gender and the strategies she used to protect her intimacy. During her second arrest in 1972, the visual aspects of Daniela's femininity were described and recorded by police officers who fixated on women's sexual emancipation. Following this trend, in the third section I look at the personal photographs confiscated from Carla, which were produced by a group of trans women who enjoyed posing in quiet settings and taking snapshots. Carla's story illustrates the disproportionate targeting of working-class trans women by police officers as well as the centrality of the *paseo* (stroll) in Spanish trans women's quotidian practices of visibility. In 1975, Carla was arrested along with her friend Romina on one of their strolls. Romina's file demonstrates the state's investment in curating trans visual culture; state agents photocopied her personal images and love poems to create montages with an implicit narrative that preserved the visual and textual semantics of intimacy from the original, confiscated materials. The last section delves into Tania's files—her photographs, memoirs, and testimony—which together demonstrate the substantive gap between official reports on trans women and the latter's relationality, self-narration, and eroticism.

Visibility and Ethics in Trans Scholarship

In Spain, most of the relevant sources for tracing trans genealogies were produced in contexts of control and coercion.[3] In response, Lucas Platero has produced imaginative work that engages with the judicial file of a person (we can use the initials M.E.) arrested in Barcelona in the late 1960s for using male clothes while being officially classified as female.[4] By writing in the first person about his investment in this story, Platero helps the reader imagine the quotidian life of M.E. in a way that subverts the logic of the extraordinary case.[5] Norma Mejía, in her ethnographic work on transgenderism and sex work in Barcelona, which is written from a first-person perspective, highlights that the "first generation" of transgender people to become visible in Spain expected that the democratic system installed at the end of the 1970s would protect them but were instead confronted with "marginalization, mockery, humiliations, and discrimination."[6] Mejía's work tempers any romanticization of trans experiences, as she cautions that transgender people's performance of joy should not detract attention from their extremely low life expectancy and argues that solidarity among trans people is "almost non-existent."[7] Finally, Rafael Mérida Jiménez describes trans women's experiences as commonly shaped by "an early self-recognition, rejection and fleeing, prostitution, hormones, drug-addiction, surgery, police raids, illness, money, joy and loneliness."[8] These factors produced a shorter-than-average life expectancy in the trans community that had particularly negative effects on the preservation of their historical memory. In addition, the decentralized network of public archives lags behind in the identification, acquisition, and cataloguing of archival materials produced by trans people. The fate of the personal belongings of the well-known performer Carmen de Mairena, found in a dumpster after her death, illustrates the consequences of this form of institutional neglect.[9]

In connection with the issue of historical preservation, the politics and ethics of visibility center much recent work by trans scholars and activists. Tatiana Sentamans argues that the ranges of the visible and the livable expand hand in hand and that "visibility means existence."[10] Cyle

Metzger and Kirstin Ringelberg define the visible not only in terms of "that which can be observed by the eye" but also as a "metaphorical tool" that points to "the inseparability of visibility from materiality in transgender existence."[11] This inseparability produces a relationship with visibility as a sort of double-edged sword. Invisibility blurs the past and makes the future impossible, while hypervisibility relates to the trope of monstrosity.[12] Subjects' agency in their own representation is key to resist the extractivist and instrumentalizing approaches to the "artwork and experiences of marginalized peoples."[13] This attention to agency becomes, if anything, more pressing when dealing with photography, which was historically constructed "as a privileged medium for situating the truth of deviance."[14] Hence, I am here interested in the agency of self-representation through photography.

Most of the images analyzed in this chapter were taken with the consent of and/or by trans women whose representational strategies centered joy, sisterhood, and intimacy as tenets of a livable life.[15] These photographs were—following Elizabeth Edwards—material performances animated by actors' desire to leave their trace in history, aware as they were of photographs' potential as objects that open a space for the exploration of subjectivity.[16] Similarly, in her study of identification photos of Black diasporic subjects, Tina Campt invites us to listen to images that register "state management" and engage with them "as conduits of an unlikely interplay between the vernacular and the state."[17] The resulting method "reckons with the fissures, gaps, and interstices that emerge when we refuse to accept the 'truth' of images and archives the state seeks to proffer through its production of subjects."[18] In this line, here I listen to vernacular photos to unravel the tension between the representational strategies encrypted at their production and the state curatorial practices. In these photographs, the models appear posing, hugging each other, smiling, exhibiting their legs, swimming, and sunbathing. As Campt points out, it is possible to recalibrate "vernacular photographs as quiet, quotidian practices that give us access to the affective registers through which these images enunciate alternate accounts of their subjects."[19] Originally, there was no obvious trace in these images of the intricate web of pathologizing and criminalizing mechanisms implemented by the Franco regime to ostracize trans people and prevent them from living their lives. Instead, these images provide a glimpse at the imagination and production of sheltered spaces, where trans women could enjoy and be oblivious of the condemning gaze of the state, at least for a brief instant. Thus, I propose that visual materials created by trans women, even when archived as part of their prosecution, provide a means to reach beyond a forensic analysis and toward trans women's reading of their own self.[20]

At the same time, archival violence cannot be erased from the present. The Law for the Protection of Personal Data (Ley Orgánica de Protección de Datos de Carácter Personal), enacted by the Spanish government in 1999, contemplates the data from these judicial records as particularly "susceptible of affecting the security, honor, intimacy and image of people."[21] This clause does *not* refer to judicial records in general, just to those from the Francoist Vagrancy and Dangerousness Courts in charge of policing "antisocial" types such as the prostitute, the drug addict, the "homosexual," the vagrant, and the mentally disabled. In other words, the premise in the 1999 Privacy Law is that the data about people who were typified as a danger to society requires exceptional protection. Arguably, some of the people convicted as "homosexuals" agree with this premise. The possibility of erasing the traces of the state persecution of sexual "minorities" remains controversial, as these traces also provide the documentary ground for keeping the state accountable for its historic crimes and building the collective memory of non-normative sexual communities.[22]

In this context, the 1999 Law aims at striking a delicate balance between public access and the right to privacy, mandating that "pertinent technical procedures" must be applied to "suppress" any personal data from the documentation if there are requests to access it.[23] The legal term "technical procedure" by itself is indicative of the kind of detached, clinical treatment of queer and trans subjects that scholar María Elena Martínez is so critical of; the implication is that archivists and historians can perform a kind of localized surgery on the visual traces of trans communities that extirpates the potential breach of privacy while preserving as much as possible the integrity of the living document.[24]

The law is intentionally vague in stipulating *how* to suppress personal data, producing significant variation in archives' interpretation of this clause. In terms of the reproduction of photographs from the files, the agreement that I initially reached with the archive of Barcelona was to follow a long-established convention of anonymization, by covering subjects' faces with a black bar.[25] However, as T. Benjamin Singer points out, this convention perpetuates problematic, if not overtly violent, visual representations of trans subjecthood:

> [A]t first glance the bar would seem to indicate respect for the privacy of the person pictured. However, even as it ensures anonymity, it also creates the effect of scientific objectivity through de-sexualizing, de-familiarizing, and ultimately depersonalizing the represented figure. This visual strategy makes clear that these are medical photographs, rather than pornography, or snapshots for a family album.[26]

In the case at hand, to follow the law, I would be adding a black bar on photographs that were, in their origin, ordinary snapshots or charged with erotic and familiar meanings. In fact, their visual language included the elements that Singer and others identify as the opposite of the silence and passivity produced by medical representations: the subject looking directly at the camera, returning the gaze and resisting objectification; the snapshot amateur qualities that capture a "fleeting moment"; and social settings with people in the background, demonstrating subjects' participation in public spaces and social networks and their own very existence in contexts other than the "the clinic or the prison."[27] Singer emphasizes that photographs have "a profoundly ethical dimension" insofar as their visual language communicates how to relate to another person and properly regard their claims for recognition.[28] The sole image I reproduce in this chapter is a photocopy of multiple photographs, traces of daily encounters in public spaces where trans women exhibited their physicality. Yet part of my argument is that—even without the photographs themselves—trans women's statements and the texts produced to denounce them orient the archive toward the potent visibility of their bodies and affects.

Daniela: Intimacy and Aesthetics

The cover of Daniela's file announces it as a case of "HOMOSEXU-ALIDAD (TRAVESTISTA)," a typology through which the authorities implied that she presented a variation of homosexuality characterized by cross-dressing.[29] At the time of her first arrest, she was traveling to Spain in order to get married to her French fiancé.[30] They stayed in a boarding house in Aranjuez until someone reported them to the Guardia

Civil on account of her appearance. The visual evidence from this first arrest includes an ID photo of the fiancé, who was quite attractive, and a transcript of Daniela describing her own appearance. While this transcript is not visual evidence *per se*, it was meant to play the role of photographic evidence by painting and invoking an image of her before she was arrested: "When she was fourteen, she felt that she had the sensibility of a woman, even though she had male genitalia, but smaller than average and never having an erection. Her voice, her body shape from the wrist up, and her breasts were characteristic of a woman, and she used female underwear, both bra and panties" *(A los catorce años sintió que su sensibilidad era la de una mujer, a pesar de tener sus órganos genitales masculinos, si bien más pequeños que los normales, sin que se haya erreccionado nunca; que la voz, la forma del cuerpo de cintura para arriba y los senos, eran los característicos de una mujer, usando las ropas interiores de la misma, tanto de sujetador como de bragas).*[31]

The authorities transcribed depositions by defendants using the grammatical third person, which produces a slippage between the male and female genders in the document. In Spanish, nouns and adjectives are gendered, and nouns are often implicit in the verb. The person typing the transcript used male nouns for Daniela. However, she inscribed her gender in official records by using female adjectives for herself ("documentada," "enferma").[32] Similarly, she was registered as living in a town in France, on a street she reported as being named "Desire." When she was arrested again months later, she reported her address in France to be on a street named "Enjoy"—in English in the original—suggesting that she might have been providing the authorities with an imaginary and erotized street map and mocking their lack of language skills.

On a couple of occasions, the person transcribing Daniela's deposition "corrected" her grammatical gender by crossing out "la dicente" (deponent, female noun) and writing "el dicente" (male noun) over it. Thus, judicial records capture both authorities' visual and linguistic strategies to erase trans subjectivities and, more important, the underlying presence of trans people's use of grammatical genders as it was originally transcribed.[33] Likewise, forensic doctors saw their own role as the "uncovering" of defendants' biological sex based on their observation and visual description of the defendants' secondary sex characteristics. The forensic report on Daniela reads: "This is a man of normal constitution,

with perfectly shaped male genitalia, although his voice is slightly effeminate. Examining the thorax, we find a purely masculine thorax, without
hair and with pigmented mammary areolas and protruding nipples. No
gynecomastia—i.e., protruding breasts—has been observed" *(Se trata de
un varón de constitución normal, con un aparato genital masculino per-
fectamente conformado, si bien la voz es ligeramente afeminada. Exam-
inado el tórax, nos encontramos con un tórax netamente masculino, sin
vello y las areolas mamarias pigmentadas y pezones salientes. No observa
ginecomastia, es decir abultamiento de las mamas).*[34]

Forensic violence was exerted by means of reports that intended to
deprive subjects of their right to give meaning and represent their own
bodies. Obviously, there were drastic discrepancies in the way in which
the defendant and the forensic doctor described the former's body. The
issue for historians regarding these discrepancies is not to resolve them;
there are no photographs of Daniela's full body in the file and—even if
there were—examining them would only perpetuate the kind of forensic violence facilitated by the Francoist authorities. In other words, the
absence of visual evidence in this context means that different actors'
visual descriptions of trans physicality remain contested. Hence, and
given that bodily semantics are culturally constructed and subjective to
a certain extent,[35] we can foreground Daniela's self-representation; her
reported erotic experiences (i.e., her stated lack of "erection") and relationship with her body through intimate aesthetics ("bra and panties")
constructed a physicality described by her fiancé and others as feminine.

In his ruling, the judge established that Daniela was a danger to society: "he feigned to be a woman, using his sister's birth certificate for that
purpose, married with [her partner], with whom he had an intimate life
of the homosexual kind" *(Aparentando ser mujer, a cuyo efecto usaba la
partida de nacimiento de una hermana suya y que estaba casado con [su
pareja], con el que hacía vida íntima de tipo homosexual).*[36] According
to the sentence, Daniela was to spend from six months to three years
in prison, one year of exile from Madrid, and three years of probation.
After serving her time in prison in Segovia, she was arrested on probation while in the Basque Country for dressing like a woman. The records produced at this time include a photograph of a middle-aged man,
likely arrested for being with the defendant.[37] The subsequent arrest
records, from 1972, showcase the effects of the application of the "security measures" of prison, exile, and probation on defendants' personal

and professional options. At the time of her first arrest in 1968, Daniela worked at a factory and was planning to get married with her fiancé; by 1972 she was a sex worker in Madrid.[38] This is the moment when the booking photographs analyzed in this article's first lines were taken. The lines of running mascara on her face, her moving stare, and her disheveled wig are visual testimonies to the effects of state persecution. Using the pretext of a law supposedly aimed at protecting national mores and the ruse of "rehabilitation," the authorities prevented the targeted subjects from living their lives—imprisoning, exiling, and surveilling them and forcing them into social ostracism—so that they would conform to the image of them that the law was intended to create.

However, I suggest that the 1972 photographs also show that authorities were not able to subjugate the people they arrested as much as they wanted. To me, Daniela's expression captures a feeling that there is nothing left to lose as well as her disdain and defiance of the police officers. In a similar vein, Jun Zubillaga-Pow describes how Singaporean trans women "put on a fierce facade to stare back" using "facial position and expression" to "convey a specific message, one that could be read as either arrogance or resignation."[39] I would situate Daniela's photo at that point when resignation meets and becomes arrogance. Her facial expression is testimony to her resolve to carry on with her life regardless of her constant arrests. Amidst the pain conveyed by the running mascara on her face, she looks directly at the police photographer, her eyelashes framing her stare. Her tensely pursed mouth tells the cameraman that she is immunized by years of continuous police abuse. Campt argues that quiet photographs like this one generate levels of intensity at the lower frequency of infrasound, which touches us even though it is not audible.[40] Even though her mouth is sealed, we can perceive and feel Daniela's refusal to be fixed by the lenses of the state.

Still, relentless police harassment took a physical toll on her. As Nancy Scheper-Hugues might put it, violence became a daily lived experience for Daniela and shaped her "body-self."[41] Even though she was in her late twenties or early thirties in 1974, police officers described her as an "elderly miss" who was arrested while entering a boarding house with a young man.[42] During this last recorded arrest, police officers repeated the mortifying operation of taking her wig off and paid close attention to her looks, which they described as those of a "modern girl" (niña moderna): "She exhibited a small pair of panties and stockings of the kind vulgarly called *pololos* or leotards. Her face and eyes were adorned with feminine makeup and she wore black suede boots of the kind that reaches up to the knee, with a short skirt showing off her thighs and with her breasts accentuated with a woman's bra" *(exhibió una pequeña braga con medias de las vulgarmente llamadas pololos o leotardos. Que así mismo se hace constar que su cara la llevaba pintada con masajes y sus ojos adornados con maquillajes propios de mujer y calzada con botas negras de "ante" de las que llegan hasta la rodilla, con falda corta exhibiendo sus muslos y sus pechos apoyados con un sostén propio de mujer).*[43] Whoever wrote this report was well versed in the latest women's fashions and used a very specific vocabulary for Daniela's clothing and fabrics. As the editors of *Trap Door* point out, "fashion and imagery hold power, which is precisely why the state seeks to regulate and constrain such self-representations to this very day."[44] By fixating on the defendant's miniskirt as a core element of the "modern girl" phenomenon, the officer participated in the authorities' contemporary concerns about women's self-eroticization. In their annual reports, local district attorneys, for instance, advanced the hypothesis that there was a correlation among tourism, transactional sex, and modern fashion.[45] In view of these reports, police officers' vigilant observation and description of feminine aesthetics might respond to authorities' directives. The officers' zeal led them to violate the intimacy of people like Daniela by observing and describing her taste in underwear.

Throughout her judicial file, Daniela's intimate life was as much recorded as shaped by Francoist policies. The file not only captures her emotional investments, erotic life, and aesthetics but also the ways in which the production of the file itself is imbricated in these intimate aspects of her life. In other words, the file indirectly suggests the potentialities of her physicality and her plans to get married by adopting her sister's identity but also the ways in which these potentialities were curtailed by police arrests, forensic reports, and prison sentences. In brief, the file does not passively record her life trajectory; it actively shapes it by violent acts of intrusion that led her to an outcome—a recurrent cycle of imprisonments, release, sex work, and subsequent arrest, reinitiating the cycle—that the file's inception had to some extent predetermined for her. Yet Daniela's agency and way of expressing herself also resurface in the archival materials. She keeps a firm expression while posing for her identification photographs and refuses to adopt the physicality and gender that authorities and forensic doctors ascribe to her. What is more, that she borrowed her sister's legal identity points to the centrality of sisterhood as a strategy of survival that unsettled the state's taxonomic division between kinship and sexual "dangers," as the next section explores in more detail.

Carla and Romina: Posing and Togetherness

Photographs and intimate materials that were produced by trans women before their arrest provide a window onto their representational practices. One file, initiated in 1974, includes several such photos confiscated from Carla. These are powerful images that shed light over how persecuted individuals carved out social spaces and decided how they wanted their femininity, sexuality, and eroticism to be captured by the camera. In these images, models pose for an unknown photographer. There are multiple photos of the same woman posing alone in different settings, with various clothes and postures: against a background of dense vegetation, while confidently smoking a cigarette, wearing a nice, short dress, and exhibiting her shaved, long legs; lying barefoot on the grass in a park with one leg over the other; wearing bell-bottoms and a shirt in a field with her hands framing her hips; standing sideways against a backdrop of small bushes and trees while wearing a bra and a skirt; and looking frontally into the camera in an empty street, with her arms resting by her side.

These portraits are key to understanding the self-representation of trans women. As Gabriela Cano has noted: "Photographic portraits transformed visual body culture and made it possible for common people to fix their desired physical images in lasting prints. [. . .] Each time the portrait was viewed by oneself or someone else, the body image and the identity created by the photograph was confirmed."[46] The images from this file have in common an emphasis on *naturalness* and the focus on the model's legs as a metonymic attribute of her femininity. These visual codes correspond to the "logic of *sacar el cuerpo* [bring out the body," which Marcia Ochoa describes as a series of "technologies to allow the feminine body to emerge," according to a "notion of nature as both inherent and in need of collaboration" (namely, "nature" as a device of constructionism).[47] Posing and background are the technologies used in these photographs to bring out the model's feminine body by

foregrounding her beautiful legs and silhouettes in static landscapes. In
a photograph of an urban beach, people's faces are less clear than the rest
of their bodies (especially the bottom half of a woman's body, maybe part
of the group of trans women friends). They appear frozen in a repose-
ful summer moment; no one in the photo gives any sign of caring about
others' physicality or the body in its indexical relation to gender identity.
The ordinariness of the image is indeed special; it gestures toward the
possibility of a nonthreatening public.

There are also confiscated photographs that reflect defendants' relationality. In a foreground image, a handsome young man with sideburns
closes his eyes and kisses a woman on her chin while putting his arm
around her. Her wide smile as well as the physical intimacy conveyed by
their posturing suggests that they might have been emotionally or sexually involved in some way. The file also includes an image of two women
playing with some props in a photo booth and an image of a blond woman
with short hair wearing lipstick and a leather jacket, among many other
visual traces of a sort of community or network formed by a group of
people who enjoyed taking photographs of themselves to capture their
bodily aesthetics and shared moments of joy and intimacy. These photographs are "gestural documents," which Tonia Sutherland defines as
a "codified, culturally informed, and embodied record capable of being
engaged at the archival threshold."[48] These documents record affective
and political body gestures entangled with cultural frameworks that
invest the documents with meaning in the past and the present. The
context of criminalization, the confinement of trans visibility to the
margins, and intimacy as survival are embodied and encoded in these
files, re-envisioned in their custodial relations such that they are rightly
committed to trans genealogies and the praxes of self-determination.[49]

These photographs contradict the legal documents included in the
files, which reduce and confine defendants' social roles. To begin with,
the files are titled using the defendants' legally assigned names, which
were not the names that they used in their daily life. Carla was first arrested when she was a minor of only sixteen—a fact that apparently was
never taken into consideration when adjudicating her sentence—and accused of prostituting herself in a street called Pasaje Domingo, which at
that time was a known locale for transactional sex.[50] She explained that
she had worked in different factories and in construction as well, but
since she could not find a job for the last six months she had dedicated

herself to "homosexuality" (referring to prostitution).[51] She was arrested at a moment when the effects of the 1973 oil crisis were rippling through the Spanish economy, causing high rates of unemployment and inflation, while the Franco regime used increasingly repressive measures to contain social unrest. This socioeconomic and political context shaped working-class trans women's experiences by adding multiple layers of vulnerability to their already precarious economic survival strategies.

The judge levied a harsh sentence requiring that she had to pay a fine as well as cover the state's trial expenses, spend several months in prison, be exiled for a year, and endure surveillance after her release.[52] Exile sentences were particularly harmful and impractical for working-class families that relied on the labor of every family member in order to earn the minimum income to sustain themselves. In this line, Carla's mother declared in 1975 that Carla had come back to their family's home so that she could help them financially.[53] However, constant police surveillance prevented her from carrying on with her life. Arrested for the second time, she was asked about her appearance and sexual practices and clarified that she dyed her hair and plucked her eyebrows because "she liked it," in much the same way that she had sex with men whom she liked without charging them.[54] Taste and aesthetics as a matter of choice resurfaced in the testimonies and photographs of trans women even though official documents presented them as a question of "sexual inversion."

Most important, by looking at trans women's declarations and photographs together we can appreciate how *sisterhood* figured in their cultural and social practices. Carla and one of her friends, Romina, were arrested in May 1975 in one of the industrial suburbs of Barcelona. According to the arrest report, the two of them were out taking a stroll when neighbors started to crowd around them to discuss whether they were male or female; at this point the Guardia Civil intervened and arrested them.[55] Carla declared that she "did not have carnal knowledge of her friend [Romina]. The affection she felt for her was proper of a sister" *(No ha tenido contacto carnal con su amiga [name/nombre] y que su afecto es de hermana).*[56] As Franco lived his last days, trans women vocally and visually asserted themselves by taking to the streets and demonstrating the role of affect in building alternative forms of kinship.[57] *Pasear* (strolling) has multiple connotations in Spanish that here suggest defendants' determination to be part of the public sphere. *Pasear* is the quintessential form of community sociability in Spanish towns; after work, people take to the streets and squares, sit on benches, greet other passersby, exchange news and rumors, tell jokes, and play music, share information about their relatives and neighbors, and discuss sports and politics. To participate in the daily stroll or *paseo* for these women meant to reclaim their right to belong, to well-being, leisure time in the public sphere, to see and *be seen*. In this sense, *pasear* as a quotidian practice was inscribed "in the struggle to create possibility within the constraints of everyday life" by using a "strategy of affirmation and a confrontational practice of visibility," as Campt puts it.[58]

This desire to be seen drives my engagement with this visual archive. In the view of the Francoist authorities, the confiscation, filing, and archiving of these portraits neutralized the potential "danger to society" of the models and other people looking at these objects in a way that confirmed models' body image and identity, per Cano's analysis. The incorporation of the photographs in the judicial file was a hermeneutic practice, a "taxonomic tool" meant to insert these images into a transphobic narrative. Their preservation was aimed at retaining for posterity the moment of exposure of gender nonconformity, of inscribing the stigmatization of trans subjectivities both in institutional archives and on the bodies of the violators. Yet, as Edwards points out, the archive remains unstable: "the very fact of public access, present and future, threatened to destabilize preferred readings [. . .] as archives were subject to small acts of re-ordering, re-captioning, and re-interpretation, fostering 'myriad of random encounters with objects of knowledge rather than singular linear narratives.'"[59] One of the ways of un-setting the reading of trans bodies by Francoist curators is to fully engage in a horizontal encounter with the images that trans women took of themselves in order to preserve their desired body image.

Along with their *paseos*, the photographs suggest that they also spent their spare time in photobooths, parks, beaches, and natural spaces. In other words, their presence was not exclusively confined to those areas that the authorities associated with homosexuality or transactional sex. At the same time, while they certainly frequented public areas, natural backgrounds stood for a sort of shelter where they could fully show their bodies without being afraid of the social and legal consequences. The opposite of these women's self-representation was the image imposed on them by police officers during their arrest. A face streaked with running mascara epitomized the consequences of police violence, both in Carla's and Daniela's files. Carla's friend Romina declared that, while the police officer was making a phone call to report them, she had ducked into a public bathroom "and took the mascara off her face, because she had been crying a little bit."[60] There are two possibilities here. She might have taken the mascara off so that it would not be used as evidence against her (by means of photographing her with makeup). However, this possibility is unlikely, since she admitted that she was wearing mascara anyway. Most likely, she did cry when arrested for the simple act of strolling with her friend, and perhaps she cleaned up her face so as to not give police officers the satisfaction of seeing and photographing her spoiled makeup. The police report on Romina's arrest pays striking attention to aesthetics: "She had makeup on her face, with lipstick and a mole next to the lower lip, wearing red pants and a red sweater without sleeves and showing her cleavage. She also wore women's shoes, four rings on her hands, and a lady's wristwatch on her left wrist" *(El que tenía la cara pintada, con lunar junto al labio inferior y estos pintados, vistiendo pantalón rojo, suéter rojo sin mangas y escotado y calzando zapatos de mujer y cuatros anillos en las manos y reloj de pulsera de señora en la muñeca izquierda).*[61]

When opening Romina's file, one encounters a photocopy of all the photographs and intimate materials that were confiscated from Carla and kept in her file. Media scholar Kate Eichhorn argues that Xerox's launching of the first copy machine in 1959 reshuffled the conventions of print culture and facilitated new expressions of collective authorship (a pre-web social media) by zine and experimental communities. With xerography, author and publisher could become one and the same, copyright was harder to trace, and countercultural networks were able to circulate subversive ideas without corporate oversight.[62] Eichhorn highlights the copy machine's emancipatory potential, but the same form of media also expedited the bureaucratic processing of state violence. In creating a file for each targeted person, copy machines allowed officers to duplicate and reproduce the profiling of maricas and trans women, streamlining the processing of incriminatory evidence, extracted by breaching subjects' privacy. Xerography as countercultural social media was marked by ephemerality, but the files of institutionalized transphobia were meant to perdure as policing devices. Yet there is a third act for the polyphonous role that photocopying plays in the relationship among

FIGURE 12. Photocopy of photographs from File 416/1974, included in File 442/1974. Printed with permission by Arxiu Central dels Jutjats de la Ciutat de la Justícia, Hospitalet de Llobregat, Spain.

gender transgression, state repression, and our capacity to touch and be touched by these images; insofar as copying entailed pixelation, which, among other things, renders subjects' faces virtually unrecognizable, the copy can appear in print in this book, while the originals are yet not reproducible, according to the law.

Francoist officers created surrogate records by carefully arranging the personal photographs and letters confiscated from Carla into derivative montages, in a curatorial practice that goes beyond the logic of destruction and erasure. If we concretize the definition of photocopy as the creation of new but unoriginal images "by the action of light [. . .] on an electrically charged surface"—state agents superposed the personal photographs that these trans women had taken of themselves to an electrically charged surface so that light could form new images.[63] Thus, far from erasing the confiscated photographs, light circulated through them to form a sequential series of vignettes with their own implicit narrative, but as joyful and enticing as the original images. The visual narrativization of trans experiences is even more evident on the next page in the file, in which the state agent who selected, produced, and arranged the photocopies apparently had decided to visually connect intimate materials to depict and narrate an intimate relationship. At the top of this page there are two images taken in a photo booth. Underneath these images, the curator had included an address and a love poem to imply some sort of link between the poem and the individual(s) in the photographs:

> Por qué no vuelves a mi lado
> sí me consumo de ansiedad
> es que tal vez me has olvidado
> más no lo quiero ni pensar
> echo de menos tus caricias
> la soledad de nuestro amor
> echo de menos tu sonrisa
> y el eco dulce de tu voz
> esperaré que vuelvas
> nuevamente lo mismo
> que otras veces espere
> qué importa que yo sufra
> intensamente
> te quiero más que ayer

más cada vez
y si no vuelves a mi lado
de tu recuerdo viviré
triste recuerdo de un
pasado que nunca
más ha de volver.

Why don't you come back to my side? I am anxiously consuming myself [thinking] that maybe you forgot me
but I don't even want to think about it.
I miss your caresses,
the loneliness of our love
I miss your smile and the sweet echo of your voice
I'll wait for you to come back. Once again, the same
that other times I waited
no matter whether I suffer
Intensely
I love you more than yesterday, more and more
And if you don't come back to my side
On your memory I will live
sad memory of a
past that never
more shall come back.

While this poem is worth citing as a vital text that connects us with
the affective life of trans women under the Franco regime, our reading is
a result of police officers' violent intrusion into their intimacy. The poem
highlights certain significant aspects of a relationship that apparently
involved Romina (the envelope that the curator had included in the photocopy next to the poem was addressed to her, using her female name and
her legal last names). First, the poem characterized love as lonely. This oxy-
moron, especially in the Spanish original, "la soledad de nuestro amor,"
conveys that the bond between two lovers is stronger when it forces them
into social ostracism. The theme of mutual attraction that becomes more
intensely consuming by virtue of being forbidden is a common trope.
Yet, in this iteration, it becomes a forceful language through which trans
women claim intimacy as a mode of belonging. The semantic field of the
poem (caresses, smile, voice) alludes to the performance and production

of intimacy in the photographs from the same file. According to transgender studies scholar Cole Rizki, the "unassuming generic conventions" of snapshots include elements that are "universally recognizable" as a performance of intimacy, such as the "frontal pose, centered subject [and] affectionate gestures like arms around shoulders and broad smiles," all of which appear in the photos from this file. This visual language, with its focus on quotidian affects, counteracted the media spectacle of news and images that sensationalized trans people's life and death.[64] In addition, when we count on both photographic and written documents, following Singer this should be seized upon as an opportunity to temper what he calls the "tyranny of the visual" by incorporating subjects' own written statements, an approach that in this case contributes to highlight how the language of intimacy traverses both registers.[65]

Tania: Fierceness and Self-Narration against State Violence

I shared the following text with Tania, reading my Spanish translation to her so that she could confirm its accuracy and suggest changes. Tania Navarro Amo was born in 1956 in Barcelona. Her personal photographs and memories contrast with the content of the judicial files dedicated to her trajectory and foreground tensions and divergences between different means of archiving and representing transgender history. She keeps only a small fraction of the personal belongings and photographs that she treasured in her youth, because a fire in her home destroyed most of them some years ago (pointing once again to the contingencies of archival preservation/erasure). While her Franco-era files represent her as a criminal alienated from her mother and other relatives, unwilling to work, a dangerous presence in the public sphere, and provocatively pathological; her memoirs, oral testimony, and personal photographs emphasize solidarity between females to resist state and male violence; the joy of ephemeral moments when transgender visibility is celebrated rather than punished; and her resolve in leaving a historical narrative that honors trans women and sex workers who refused to be ashamed and silent. Tania was arrested and brought to court for the first time when she was just four years old. She did not even remember this arrest until I told her that the judicial archives of Barcelona had located her files from the juvenile court. In her recollection, she stole an apple from a store, was caught by the owner, and in the ensuing confrontation she kicked a clay jar full of oil.[66] On 20 June 2022, Tania and I met with the Direcció General d'Atenció a la Infància i l'Adolescència (DGAIA; General Directiorate for the Care of Children and Adolescents), which now maintains historical files from the Francoist juvenile courts. The person who represented the DGAIA in that meeting and physically handed Tania's file to her, emphasized that these judicial records showcase both the strikingly-out-of-place police handling of a toddler's misbehavior and Tania's mother's fierce determination to defend her.[67] Tania treats her mother, Juana, as the very core of her memoirs. In person, Tania smiles fondly every time she talks about Juana, referring to her as "la gordi" (endearing appellative translatable as "fatty"). Juana was born in the Andalusian province of Almería and moved to Barcelona to find a better life, becoming an industrial worker and breadwinner for the children that she had with different men. This trajectory was at odds with Francoist official discourses that represented male breadwinners as the core of normative families.[68] Maybe because her own life was marked by transgression, Juana had the resolve to support Tania (and other sex workers who shared their daily lives with her) every time she was arrested: she would go to the police station with food and male clothes for Tania to change into them before going to court (being aware that Tania's female appearance did not match legal records and would antagonize the judges); pleaded for compassion to judges and police officers; and suffered at the perspective of Tania continuously having to move from city to city to escape police harassment (apart from Madrid and Barcelona, Tania lived in Torremolinos and the Canary Islands, which were centers of sexual tourism). In her memoirs, Tania also recollects how painful it was for her mother to visit her in prison, where they shaved her head and treated her as a male prisoner.[69] Juana chose to call her daughter Toni, a gender-neutral appellative. Tania's Barcelona judicial files includes a report on her mother pleading for Tania's release. Mediated as the document is, it still indicates Juana's staunch support for her daughter. Juana allegedly declared that "her son [sic] is this way since childhood and it is impossible that [Tania] stops using nail polish."[70] At this point, in 1975, Tania supported her mother economically, since Juana had retired early due to asthma and bronchitis that she acquired at the factory.[71]

When she was a child, Tania spent a lot of time on the streets with neighbors and youth gangs, partly because her brother continuously assaulted her, once even throwing her from a dovecote. Tania's sister

Marina, on the contrary, always took her side and defended her against their brother.[72] Sisterhood and solidarity between females shaped transgender women's strategies of survival since their childhood. Neighbors in Hospitalet, the working-class neighborhood where Tania grew up, had mixed responses to her presence and behavior. According to Tania, some saw her with sympathy because she was loving and cared for her mother, while others were complicit with state repression by reporting her.[73] In an official report dated 27 March 1969, the police complained about a protest that apparently took place in the neighborhood when they went to arrest Tania (who was twelve years old then):

> He took [Tania] by the arm to prevent [her] from escaping, since [she] is an unruly and rebellious minor who has escaped multiple times from correctional institutions. Soon after, undoubtedly alerted by some neighbor, a women showed up who, while saying that she was the minor's aunt, began to utter insults, profanity, and contemptuous words towards the police [. . .] achieving with such attitude that a large group of people gathered around and visibly demonstrated their hostility towards the police officer who now testifies.[74]

The spontaneous anti-police protest emboldened Tania's aunt, who was able to release her from the police officer's arms and ended up arrested and charged with contempt. Opposition to the state and police intervention in matters that pertained to private family dynamics seemed quite strong in working-class neighborhoods, even though Tania's extended family was not otherwise particularly supportive of her gender expression. By contrast, Tania remembers very fondly the sex workers who worked and lived in Barcelona's red district (*barrio chino*) and who hosted and raised her as she was continuously expelled from her home by her brother.[75] Geoffroy Huard describes the "second family" that transgender and gay people formed by introducing each other into the sex work and entertainment businesses that were the main economic niches for those who came to Barcelona escaping sexual repression in other regions.[76] On a less bright note, Tania first experienced sex work as a child by frequenting the Apolo arcade—a known locale for underaged males' sex work—and on multiple occasions throughout her life had to escape violent clients who threatened to harm her. Responding to external pressures, Juana committed Tania to the Asilo Durán reformatory when she was nine years old. Tania would spend the next years in and out of reformatories and correctional institutions managed by religious orders in Barcelona and Madrid. She keeps vivid memories of the staff's cruelty and viciousness and her own aptitude in finding ways to escape and become a fugitive. She writes that when she was fifteen, they committed her to the Sant Boi psychiatric hospital, where they subjected her to electroshock conversion therapy and she tried to commit suicide (we have not been able yet to consult her psychiatric file, but the staff and direction of Barcelona's judicial archives are pursuing multiple lines of inquiry to locate it).[77]

Tania reached the age of full legal liability when she turned sixteen, at which moment the police officers who had been harassing her for years took her to the Social Dangerousness Court. At 277 pages, her file is one of the thickest I have seen at the Barcelona's judicial archives. In addition, she also has a file in Madrid, and probably in other cities where she was arrested, like Las Palmas de Gran Canaria. The Barcelona file documents years of police persecution sanctioned by Judge Antonio Sabater Tomás. On 24 May 1972, the police first reported her to the court, accusing her of being an "invert" and *bujarrón* (male sex worker), while she clarified that she worked as a "waiter" (*camarero*) in a bar called Nagasaki.[78] For the forensic doctor, Domingo Saumench Gimeno, she presented "all the symptomology proper of homosexuals."[79] The official reports from the Guardia Civil and the Hospitalet de Llobregat City Hall portrayed Tania as disrespectful toward her mother on account of her multiple internments, a misrepresentation that Tania finds particularly painful given how attached she was to her mother, which she now is able to correct in her memoirs.[80] Judge Sabater Tomás sentenced Tania to imprisonment for a period between four months and a year, followed by a year-long forced exile from Barcelona.[81]

However, official records do not reflect the most vicious abuses that Tania suffered and now narrates in her memoirs: the gruesome fascination that police officers and forensic experts showed toward her corporality and female underwear, forcefully stripping her and turning her into a spectacle every time she was arrested; her suicide attempt by hitting her head against a metallic file cabinet at a police station; the sexual abuses and rapes by police and prison officers; and the gang rape permitted by prison officers on her first night in prison when she was sixteen years old (which she and her mother denounced to the judge, to no avail). Likewise, her file includes no trace of her love life in prison, where she had relationships with other prisoners who protected her. In her memoirs, Tania conveys her own agency in choosing those partners, based not only on strategic considerations but also on her likings.[82]

In general, through her testimony (both in her memoirs and in our conversations) Tania emphasizes moments of ephemeral joy that disrupted the cycle of police abuse, migrations, and imprisonments that characterized her life under the Franco regime and in the earliest years of the transition. For instance, when she was still a child, she found a wedding dress in an abandoned house and put it on to dance in the main square while the neighbors provided music in the form of clapping. On this occasion, Tania's brother broke one of her ears to punish her for her public exhibition, but Tania persisted in her artistic endeavors.[83] Starting in the early 1970s, she performed as a dancer in night shows at clubs like Panam's, Buena Sombra, and El Molino. Tania's artistic debut in 1973 was a very joyful moment.[84] She was following in the footsteps of other performers whom she deeply admired—like the French international star Coccinelle (1931–2006), who had undergone gender affirmation surgery in Casablanca, Morocco, in the late 1950s and in 1960 married a man with the blessing of the Catholic Church.[85] In 1975, Tania declared to the police that her intention was to undergo gender affirmation surgery in Casablanca, which indicates that trans people's pilgrimage to this city to access medical interventions continued for many years.[86]

In 1962, Coccinelle performed in Madrid at the Pasapoga Music Hall, despite the Franco regime's contemporary persecution of sexual minorities.[87] By the same token, in the mid-1970s Tania was able to join the Manuel Castán dance company, which toured Spain's provincial cities and coastal towns. Trans women's role in these shows outside of metropolitan areas often went unnoticed, probably because of the shows' transience, but incidental exposure to the authorities entailed criminal penalties—Tania, for instance, was imprisoned for some days in Punta Umbría, a small Andalusian town, when police officers found out that the male name in her legal documents did not match her artistic female name.[88] While sex work and performing in nightclubs were Tania's main sources of income, she downplayed them to avoid a harsh police treatment. For instance, when interrogated by the police in Barcelona in June 1976, Tania admitted that she worked as a go-go dancer in the nightclub Coupé 77 but added that she also worked in trash collection.[89] In reality, she had done that kind of work only when she was a child.[90] The 1976 forensic report also reflected for the first time Tania's "gynecomastia" (breast implants).[91]

Although Tania hesitates to date a particular event in a specific year, her overall testimony points to a parallelism between political changes and the intensification of the *destape*. Before and immediately after the death of Franco in November 1975, censorship codes forbade the full exposure of female breasts. Tania laughs at the memory of the bikinis and *pezoneras* (nipple shields) that dancers had to wear to maintain the facade of censors' authority over the female body.[92] These measures contributed, if anything, to accentuate audiences' interest in residual taboos, underpinning experimentation and transgression in the scenic arts after the dictator's death. In the late 1970s, Tania left Manuel Castán's dance company to launch her own solo career. In that moment, she lacked the costly accoutrements of her profession, but Coccinelle gave her a feather adornment when they ran into each other in a theater in Madrid; Tania treasured it until a fire took it from her.[93] Being her own choreographer, Tania creatively used her few resources to put together a show that catered to audiences' interest in sexual transgression. As Mercè Picornell notes, between 1975 and 1978 the *travesti* image became "a recurring metaphor for the political transition between the Francoist dictatorship and a new democratic state."[94] This image was politically effective insofar as the staging of sexual ambiguity blurred the boundaries between private life and public space.[95]

For novelist Lluís Fernández—whose award-winning 1979 novel *L'anarquista nu* (The nude anarchist) condensed the ethos of 1970s countercultures—authentic pornography and trans and marica subjectivities were intertwined as one and the same catalyst, whereas commercial mainstream pornography was a sham. One of the characters of his novel equated the future of democracy with gender self-determination guaranteed by the state.[96] In an interview with Amparo Tuñon, Fernández discussed homosexuals' daily life as pornography that "fragmented" the experience of the body. As Fernández put it, "homosexuals are the only ones in this country that make pornography because they practice it."[97] While in the early decades of the century, fragmentation was authorities' mechanism to impose a reductionist reading of queer literature as pornography (as I traced in chapter 1); postmodernism vindicated the shattering of unified identities. Fernández and Tuñon reveled in

marica lives being saturated by pornography and assumed that maricas, being obscene by definition, were impervious to normalization.
The "pornographic poison" had to be inoculated through literature and
mass media, because images of "nude ladies" (*señoras desnudas*) were
not enough to destroy the "house" (a metaphor for the hetero-centered
status quo that is reminiscent of the Master's House in the work of Audre
Lorde). Whereas Fernández placed the burden of being obscene on maricas and trans people, he did not believe the latter had the capacity to
grasp the political framework of their transgression and *intentionally*
undermine conservative values. In the last instance, Fernández's premises reified the centrality of countercultural intellectuals like himself in
mobilizing trans and homosexual imaginaries to counter the hegemony
of accommodating, bad-taste porno. In Picornell's analysis, in this period
there was a "perverse appropriation that does not define transgender
transgression as an option or practice with a meaning in itself, but rather
as an empty emblem of counterpower."[98] By contrast, Tania's shows did
not center as much the transgressive appeal of *travesti* subjectivities as
her choreographing bizarre sexual tableaux.

Tania purchased a life-size teddy bear and "had sex" with it on stage.
One of the few black-and-white photographs that Tania keeps from the
1970s shows traces of fire on the edges and Tania at center stage with a
teddy bear underneath her simulating a sexual position. She is naked, she
wears a blond wig and dark mascara, and her facial expression (meant to
convey sexual pleasure) contrasts with the impassive presence of three
men who sit with drinks on a table in the background. This scene could
seem to reify the male gaze's dominant position, but the way in which
every other element in the image revolves around Tania's performance
and her expressiveness suggests an alternative reading: she directs both
the camera and the audience toward herself to dramatize sex within a
choreography of her design. After all, Tania was aware of a time when
transgender women could capitalize the spectacularizing of sex for their
own purposes.

In parallel to her artistic career, Tania participated prominently in
the first public demonstration to demand the abolition of the Dangerousness Law, which took place in Barcelona on 27 June 1977. In fact,
the photographs of her and other trans women leading that protest have
become nothing short of the main symbol of the LGTBQ+ movement's
origins in Spain. However, in 1977 some homosexual leaders repudiated

FIGURE 13. Photograph from Tania's personal collection. She appears naked, performing an imitation of intercourse with a life-size teddy bear, with a few members of the audience seated at a table in the background. Printed with permission by Tania Navarro Amo.

trans visibility and argued that it distorted and undermined the agenda of their movement. Historian Piro Subrat has documented these early transphobic reactions in their book *Invertidos y Rompepatrias*.[99] When

I read to Tania the passages of the book that discussed this episode, she was infuriated. As she recalls, since this and other demonstrations ended up in confrontations with the police, trans women's leading role resulted from their willingness to expose themselves and face the police who harassed them on a daily basis. Furthermore, Tania adds another reason why she appears to pose for the photographs documenting this protest: every time she was imprisoned, they shaved their head, but in June 1977 she had been out of prison for months and she felt particularly beautiful. She wore a leather jacket and jeans that highlighted her slender body, and in the photos she either looks directly into the camera or smiles and shouts as she marches along with her friends. In her recollections, that day she went from one gay bar to another shouting "let's protest, faggots" *(venga maricones, vamos a manifestarnos)* in a quasi-festive tone that convinced many people to join.[100] Yet trans sex workers were neglected as elected officials assumed the task of reforming the Francoist legislation on gender and sexual issues.

In the 1980s, Tania was still arrested quite often and had an open dangerousness file on account of her sex work.[101] Her personal photographs show her at parties and beauty contests that took place in the early 1980s, often smiling and looking into the camera. Her life in the post-Franco era was a mix of joy and tragedy: she received significant media attention and was able to save enough to open her own business; she married and had two children; and she was seemingly accepted by neighbors and relatives alike. However, bad fortune struck Tania again in middle age: she lost her house and most of her mementos to a fire; she separated from her husband; she suffered from addictions and poor physical and mental health; and she lost almost any contact with the external world for years.[102] In 2021, she published her memoirs, which allowed her to take control of her own life and narrative.

Conclusion

Taking into consideration the long trajectory of deployment of judicial evidence to subjugate and erase trans people, this chapter foregrounds how their confiscated personal photographs can be read in a way that turns the concept of "evidence" on its head. The visual materials analyzed in this chapter point to trans women's ideas of intimacy, beauty, and kinship—sisterhood, in particular, appeared to be a central value and survival strategy for trans women. Thus, these images center a different narrative than the one presented by depositions and legal documents, which generally revolve around public shaming, forensic violence, and police harassment. Through the photographs that trans women took in (semi)public and naturalized spaces and through their participation in social rituals and affective relationships, we can trace the genealogy of their experiments with visual codes, self-representation, and community building.

Tania Navarro Amo's testimony, for instance, goes beyond police violence as the structural condition for the perpetuation of the regime and its surveillance of trans communities. Tania also describes the marvels of Barcelona's nightlife, the solidarity and attachment between sex workers, the urban cartography of forbidden erotic encounters, her love interests while in prison, and her collection of feather boas and jewelry. Pain and pleasure, intimacy and violence, abjection and political mobilization coexist and merge in Tania's narrative, pinpointing the reductionism of the judicial files in accounting for the lives of those who fell under the state's purview. In sum, trans women's embodied readings of their own subjectivity defy the forensic gaze that usually permeates and dominates judicial records. The next chapter further investigates how the political transition of the 1970s affected different groups, including trans women, that had been relegated to the terrain of "deviance" and obscenity under the Franco regime.

SIX

"Frosted Glass"

THE SEXUAL POLITICS OF THE DEMOCRATIC TRANSITION

In 1978 a sex shop owner was arrested and judged at the Social Dangerousness Court of Barcelona for the crime of trading in pornography. Her case escalated into a series of institutional exchanges discussing the frosted glass through which light entered the sex shop.[1] Frosted glass protected both the anonymity of porn consumers and the values of "decent" citizens. A refractory light that both traverses and keeps apart the public sphere and the porn business is an apt metaphor for the new regime of limited tolerance that emerged in post-Franco Spain from the mid-1970s in response to the conflicting demands of different social sectors. During the trial against the sex shop owner, multiple instances of state power had to report on their role in policing the porn business. The Ministry of the Interior had issued orders for police departments nationwide to prevent the sale of pornography in public.[2] However, the governor of Barcelona pointed out that erotic publications were already a normalized consumer item and exemplary arrests had proved ineffective (as defense lawyers would also repeatedly argue).[3] The judge petitioned the governor's office for additional information on whether the sex shop merchandise was exposed to the public or only to interested consumers, to which the response was that "frosted glass" kept the inside of the store invisible to the outside world.[4] The defendant clarified that only adults were allowed to come into her store, even though the magazines she sold were available at any newsstand.[5] Since both the prosecutor and the judge agreed to drop the case, it seems that by 1978 selling pornography in private businesses was no longer considered a threat to society.[6] The case against the sex shop owner had been initiated on 22 December 1978. Just four days later, the passing of Law 77/1978 repealed the articles of the Dangerousness Law that mentioned homosexuality, which was no longer typified as a threat to society.[7]

This chapter focuses on how the interplay among public opinion, opinionmakers, media entrepreneurs, and state authorities in the 1970s shaped the image of an inoffensive porn consumer: a middle- or upper-class heterosexual male who endorsed moderate politics. In 1975 the Franco regime allowed nudity in films if the storyline demanded it. After Franco's death in November 1975, restricted sexual permissiveness became a fundamental strategy to garner support for the process of political reforms. This permissiveness, however, was initially limited to male consumers interested in female nudity. As most of the population came to support the end of censorship—affluent urban men were privileged political subjects during the transition and particularly significant in this respect—the persecution of pornography under the Dangerousness Law came to be perceived as inconsistent with democracy.[8] Criminalization generated disproportionate profits for people involved in the pornography industry, and punishments intended to serve as a deterrent did not prevent its expansion.

Eventually, the Suárez administration legalized freedom of expression in 1977, putting an end to cinematic censorship in November of that year. The publication of *Playboy* in Spain starting in 1978 epitomizes the normalization of erotic magazines that targeted straight male consumers and were defined by technical sophistication and political moderation. However, according to *Playboy*'s first editor in chief, Iván Tubau, the magazine's standard consumer—a respectable middle- or upper-class male citizen who consumed sophisticated erotica—by then had lost his role as the main agent of the transition in sexual norms, because countercultural movements were already leading the way to sexual experimentation. The articulation of a radical critique of pornography being coopted by consumerism and the state dates to the very beginnings of the democratic transition. In February 1976, Armand de Fluvià, leader of the Catalan gay movement, wrote to Héctor Anabitarte, an Argentine gay activist, describing the first signs of sexual liberation after Franco's death. Fluvià was cautious and skeptical about the possibility that there would be drastic improvements in the rights of sexual minorities:

> Things have changed a bit: there is more freedom of press and expression, nudity is already allowed in theater and cinema (never the exhibition of genitals) as well as in magazines (*Play Girls, Viva*) but at prices that make eroticism a privilege of the wealthy classes [. . .] The laws have not changed yet, despite promises in this respect, and I am afraid they will not change.[9]

Fluvià and other activists pointed out that sexual liberalization was only accessible to restricted audiences (middle- and upper-class straight men) who could take advantage of implicit state toleration without challenging the legal framework or promoting drastic changes. Still, media attention to previously banned topics would eventually allow Fluvià and other activists to advocate for a more inclusive society with greater openness. Throughout the 1970s, educated readers became familiar with nonconforming gender expressions through progressive publications such as *Cuadernos para el dialogo* and *Triunfo*.[10] Already in 1970, *Triunfo* dedicated an entire issue to eroticism in Spain. The unidentified author(s) of the preface were critical of censorship and skeptical about market-driven sexual liberalization. The preface focused on the "grotesque mechanisms" of self-repression that Spaniards had developed after decades of living under a dictatorship, which had substituted pornography with censorship—so the latter eventually acquired similar titillating effects, promoting "the anguish of seeing and not seeing, having and not having."[11] This anguish resembles what Jeffrey Escoffier has termed "the indeterminacy of pornographic media," which "reveals a gap between pornography as photographic representation of sex and the human experience of sex."[12] The *Triunfo* editors argued that censorship had taken on the role assigned to pornography in mediating between representation and experience in ways that had led Spaniards to internalize repression for decades. However, the permissive society of the 1970s valued the self-gratification of consumers, which in Spain translated into "apparent" toleration of the public visibility of sex.[13] Intellectuals who collaborated in the dossier, like Gonzalo Torrente Ballester, shared the skepticism toward sexual liberation, voicing their concern that hypocrisy and puritanism had given way to the commodification of sex spectacles.[14] Current historiographical assessments of the sexual politics of the transition somehow mirror these concerns, as the outcomes of this historical period are measured against the projects of emancipation formulated by radical and progressive activists.

During the democratic transition, the Dangerousness Courts ceased to prosecute pornography, censors lost the authority they had under Francoism, and public scandal reverted to the jurisdiction of ordinary law, undoing the frameworks of moral exceptionality that Francoism had implemented. In this new legal context, media representations became the main area of contestation among reactionary, liberal, and radical politics, which broadly correspond to the three major positions toward sexuality that cultural historian Germán Labrador has traced in the democratic transition: "nostalgic" (*nostálgica*) of the Catholic moral hegemony under Francoism, favorable to the emerging "transitional" (*transicional*) sexual regime, and "groundbreaking" (*rupturista*) and inspired by anarchist utopias. According to Labrador, the spectacular facets of sex and politics dominated the public sphere in 1976 and 1977.[15] This chapter focuses on the "backstage" of the spectacle of (sexual) democracy and on its archival traces, including censors' red markers, obscene images, and defendants' testimonies. These sources underpin a view of the transition as a contingent process in which different historical actors strategized over the meanings of modernity, civilization, and freedom in political disputes that today remain open-ended.

Reactions to Global Sexual Liberation

In the late 1960s and early 1970s there was a global transition from the "clandestine tradition" of stag films screened in brothels to feature hard-core films screened in commercial venues under conditions of relative normalcy. Softcore movies (partial nudity and simulated sexual acts) gained popularity over the 1960s, while the legalization of hardcore (full nudity and non-simulated sex) in Denmark at the end of that decade facilitated the emergence of a global market for these films.[16] In the United States, *Mona the Virgin Nymph* (1970) pioneered hard-core produced for mass audiences, while *Deep Throat* (1972) marked the commercial and mediatic success of this formula. The 1970s were the golden age of pornography (the "porno chic" era), which spread in ways that accentuated sociopolitical anxieties about the effects of North American consumer culture on European societies. According to Alberto Elena, "France was the true port of entry for American hard-core into Europe."[17] In Spain, these anxieties overlapped with state authorities' decades-old perception—not entirely baseless—that "libertine" France was the point of reference for Spanish pornographers.[18] Conservative media outlets in Spain first focused their attention on the use of the artistic alibi in French films such as *Last Tango in Paris* and *Emmanuelle*, which successfully brought soft-core to commercial theaters in other countries.[19]

These media outlets also voiced their concern regarding the mounting threat of pornography by linking it to radical politics and homosexuality. *ABC* was the oldest newspaper in the country, a media proxy for Catholic monarchical sectors. Its editorial line was to present an image of consensus across conventional ideological divisions, emphasizing how leading figures of international "leftism" and the pope converged in their opinions regarding obscenity. In 1971 *ABC* published an article by Jean Cau, presenting him as a noted French "leftist" (Cau had been Jean-Paul Sartre's personal secretary) even though he had by then become a reactionary who advocated for ethnic nationalism and criticized the lack of spiritual ideals in the West.[20] The same issue of *ABC* printed a speech by Pope Paul VI, sharing many points with Cau's article. Paul VI warned Catholic believers about a "plague of eroticism" that was an "aggressive threat" with "unbridled and repugnant manifestations" that built on the liberationist theories of Freud and Marcuse. The pope stated that eroticism (promiscuity and pornography) led to drug addiction, the "dumbing down of the senses," and ultimately, abjection against God. Alfonso Barra, the journalist who wrote the preface to the pope's speech for *ABC*, struck a nationalistic tone when he asserted that Spain remained a haven from the "morbid excitement of sexuality" and "blatant pornography" that had taken over other European countries. Barra advocated for a "balanced surveillance" that neither allowed pornography nor reverted to the prudish policies of earlier decades.[21] This middle-ground position aligned with the regime's modernization project without questioning its ideological foundations.

In 1972 *ABC* dedicated a multi-page report to the Nationwide Festival of Lights, a demonstration in London organized by evangelical Christians and attended by approximately thirty-five thousand people protesting pornography. This protest catalyzed internal debates within

the convening platform about whether opposition to sexual liberalization should be articulated in Christian or "religiously neutral" terms
to expand the social basis of the movement.[22] In the 1970s, antipornography activists learned to combine religion as a mobilizing force with
the outfacing projection of a modern secular discourse. Ben Strassfeld
argues that the "potent new antiporn discourse" that emerged in the
United States in the 1970s "eschewed the overt moralizing of previous
antiporn efforts in favor of economic and rights-based arguments rooted
in concerns about urban decay."[23] As public opinion increasingly turned
against censorship in the permissive society of the late 1960s and early
1970s, pornography became a mainstream, almost respectable phenomenon. In response, grassroots antiporn activism and media campaigns
downplayed "the religion-infused moralizing that had long typified antiporn political discourse" in favor of pragmatic considerations.[24]

Antiporn opinionmakers in Spain also reacted to the public's antagonism toward outdated moralism by modernizing their discourse and
representing their platform as mainstream and youthful. In his coverage
of the protest in London, Alfonso Barra reiterated his position in favor
of "moderate" modernization, rejecting "immorality as a system" while
normalizing modern fashions that broke away with old propriety norms
by exhibiting the body.[25] He also claimed that the Nationwide Festival
of Light was fundamentally a youth movement. The organizers of the
festival indeed did put the emphasis on the mobilization of youth, to generate the impression that opposition to obscenity created a consensus
among people of all ages and ideologies.[26] One of the main goals of the
antipornography campaign by British evangelical groups was to prevent
positive representations of homosexuality. However, Barra described
ultraconservative activist Mary Whitehouse, who waged a series of legal
battles against British gay publications, as a "standard-bearer for wom-
en's rights."[27] Antipornography activists appealed to a so-called silent
social majority that opposed the sexualization of mass culture yet embraced other aspects of modern politics.

Barra acknowledged the difficulty of conveying the threat of obscenity (encompassing queerness) without falling into it. To provide Spanish readers with a vivid impression of the perversion taking place in
British cinema theaters, Barra cited the film *Myra Breckinridge* (1970),
describing it as "a homosexual fantasy, with a hero changing his genetic
identity."[28] This film focuses on a transgender woman who, in the most

controversial scene, anally rapes a young man, interspersing images of classical Hollywood stars with the protagonist's speech, while she explains that this is an educational act to deconstruct a conventional masculinity anchored in notions of normality and fears of emasculation.[29] Barra was well aware that reporting on the widespread presence of pornography in London could potentially lead to his own writings becoming obscene. He continuously emphasized his own visceral sense of disgust: "my pen trembles with disgusted amazement and indignation when referring all these irreverence, sacrileges, and obscenities."[30] He presented himself as a martyr of the cause forced to expose himself to obscenity to inform and warn Spanish readers of the depravity that had taken over European societies.[31] He criticized young leftists who merged psychoanalysis, sexual freedom, and socialism despite the strict Soviet policies to protect traditional family structures. This was an argument commonly used by Spanish conservatives to oppose the New Left and sexual liberation. For his conclusion, Barra advocated for the freedom to defend "beauty, decency, and the affects and ideals of human life," namely, the freedom to censor.[32]

The Legalization of Softcore in Spain and Hardcore in France

The year 1975 marked the introduction of hard-core in French theaters—the film *Exhibition* sold six hundred thousand tickets in Paris in 1975—as well as the massive arrival of American hard-core in France.[33] President Giscard d'Estaing promoted, since his election in 1974, a policy of moral "relaxation" that he conceived as a central factor in building an "advanced liberal society." In 1975, the French government lifted all censorship—which moved many Spaniards to cross the French border to watch *Deep Throat*—while General Franco's deteriorating health made it clear to all that his personalist regime was about to end.[34] The French government's liberalism in sexual matters affected gay pornography. The 1975 film *Good Hot Stuff* avoided censorship by using the alibi of a "documentary" on the American studio Hand in Hand, introducing gay hard-core in French commercial theaters.[35] Gay pornography captured an urban transition between the "declining industrial past" and the "neoliberal future" of Western metropolises like New York.[36] From the early to the mid-1970s government policies shaped the agenda of centrist liberalism—first in the United States and later in France—in a way that combined moral permissiveness with a transition from industrialism to economic neoliberalism, validating consumers' interest in technical and commercial innovation. The pornography business's technical sophistication and large profit margins—which centered the debate on the Dangerousness Law in 1970—remained central to Spanish hardliners' arguments in the mid-1970s. Antonio Colón in *ABC* echoed the opinion of French journalists who warned readers about the "assault" of American hard-core of relatively high technical quality and low cost.[37]

As hard-core became mainstream in neighboring countries, the reformist minister of information and tourism Pío Cabanillas promoted a law (passed in March 1975, when he had already been demoted) that relaxed censorship by allowing filmmakers to include partial nudity if it was necessary for the development of the story: "nudity will be allowed if the wholeness of the film demands it, but will be rejected if it intends to arouse the spectator's passions or incurs in pornography."[38] This law still banned films that justified:

A) Suicide and homicide out of compassion [that is, euthanasia];
B) Revenge and violence as a means to solve social and human issues;
C) Prostitution, sexual perversion, adultery, and illicit sexual relationships;
D) Abortion and anything that undermines the institution of marriage and family; and
E) Drug and alcohol addiction.[39]

Reformist policymakers proposed a paradigm of sexual modernization that would satisfy male straight consumers' interest in female nudity while banning any attempt at openly normalizing nonreproductive sexualities or sex outside of marriage. The new censorship code guaranteed that the heterosexual nuclear family remained the only acceptable societal paradigm but legalized soft-core under the alibi of narrative unity. These legal reforms infuriated hardliners, who convinced Franco to demote Cabanillas.[40] Films that included scenes of nudity as part of a moralistic narrative were likely to pass through censorship under the Cabanillas law. A paradigmatic example was *Las adolescentes* (1975), which told the story of a good girl who was perverted by her classmates in a boarding school and ended up in the hands of a criminal gang that produced pornography. A key moment in the story involved a Black man trying to rape the protagonist, in a way that merged racial and sexual anxieties to incite viewers to be vigilant regarding the threats of pornography and perversion by youth subcultures, represented as alien to Spain.[41] The government allowed scenes of nudity and sexual violence if they were subordinated to the promotion of traditional mores, and some filmmakers adjusted to this scenario by crafting reactionary narratives. The goal was to satisfy moviegoers' sexual curiosity while reconciling it with a moralizing agenda that would appease censors.

In the last days of the Franco regime, works that discussed nonreproductive sexual activities provoked a visceral reaction among censors, even when written in a clinical tone and from a moderately liberal perspective. In April 1975, the publisher Sedmay submitted *Las españolas en secreto* (Spanish women in secrecy) to be approved by censors. This book was based on the clinical experience of gynecologist Adolfo Abril and a series of interviews conducted by journalist José Antonio Valverde. The male authors advocated for open discussions of sexual matters to overcome the negative effects of ignorance and repression but still treated heterosexuality as a normative ideal. In fact, they theorized lesbianism as a byproduct of repression.[42] While the book's perspective was anything but transgressive, one of the censors reporting on it categorized it as scandalous because it praised "liberated" women interested in experiencing sexual pleasure and able to use contraceptives, dismissing the Catholic ideal of female chastity. The censor used racialized language by equating excessive sexual freedom with primitivism he attributed to African Pygmies.[43] The authors and the censor defined Spain's civilized status through sexuality but in different ways, either as the overcoming of taboos through specialized expertise (in the authors' view) or in terms of traditional religious and moral norms (in the censor's view). Sedmay also consulted the Ministry of Information about *Convivencia: Cuadernos de orientación para la intimidad de la pareja* (Coexistence: Guidance notebooks for the intimacy of the couple), a magazine that often addressed the issue of non-normative sexualities. Through these consultations, these materials were deposited in state archives, where they remain to this day. The May 1976 issue of *Convivencia* was a monograph on lesbianism. The censor objected to its lighthearted and noncondemnatory treatment of the subject and to the dissemination of information on contraceptives, which was prohibited by the penal code.[44] *Convivencia* editors adopted a moderately liberal position, stating that their intention was neither to condemn nor to celebrate lesbianism but rather to attain veracity through informed analysis in an almost clinical manner. The images that illustrated the monograph were not particularly provocative, with the exception of a painting by Leonor Fini depicting two women, one of them lying down while the other separates her legs to dip her face between them (the censor used his red marker to block this image).[45]

Sexual liberalization was gaining ground in Spain before Franco's death as the result of Francoist reformist politicians' initiatives to direct this process on their own terms—maintaining their core moral values, favoring straight male consumers, and excluding everyone else. Reformers' willingness to compromise in matters of sexual morality led significant actors to reassess and restate their priorities after the death of Franco on 20 November 1975. The cardinal-archbishop of Madrid, Vicente Enrique y Tarancón, issued a pastoral letter on 22 November 1975. Throughout the 1970s Tarancón had acquired a well-deserved reputation for his critical stance on the dictatorship. However, in his 1975 letter he adopted an alarmist tone to discuss the sexualization of consumer culture. Tarancón expressed his concern that Spaniards—set as they were on overcoming underdevelopment caused by decades of authoritarian rule—would open the floodgates to a "current of immorality" and "escalation of pornography" coming from Europe. Tarancón, despite his antiauthoritarian credentials, had joined the front lines of the "war on pornography" that intensified after Franco's death.[46]

Sex in Transition

The sexualization of democracy—the widespread notion that political and sexual freedoms went hand in hand—played a central role in the political reform process that started in 1975 and culminated in the passage of the democratic Constitution in 1978. From a critical standpoint, Alberto Cardín and Federico Jiménez Losantos, leading figures of the left-wing Barcelona intelligentsia in the 1970s (Losantos would eventually become a well-known right-wing radio host), edited a volume on porn theory in 1978. They saw pornography as the "touchstone" to understand the subject's cultural integration in advanced capitalist societies and criticized the "state apparatus' operation to integrate pornographic products, from movies to vibrators."[47] They focused on the top-down process of sexual liberalization tacitly accepted by the right, depicting porn as "substantially anti-ideological" and contemporary permissiveness as an "antidote" inoculated in Spaniards to convert them from Francoism to European democracy.[48] In the previous chapter, I discussed how Lluís Fernández advocated for inoculating porn (understood as cultural and gender transgression) on people, whereas for Cardín and Losantos this metaphor referred to the reshuffling of the boundaries between the private and public realms through pornography's genital fixation and spectators' voyeuristic satisfaction.[49] In both cases, Spaniards were seen as passive receptacles of a sexual revolution in the media; their bodies were not immunized because the Franco regime kept them isolated from "contagion," and with Franco's death the main question was whether that media and erotic contagion was going to contribute to sociopolitical continuity or rupture. In a related but recent critique, Labrador argues that in the 1970s political elites intended to demobilize citizens by offering parliamentarian representation as a substitute for participatory democracy. For Labrador, this process of liberalization—represented in popular erotic magazines like *Interviú*—atomized politics and sexuality, offering citizens spectacles of liberation (masturbatory pleasure and elections) in lieu of actual emancipation. Radical satirical publications like *Por favor* (1974–1978) and protest youth movements criticized the top-down design of these policies and the use of female nudity and other superficial expressions of sexual liberation to legitimate a system of limited democracy.[50] Jorge Marí argues, on the contrary, that the *destape* was "inherently political," even an engine of democratization, precisely because the ubiquity of Francoist censorship had politicized banned content. For Marí, the "symbolic violence" of censorship was an extension of the "physical violence" that had originated the Franco regime.[51] From a celebratory standpoint, Carlos Santos, who was very active as a journalist during the democratic transition, suggests that many Spanish citizens experienced democracy first and foremost through sexual freedom.[52] During the transition, sexuality was not equated with procreation anymore. According to Santos, most Spaniards did not make "distinctions between sexual repression and political repression" when they expressed their desire to overcome the Franco era.[53]

In September 1976, the cover of *Interviú* was a nude photograph of the actress and singer Pepa Flores, once a celebrity child (she launched her film career in the 1950s, when she was eleven years old). The issue had record sales of over a million copies. According to Santos, Pepa

Flores was a symbol of tenderness and candor, which is why "Spaniards lost their innocence on that day, defeated in an unequal battle with freedom."[54] Santos's use of "innocence" implies that sexual naivete was the correlate of the population's disenfranchisement under the Franco regime. The role of political violence as the foundation of "innocence"—a term that has a telling parallelism with defendants' self-representation in cases of pornography—goes virtually unnoticed in Santos's narrative, which romanticizes the tensions inherent to post-dictatorship regimes. Labrador interprets the *Interviú* cover in a diametrically different way, as a "porno-democratic muse," an allegorical image of democracy's body politic, which reduces male voters to the condition of voyeurs.[55]

Tania Navarro Amo was interviewed and photographed for *Interviú* in April 1982. Her testimony was framed in sensationalist terms, with the title "Tania, el travesti más humillado: 'Me penetran 15 veces diarias'" (Tania, the most humiliated travesti: "They penetrate me fifteen times a day").[56] While Tania recognizes that the journalist distorted her story to exaggerate the most shocking elements—especially sexual violence and abuse—she also emphasizes that the interview gave her the opportunity to be generously remunerated (at a moment when the state did not contemplate any reparations for people victimized under the Dangerousness Law) and also to choose how she wanted to be photographed to highlight the aspects of her body that she liked the most.[57] The branch of the *destape* represented by *Interviú* was both reductionist in its approach to state violence and discrimination issues and a framework of opportunity for people like Tania who did not count on many other venues or institutional channels to denounce their situation and make themselves visible.

Disagreements over the interpretation of the *destape* correlate with the assessment of the post-transitional system as either a failure to radical popular expectations (Labrador's view) or a successful model of management of political conflict (Santos's view). Rather than discussing the transition period in view of its outcomes, judicial records and censorship files reveal the contingent negotiation of the boundaries of state permissiveness by editors, authors, and newsstand and sex shop owners, among others, as well as authorities' double standard in differentiating between mainstream and transgressive materials.

Starting in the mid-1970s, defense lawyers at Dangerousness Courts drew attention to the gradual changes in government criteria for the treatment of pornography trafficking. In December 1976, in the case of a defendant accused of trading in pornographic tapes, the defense lawyer requested that an official of the Ministry of Information and Tourism rule on "the moral qualification of the confiscated films, according to the current criteria of the Ministry, taking into account that these have suffered notable changes in the last twelve months."[58] This line of defense pointed to significant inconsistencies between the legal and institutional frameworks that regulated media contents. As I noted before, incorporating pornography into the Dangerousness Law created jurisdiction issues, since the dissemination of obscenity was already punishable through the censorship apparatus (according to the 1966 Press Law) and through the articles of the penal code covering public scandal (overseen by the Supreme Court). This duplication of functions and the overlap between the Press and Dangerousness Laws allowed defense lawyers to question the classification of pornography as a threat to society, since the Suárez administration was adapting to the formal requirements of liberal democracy. In October 1976, Minister of Information and Tourism Andrés Reguera Guajardo extended an amnesty to journalists who had been prevented from working for political reasons.[59] In 1977, Royal Decree 24 abolished the government's power to "suspend" publications based on political criteria. This measure was a prerequisite for holding democratic elections with a plurality of opinions and freedom of expression.[60] Even though the law's stated intention was to guarantee freedom of expression, it preserved the inviolability of institutions like the monarchy and the armed forces. After the passing of this law, the first democratic elections were held in June 1977, continuing the political transition process that culminated in the Constitution of 1978, which recognized freedom of the press and freedom of expression as constitutional rights.[61]

The legalization of freedom of expression to normalize political pluralism during the democratic transition had as a correlate the de facto recognition of freedom to commercialize soft-core. This phenomenon manifested itself in the Dangerousness Courts, where judges increasingly chose to dismiss the few cases of pornography that were presented to them. For example, the case from December 1976 that I mentioned earlier does not have any sentence, because Judge Álvarez Cruz opted to dismiss it.[62] The lack of judicial and governmental action constituted a policy of normalization. Moreover, defense lawyers demanded that judges acknowledge that consuming soft-core had increasingly become normalized. In 1976, the Barcelona police arrested a man for trying to sell three pornographic magazines (two issues of *Color Sperma* and one issue of *Erotica*) in an alley near the port, hiding them in a newspaper. The defendant stated that he had bought them from a sailor for his own recreation, not in order to sell them.[63] This statement made sense as a defense strategy, given that only trafficking in pornography was typified in the Dangerousness Law. However, in this case the judge sentenced the defendant to go to prison, pay a substantial fine, and leave Barcelona.[64] The defense appealed, arguing that it was absurd to prosecute—even selectively and to set an example—the distribution and consumption of pornography, since this had become such a widespread phenomenon. According to the lawyer, the type of magazines confiscated from the defendant "are currently in all newsstands and in the San Antonio market on Sundays."[65] In 1978, the Special Dangerousness Court of the Audiencia Nacional overturned the ruling on the grounds that there was no conclusive evidence of the magazines' pornographic nature or the defendant's intention to sell them.[66] By questioning whether magazines such as *Color Sperma* could be classified as pornography, the Audiencia limited the scope of this legal figure and legitimated the public visibility of soft-core.

Meanwhile, conservative media outlets like *ABC* advocated for an alliance between the Catholic Church and the state to put limits on the "pornographic wave." The same articles that established the unequivocal rejection of pornography as *ABC*'s editorial line included images that illustrated society's sexualization—women in underwear, couples in intimate positions, and so forth—appealing to readers who were potentially more interested in these images than in the texts that condemned them. In February 1976, an *ABC* article claimed that publishers and theater and movie producers were taking advantage of the ambiguous boundaries between eroticism and pornography to normalize the latter and transform it into the most visible and tangible manifestation of democratization. According to the article, one of the most alarming consequences of this phenomenon was that it encompassed homosexuality, hitherto represented as marginal or shameful, but was now featured in sympathetic storylines, as in the movie *The Boys in the Band* (directed by William Friedkin, 1970). This was an explicit acknowledgment that marica culture—more than nudity or eroticism by themselves—was the primary target of reactionary groups.[67] The article also reported on the government drafting a law to ban hard-core pornography and impose fiscal disincentives on soft-core pornography, as a formula to reconcile the sexual promises of democracy with social conservatism. Soon after, *ABC* published letters from readers who expressed their support for the enactment of antipornography legislation.[68]

However, these measures were never implemented, probably because most of the population was in favor of ending censorship. According to a poll conducted in early 1976 and published in the Catholic newspaper *Ya*, most respondents (52 per cent) supported the end of film censorship, compared to 35 percent who supported content policing by the state. The demographic group that became a privileged political subject during the transition process—educated middle- and upper-class men in urban areas—was overrepresented in the anticensorship side.[69] This demographic group was the "mesocratic" subject on which the political elites deposited their hopes to lead a transition process characterized by moderation.[70] The selective eradication of censorship contributed, then, to strengthening the agenda of reformist elites.

Despite perceptible changes in social attitudes and state policies, marica pornographers were still targeted as essential transgressors. In May 1976, a man was brought before the court of Barcelona accused of conducting clandestine sessions in which he would project porn movies for small audiences in a room with walls covered with photographs of nude men and women. Significantly, the focus of the police report was primarily the gender performance of the defendant and his acquaintances: "He has friends of little note and effeminate aspect, who externalize their [care for] good dress; [they look] neat, with a [clean] haircut, and use perfume. Up until now, we have not had to warn them about these circumstances. Regarding socio-political issues, he is classified as suspect because of his family background, since his father was shot for his relevant role in the Red Zone," referring to the territory controlled by forces loyal to the Second Republic in the Civil War.[71] According to this report, caring for one's appearance (perfume, haircut, and overall neatness) was a feminizing trait among poor males, who were then treated as maricas, but these same criteria arguably did not apply to upper-class men, from whom neatness was socially expected and codified in class terms. In addition, the defendant was assumed to be politically suspect based on the view that working-class subversiveness was hereditary, transmitted along bloodlines from the generation of antifascist fighters defeated in the Civil War (father who fought in the Red Zone) to their children (marica offspring). Despite these factors, the judge acquitted the defendant, taking into consideration that he suffered from a partial mental disability that reduced his liability.[72]

Newsstand owners were also at a border zone regarding the newly official permissiveness, as they were exposed to complaints by citizens who opposed the public visibility of pornography. In June 1976, one such citizen reported to the Barcelona police that, while taking a stroll, he saw a newsstand that "exhibited, together with toys for children, calendars of nude and semi-nude women." He bought five of them, at which point the newsstand owner asked if "he wanted something stronger" for a higher price, referring to hard-core.[73] The complainant refused to pay that price and went to the police to report the incident. It is unclear what his motivations were; either he was offended by pornography, or he was upset by the prices set by the defendant. His statement, in any case, reveals the daily negotiation of the boundaries between soft-core (sold publicly) and hard-core (sold clandestinely) as well as the correlation between secrecy and a higher market value. Nude calendars had become affordable and easily accessible at this point, while displaying them could potentially attract consumers interested in more explicit and unaffordable materials that remained illegal. The police officers followed the complainant to the newsstand and observed him as he bought one of the illegal magazines. At that moment, they arrested the defendant and confiscated a series of publications: *Sex Bizarre, Slave Girl Terror, La viciosa* (Vicious woman), *Incestuosamente vuestra* (Incestuously yours), *La folladora* (The woman who fucks), *Sexy Girls,* and *Sex Delight.* The titles of confiscated films include *Mujeres ardientes* (Ardent women), *Discovering Orgasm*, and *Sex on the Motorway.* Having been arrested *in flagrante*, the defendant could not deny the accusations. He admitted that he had been engaged in the pornography business for three months, by importing magazines and movies from Perpignan, France. Another facet of the business was exchanging secondhand materials with customers. In his defense, he emphasized that, after all, the hard-core materials had not been exposed to the public but were only available for a chosen clientele of adult men.[74] Similar to the "frosted glass" case, from the mid-1970s the primary legal issue was not the consumption of pornography but rather the establishment of the proper mediating role for businessmen who should guarantee that minors (and implicitly women) did not have access to it.

Defendants acknowledged that the clandestine distribution of pornography produced a very high profit margin. According to the newsstand owner, he earned on average 500 pesetas for each magazine,
while the legal minimum wage at that time was 345 pesetas per day.[75] By
selling a single magazine, he earned an income 40 percent higher than
someone working a full day for the minimum wage. The legal framework
of censorship produced a clandestine market with profit margins that
provided a strong incentive to get involved in the business. In addition,
the dismissal of many of these cases amounted to a policy of permissiveness. The prosecutor in 1977 requested that the security measures
established by law be applied to the defendant, including imprisonment
for up to three years, but the court ignored the request.[76] Instead, the
court focused on locating the confiscated materials, which apparently
at some point had been lost in the chain of custody, probably to police
officers who used it for their own recreation or profit.[77] After months of
futile attempts to locate the evidence, in 1978 the prosecutor withdrew
its previous request and recommended the dismissal of the case (confirmed by the judge).[78] It was a lost cause: lower-tier state agents' interest
in pornography made the apparatus of repression close to inoperative.

Even when judicial authorities were able to oversee the chain of custody, they produced documentation that testified to their concern about
state agents' potential interest in pornography. The last catalogue entry
related to pornography at the Barcelona judicial archive corresponds to a
series of police proceedings in 1979. An antidrug patrol, having infiltrated
a large nightclub, reported that part of the clientele smoked marijuana
while pornographic films were screened. Since some of the clients were
minors, the manager was arrested and the police confiscated a projector
and seven films.[79] To verify that the films were indeed pornographic, the
Guardia Civil screened them in the "weaponry room of these barracks."
The report refers to "due formalities" that were used in this screening
(probably so that no one questioned officers' motivations in organizing it)
without further explanation.[80] The proceedings did not lead to a formal
trial. The owner of the nightclub alleged that the minors had managed
to enter because of an oversight by the doorman, acknowledged that pornographic films had been screened for months, and claimed ignorance
on attendees using or selling drugs. No judicial action was taken by the
Dangerousness Court until a few years later, when a judge ordered the
case to be closed in 1985.[81] Starting in the late 1970s, judicial inaction in

the Dangerousness Courts reflected judges' decision to leave the prosecution of pornography to ordinary courts, which would apply the penal code to decide cases classified as public scandal, under the authority of the Supreme Court.

Selective Censorship and the *Destape* Iconography

In July 1977, the government dissolved the Ministry of Information (replaced by the Ministry of Culture) that had overseen censorship during the Franco regime.[82] This milestone—along with the law on freedom of expression and the November 1977 law on the distribution of films—put a formal end to censorship. However, state employees were still submitting reports on cultural products for the democratic Ministry of Culture as late as 1982.[83] They could pass their reports to the prosecutor's office if they considered that a publication or cultural production was involved in a crime such as public scandal. According to Santos, the most common resolution was a monetary fine of 10,000 pesetas and the editor in chief's forced admission of responsibility.[84] Amid these institutional changes, civil servants (officially not called censors anymore) in charge of identifying potentially illegal publications targeted contents in ways that reflected the lasting effects of Francoism on post-dictatorship state policies. Criticisms of state authoritarianism or police abuse and open discussions of nonreproductive sexualities (including contraception and homosexuality, both criminalized until 1978) were still targeted as public scandal or contempt.

One of the most controversial cases of post-Franco censorship involved the banning of Eloy de la Iglesia's *Los placeres ocultos* in 1977 on the grounds that the film portrayed homosexuality without moralizing about it. The film's protagonist is a banker who engages in transactional sex with working-class youths, until he falls in love with one of them, who does not reciprocate. They maintain a platonic relationship that involves the youth's girlfriend, but the story open-endedly concludes with a fight between the protagonists and the exposure of the banker as a homosexual. Shortly after the banning of the film, Eloy de la Iglesia, in an interview published in February 1977, argued that the film gave visibility to gay people's issues, rooted in marginalization and conservative morality, to demand that democratic parties, particularly on the left, embrace the fight of sexual minorities against discrimination.[85] The government finally allowed the screening of the film in April 1977 to silence the critical voices demanding an end to censorship. Historian Geoffroy Huard analyzes the controversy around this film as a sort of "Spanish Stonewall" that played a pivotal role in raising awareness about the discrimination of LGBTQ+ people.[86]

By the late 1970s, while the exhibition of female nudity for the male gaze had been normalized, civil servants in the Ministry of Culture still classified homoeroticism as obscene. In 1979, already under the democratic Constitution, the publisher Permanencias printed a short volume of illustrations by Tom of Finland, who pioneered gay porn for mass consumption starting in the 1950s. A civil servant reported: "My opinion is that they are pornographic, for male homosexuals. [. . .] All pages, without exclusion, are obscene. Judicial communication."[87] The report was passed along to the prosecutor's office to take legal measures. These drawings eroticize and fantasize situations involving sexual abuse between prisoners and by police officers. Although all illustrations showed hyper-muscular men with disproportionately large genitalia, none of them included images of anal or oral sex but rather a positioning of the bodies that evoked the possibility of sex between men. The male gaze functions in these images as a substitute for sex; there are no sexual acts, but men desire and penetrate each other with their gaze.[88] Under the new constitutional regime, homoerotic images could still be denounced by state employees as criminal, which contrasted with state policies that normalized pornography for straight male consumers as a central element of democratization.

Amid the rapid changes of this period, porn as media was remarkably self-reflexive as a historiographical and cultural intervention.[89] As I embarked on this book project, friends who knew of my passion for the subject matter gave me presents that I treasure as a small but representative collection of "obscene" materials from the 1970s and 1980s. My friend Joaquín found a copy of Félix Llaugé's ¿Qué sabe de sexología? (What do you know about sexology?), published in 1971, that caught his attention because a reader had altered it in ways that illustrate my argument that even the most inoffensive-looking materials could be erotically appropriated. The text of the book is a prudish take on sexology, but someone had colored the anatomical illustrations of genitals and full nude bodies. As previously argued, in the early 1970s clinical and/or condemnatory texts on sexual behavior were the ones most likely to pass censorship; in this

FIGURE 14. An illustration criticizing the hypocrisy of homophobic men who harass maricas while participating in clandestine sexual markets. The same man who yells "Marica" at a passerby then goes home to inflate a sex doll imported from Perpignan (France). Included in the March/April 1977 issue of *Marginados*.

case, however, the coloring was meant to bring flesh into the page, transposing the book from the realm of expert-guided self-discipline to the haptic/erotic realm. I also acquired a few items myself in flea markets and secondhand bookstores, including a few late-1970s reprints of *The Pearl* by Ediciones Polen, a collection of erotic tales originally published in Victorian England. In the Spanish edition, the back cover of each volume contains information on the historical context and a vindication of the long-lasting cultural and sexual potency of this illustrated tales: "Almost hundred years later [these booklets] come to light in Spain, because EDICIONES POLEN believes that their merits are still alive and must be known [. . .] we hope to edit THE PEARL fortnightly in the book format, because undoubtedly its content deserves this lasting format and not the magazine's volatile character."[90] These editors' uncanny desire to leave behind a lasting oeuvre is a byproduct of their historical reflexivity.

Those editors wanted to reactivate the pre-Franco sycaliptic tradition, honor their predecessors in the fight against puritanism, and make collectors and readers aware that obscenity is worth preserving. They formulated a praxis of preservation that involved touching and transforming the curated text; each booklet was illustrated with images that the Spanish editors handpicked from multiple contexts, from classic Japanese prints and French eighteenth-century drawings to avant-garde art of the interwar period. The addition of this imaginary made the booklets more marketable, yet still historically oriented; while the covers reflect that censorship contemporaneously lingered in Spain—black stars cover any genitals and there are trigger warnings for minors and sensitive readers. Broadly speaking, the placing of censor-mandated stars is central to the marketing of 1970s obscenity. In a flea market in València, I found a copy of *Camilo Bolas: El Socialista*, part of a series of comic books inspired by the Italian character *Il montatore* (The mechanic). The back cover introduces Camilo Bolas as a "rabid socialist [. . .] he fights against the capitalist right but also defends the company as far as it belongs to everyone." The politics of erotic identification between working-class readers and the comic's main character were channeled through masculinity; Camilo Bolas is a womanizer always willing to take risks as a skilled manual laborer. As I will elaborate, sexual populism imposed itself over *Playboy*'s elitism during the *destape*. Camilo Bolas's price is marked as "50 pesetas"—quite affordable compared to the prices listed in judicial records—in a star-shaped tag that simultaneously covers part of a woman's buttock—the character's zealous socialism is in tension with the commodification of female nudity. Publishers turned visual markers of censors' lingering presence into titillating signs of what could be discovered beyond the cover; this was the print version of frosted glass. This is also true for a series of magazines that another friend, Piro Subrat, gave me. *KISMI*'s cover is simply green, with no images, no date of issue, only the warning "banned for minors." Along with a short text, it contains photos of an orgy in which the participants' clothing and the decoration of the space are inspired by psychedelics and hippie trends, much as in that *guateque* of young people judged by the Supreme Court in 1971 (see chapter 3). The *mise-en-scène* in all these magazines includes 1970s fashion codes and aesthetic schemes: from the color palettes to the hairstyles, porn's contemporaneousness betrays that it is meant for immediate consumption. Likewise, for Spanish publications, the extent to which

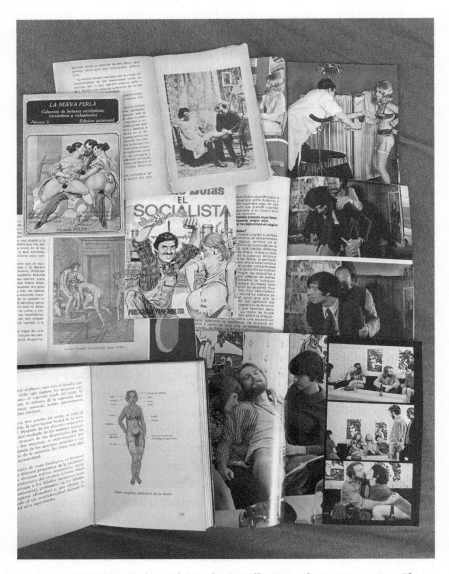

FIGURE 15. Some items from the author's collection of vintage erotica. Photograph by the author.

non-straight sex is visible is an index of different stages of the democratic transition. The booklet *El campesino insaciable* (The insatiable farmer) is clearly from the late 1970s or early 1980s; prior to that, the cover's explicit depiction of the farmer anally penetrating an elegantly dressed man and kissing a woman's breast would not have been allowed. The trigger warning is a mockery of the censorship of yore: "The reader is warned that this facsimile, because of its theme, may make him HORNY!!!"

Despite state employees' persistent fixation on the "threat" of homosexuality, 1977 was a turning point in this regard because editors started to publish explicit depictions of homoeroticism that went hand in hand with radical demands of sexual pluralism. The eighth issue of *Hip,* published that year, included explicit images to illustrate a monograph on homosexuality, going beyond the liberal/clinical tone of pre-1977 publications. A civil servant at the Ministry of Culture reported that the magazine intended to legitimate homosexuality, which along with its photographic content could constitute a crime.[91] He crossed out with his red marker those photographs that he considered obscene, materially setting the boundaries where consumers' interests and desires would meet his prudishness. These photos depict a Black man and a White man taking turns rimming each other, anal sex, erect penises, drag performers, women kissing and performing oral sex on each other, and so forth. The headline on the cover is "We are all born bisexual," with the subtitle announcing that 30 percent of the population has engaged in homosexual practices. This framing questioned the rigid sexual identities that undergirded the clinical approach to sexual matters. Furthermore, *Hip* published first-person accounts of homoerotic encounters, departing from the tendency of earlier magazines (like *Convivencia*) to present maricas as objects of analysis instead of subjects of desire.[92] Maricas were also vocal in denouncing state violence. Given that the penal code categorized "slandering" (*calumniar*) police officers on duty as contempt, publishing first-person accounts that reflected those officers' abuses of power could make publishers liable.[93] In 1978, a civil servant at the Ministry of Culture objected to the publication of *Homosexualidad y represión* (Homosexuality and repression), authored by psychologist Manuel Ángel Soriano Gil, on the grounds that the book advocated for homosexual people's right to be visible and included transcriptions of interviews with homosexuals who complained of "ill treatment by the *Guardia Civil* and the Police," but the book was published nonetheless;

a second civil servant reported that news of these abuses were public knowledge and therefore their dissemination could not constitute a crime.[94] One of Soriano Gil's interviewees described how the Guardia Civil patrolled a nudist beach, enjoying the view of nude bathers and occasionally arresting and physically abusing the maricas who frequented the beach.[95] This anonymous interviewee identified moral policing with voyeurism, manifested in officers' cynical use of violence.

The police targeting of maricas contrasts with the equation between democratic politics and female nudity in the iconography of the transition. The image that for many contemporary observers came to encapsulate the ethos of the transition is a photograph, published in *El País*, Spain's major progressive newspaper, of a ceremony in 1978 in which actress Susana Estrada exhibited her bare chest while receiving an award from the mayor of Madrid, the socialist intellectual Enrique Tierno Galván. One of the men smiling complacently in the background of this scene was the owner of the company Planeta, which published *Playboy*. For Jorge Marí this image symbolized the "alliance" between male leftist intellectuals/politicians (Tierno Galván) and *destape* female performers (Estrada) that brought together the legitimacy of high culture and the popularity of sexual liberalization.[96] Estrada had performed in a show called *Historias de striptease*, a parody of censorship that included scenes of full nudity. Francoist censors had banned the famous scene in the 1946 Charles Vidor movie *Gilda* in which Rita Hayworth takes off her gloves, while in her show Estrada stripped herself completely— except for her gloves. This was a political act that revealed the paradoxical nature of censorship, which accentuated the eroticism of gestures like Hayworth's precisely by banning them. Estrada's interpretation of her own agency has added a different layer to scholarly readings. She clarified that, as she moved to the stage, her dress accidentally opened up to reveal her chest: "I could have covered myself, but that would not have been true to myself, there was nothing to be ashamed of."[97] Tierno Galván told her to stay calm and cover herself, but she answered, "I am very calm, Professor." She refused to be patronized, as she was aware of what her gesture meant. Not in vain had she experienced the consequences of actively demanding and performing sexual liberation—she had been sentenced for public scandal because of her sex advice column in *Playlady*, the authorities took away her passport and right to vote until 1987; she had to escape from a man who tried to shoot her on stage in

Bilbao; she strolled nude with a man in a submissive role on Madrid's major boulevard to make BDSM culture visible; and she wrote a song supporting same-sex relationships.[98] Estrada does not perceive herself as an icon of the institutionalization of eroticism but rather as a historical agent who contributed to the cause of sexual liberation. By the same token, the interplay between top-down market strategies and consumers' preferences shaped the pornography industry, as illustrated by the trajectories of *Playboy* and *Interviú*, epitomes of the elitist and populist paradigms of porn publishing, respectively.

Playboy's Debacle and *Interviú*'s Success

Playboy was first published in Spain in 1978 with the full and enthusiastic backing of advertisers. Its financial debacle suggests that a significant segment of its potential consumers aspired to drastic changes in sexual mores that went unmet by the publication's editorial line (which aligned instead with political elites' schemas). Iván Tubau, editor in chief of the Spanish edition of *Playboy*, summed up the magazine's ethos: "What distinguishes eroticism from pornography? In the world of publishing, it's basically literary or artistic quality and, in many cases, the quality of paper or photo-mechanical reproduction, plainly speaking. In other words, eroticism protects itself through a luxurious cultural alibi. [. . .] Hefner sells the respectability of sex, more than raw sex."[99] A luxurious format and high-quality printing undergirded the editorial strategy to present *Playboy* as respectable erotica rather than "raw" pornography. During the 1970 debates on the Dangerousness Law (discussed in chapter 3), Pilar Primo de Rivera had already identified technical sophistication and luxury as key alibis through which pornographers could outwit the Francoist legal regime. The Spanish edition of *Playboy* printed primarily photographs of "flawless" women with "satin-like" white skin, perfectly proportioned bodies (according to Hugh Hefner's conceptions) and complacent smiles. For Tubau, these women had to be both beautiful and "liberated" (in the sense of sexually accessible but subordinated to men) to fulfill their role as "gadgets" that attracted readers to a larger world of consumerist gratification. In Tubau's words: "the fat, the skinny, the long-legged, the small, the resentful, the small-chested and other abnormal women are, of course, excluded from this satiny-paper paradise" (*Gordas, flacas, zanquilargas, enanas, despechadas, escurridas y otras anormales*

quedan por supuesto excluidas del satinado paraíso de papel).[100] The
Spanish edition of *Playboy* also republished canonical literature by
"scandalous" authors such as Henry Miller and Vladimir Nabokov and
political commentary representing a range of positions from Francoist
nostalgia to Eurocommunism (a moderate brand of communism that
accepted the parliamentarian rules of Western democracies), cementing
the magazine's centrist liberal reputation and contributing to the culture
of moderation and consensus favored by political elites.[101]

According to Tubau, *Playboy* did not reach its sales target in Spain
due to a sort of asynchrony. It was both "too late and too soon" for its formula to be appealing.[102] Hugh Hefner came up with this formula in the
"mesocratic" and puritan U.S. context of the 1950s. Tubau shared with
Pilar Primo de Rivera their belief that *Playboy* represented the golden era
of liberal capitalism, an ethos of prosperity and unlimited expectations
of socioeconomic progress. *Playboy* was born as the Western world tran-
sitioned from production to consumption as the main economic engine,
which translated into the promotion of "reasonable hedonism" (Tubau's
phrase) as a societal ideal. *Playboy*'s editors had no qualms in objectify-
ing women and did not address them as potential consumers. For Tubau,
Playboy's politics aligned with U.S. centrist liberalism, which pursues
gradual progress and avoids social conflict.

Spanish editors were very optimistic about *Playboy*'s potential market,
since it had been the most emblematic and sought-after erotic magazine
for Spaniards traveling abroad during the Francoist period looking to
buy censored publications. They published a run of three hundred thousand copies, of which more than half did not sell. Following a liberal
logic, Tubau conceived the Franco regime as a historical anomaly that
prevented the formation of the normative democratic citizen, expressing
his hope that, in the postdictatorial era, the leadership of mainstream
political parties would reach a consensus to empower a mesocratic political subject, who would read *Playboy*.[103] However, by the time *Playboy*
could be legally published in Spain, its target readership—liberal-leaning,
affluent men interested in "tasteful" erotica and opinion and lifestyle articles—was not a consolidated market. According to Tubau, the Spanish
edition of *Playboy* targeted married men and offered them erotic entertainment and exclusive consumer habits compatible with a domestic life
organized around the nuclear family. As philosopher Paul B. Preciado
argues, *Playboy* had appealed to U.S. male readers in the 1950s and

1960s precisely because it offered them a "sexual utopia" that was an alternative to suburban family life. This was a paradigm of "masculine sexual liberation" that fostered men's complete autonomy by providing heterosexual bachelors with an ideal image of domestic management. To dissipate any fear that men's enjoyment of domestic consumerism was feminizing or queer, the magazine reified the centrality of the male gaze directed toward female bodies. Hefner also claimed that the healthy, rational, polygamous masculinity he proposed was an antidote to perversions like homosexuality, which flourished in repressive contexts.[104] This paradigm of domestic heterosexual masculinity was disseminated by *Playboy* in other countries. Verónica Giordano has studied the cooking section of the Brazilian edition of *Playboy* (called *Homem* and founded in 1975), which provided male readers with recipes for a "good life" as well as political commentary that was critical of the Brazilian military regime (1964–1985).[105] The Spanish edition of *Playboy* avoided the cult of bachelorhood that informed other national editions and Hefner's philosophy. The explanation might lie in a prevalent social model in Spain that normalized married men's extramarital sex, as Tubau himself pointed out.[106] By the time *Playboy* came out in Spain, most potential readers were not interested in a respectable "cultural alibi." They sought groundbreaking and sexually explicit publications, the "gross emphasis on the body's materiality" (including pubic hair) and the "absolute proximity" to consumers that *Hustler* introduced to U.S. consumers in 1974, undermining *Playboy*'s niche market of idealized soft-core.[107]

In Spain, *Interviú* was quite aggressive in its approach to the politics of the transition, publishing sensationalist headlines on scandalous news along with nude photographs of celebrities in its covers, a formula that suited this magazine very well.[108] For Marí, the central paradoxes of this formula—embracing eroticism as both liberation and the perpetuation of male domination; exalting democratic values while equating journalism with sensationalism—are inherent to the *destape* and the process of political transition.[109] The renowned writer Francisco Umbral described *Interviú* as "*Playboy* for poor people" *(el Playboy de los pobres)*. Working- and middle-class consumers were the leading demographic sector in this market, versus Tubau's interest in affluent consumers. The Spanish edition of *Playboy* published photographs of U.S. models (it took the magazine a whole year to recruit Spanish models), which did not line up with Spaniards' erotic fantasies.[110] *Interviú* opted for models who looked like "accessible and approachable goddesses," according to former president of Zeta press Francisco Matosas.[111] As historians Pablo Ben and Joaquín Insausti argue in their history of 1980s Peruvian porn, idealized images of U.S. White models were not appealing to male readers, who were instead enticed by realistic representations of local, racialized women.[112] In post-Soviet Russia, local erotic magazines like *Andrei* were also more successful than *Playboy* by stressing the "Russianness" of models and settings.[113] Similarly, Spanish readers were more attracted to the local models of *Interviú, Macho,* or *Penthouse* than to *Playboy*'s U.S. models. In sum, readers aimed for the real rather than the ideal, for sex rather than eroticism, and for rupture with Francoist moral norms rather than compromise.[114] The first issue of *Interviú* was published in May 1976, which means that the explosion of obscenity that Francoist *procuradores* had feared took over newsstands and daily conversations just six months after the death of Franco.

The judicial apparatus forcefully resisted this trend throughout the late 1970s. The table below illustrates the explosion of cases of pornography judged at the Supreme Court during the democratic transition. The number of rulings for the period between 1978 and 1983 is 182, a figure that more than doubled the total number of rulings for the entire preconstitutional period (83 through 1977). The percentage of defendants prosecuted for pornography who appealed their convictions to

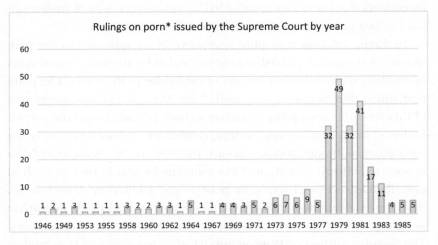

FIGURE 16. Rulings on porn* issued by the Supreme Court by year. Figure elaborated by the author based on data taken from the CENDOJ database. Searching the database for "porn*" with the asterisk included yielded the broadest results for cases related to pornography.

the Supreme Court during the Franco regime is probably low. They may have accurately perceived the judicial system as unsympathetic to their predicaments. By contrast, starting in the late 1970s editors, authors, and photographers continuously appealed their sentences to challenge the legal framework that treated obscene publications and films as an issue of liability for public scandal. As different historical actors perceived a framework of opportunity for sexual liberalization during the political transition, the judiciary (and the Supreme Court in particular) remained invested in policing public scandal. Many Franco-appointed judges remained in their positions, since the Spanish transition model did not lead to a systematic reevaluation of the role of civil servants appointed by the dictatorship.[115] The executive branch took the initiative in adjusting the legal framework to majority mores and the European context. On 24 February 1982, the government legalized X-rated theaters, sanctioning the consumption of pornography by adult audiences insofar as it remained circumscribed to specialized spaces and hidden from plain sight (the "frosted glass" model).[116]

Conclusion (and a Recapitulation)

Even though the chapters of this book are organized chronologically, they do not present a teleological view. The previous scholarship on obscenity in Spain has focused either on early twentieth-century literature or on the democratization of mass culture starting in the 1960s. Looking at anonymous pornographers and obscenity preserved in state archives, I bring these periods together to understand the continuities and ruptures throughout the century. Reactionary regimes used multiple formulas to target obscenity: from relative sexual freedom in the 1920s and the burning of books in the late 1930s to the 1975 law that legalized nudity for the sake of maintaining films' narrative cohesiveness. These formulas showcase authoritarianism's multifaceted nature and the complexity of state policies on the ground.

I have traced change over time but maintained the thematic focus on the paradoxical archival praxis of preserving the objects of one's loathing. The construction of obscenity in the archive brings together legal surveillance, theories of deviance, fascist politics, and the social influence of the Catholic Church but also lived experiences and the visual economy of pleasure. The policing of obscenity (public scandal, pornography, and "homosexuality") became a fundamental terrain in which authorities could concretize their claims over conflicting legitimizing discourses (traditional morality and socioeconomic modernization) while preserving the privileged status of "real men." Spain's antiliberal regimes fashioned a relationship between masculinity and obscenity that contrasts with historical narratives on obscenity in contemporary liberal democracies.[117] *Playboy* epitomizes the Sexual Revolution initiated in the United States in the 1950s: single men were set free from the demands of suburban family life by cultivating polygamy, consumerism, and their own domestic spaces. *Playboy* culture allowed men to be perpetual adolescents, focused on hedonism and released from family obligations and military citizenship.[118] The *Playboy*-era ideal of the eternal bachelor/adolescent made less sense in Spain, where married men's infidelities were tacitly tolerated and the political system infantilized citizens.[119] Men charged for the illegal possession of mainstream pornography, in their defense, commonly presented themselves as family heads while using a self-infantilizing terminology of sexual naivete—a double-edged performance that resonated positively with judicial authorities and resulted in leniency.[120] By contrast, maricas and sexually empowered cis and trans women became the primary targets of state surveillance because they challenged the equation between virility and Spanishness. Prior to being confiscated, erotica played a central role in the social fabric and intimate practices of these disenfranchised groups.

The transition of the 1970s made open and explicit the toleration of sexual entertainment, including *travesti* shows. The new paradigm implied the eroticization of democracy, namely the use of restricted permissiveness to generate support for the political reform process. Porn magazines proliferated, many of which are preserved in the censorship files along with the annotations by censors whose main concerns included women's liberation, homosexuality, and antiauthoritarianism. Until the mid-1970s, authors and editors used different alibis to publish on transgressive sexualities, such as the use of a clinical tone appropriate for a centrist liberal position. Radical demands for sexual freedom took center stage in new magazines that used visual materials and first-person testimonies to present maricas and trans people's perspectives. In parallel, the Dangerousness Courts became unwilling or unable to fulfill their role of destroying confiscated pornography.

Hence, the implementation of the framework of dangerousness to censor pornography ended in the 1970s, giving way to new regimes of regulation in which opposite social sectors and state actors continue to battle each other over which representations and experiences of sex and gender belong in the public realm.

NOTES

Introduction

1. Pierre Bourdieu, *Science of Science and Reflexivity*, trans. Richard Nice (Chicago: University of Chicago Press, 2004), 4.

2. George Steiner, "Ten (Possible) Reasons for the Sadness of Thought," *Salmagundi*, no. 146/147 (2005): 22.

3. Linda Williams, "Porn Studies: Proliferating Pornographies on/scene: An Introduction," in *Porn Studies*, edited by Linda Williams (Durham, N.C.: Duke University Press, 2004), 3.

4. STS 2546/1974 (STS stands for *Sentencias del Tribunal Supremo*, which signifies Supreme Court cases). Histórico del Tribunal Supremo/Centro de Documentación Judicial (digital database, hereafter CENDOJ).

5. As Matt Houlbrook affirms: "Queer lives always occupied spaces that were simultaneously and to varying degrees public *and* private, subject to surveillance *and* invisible, dangerous *and* safe." See Houlbrook, *Queer London: Perils and Pleasures in the Sexual Metropolis, 1918–1957* (Chicago: University of Chicago Press, 2020), 41.

6. File 93/1963, Signatura 8935, Archivo Histórico Provincial de Sevilla, Sevilla, Spain (hereafter AHPS). These photos had been kept by a British subject who had been deployed in Africa (most likely Nigeria, where he returned after being expelled from Spain). At some indefinite moment after Nigeria gained its independence from the United Kingdom in 1960, he moved to Spain. There he established a relationship with the arrested Moroccan. Both the Moroccan and

the British were eventually declared to be threats to society and expelled from Spain.

7. Ruling on April 28, 1969, cited in STS 2546/1974, CENDOJ.

8. Luis Vivas Marzal (Speech of 26 de November 1963, reply by Eduardo Molero Massa), "Contemplación jurídico-penal de la homosexualidad. Discurso de ingreso en la Academia Valenciana de Jurisprudencia y Legislación," *Publicaciones de la Academia Valenciana de Jurisprudencia y Legislación* 53 (1963): 19.

9. Vivas Marzal, "Contemplación jurídico-penal," 21.

10. STS 730/1961, CENDOJ.

11. Judges treated homoerotic images inconsistently: while the Barcelona Vagrancy Court preserved explicit photographs confiscated from homosexual defendants as evidence, the Madrid Vagrancy Court destroyed them. See Ruling on 20 May 1967, File 326/1967, Legajo 1830, Juzgado Especial de Vagos y Maleantes de Madrid, Archivo General de la Administración. Alcalá de Henares, Spain (hereafter AGA).

12. Vivas Marzal, "Contemplación jurídico-penal," 23–24.

13. Javier Fernández-Galeano and Mir Yarfitz, "Serious Maricas and Their Male Concubines: Seeking Trans History and Intimacy in Argentine Police and Prison Records, 1921–1945," *Hispanic American Historical Review* 103, no. 4 (2023): 654.

14. This is the central argument in Javier Fernández-Galeano, *Maricas: Queer Cultures and State Violence in Argentina and Spain, 1942–1982* (Lincoln: University of Nebraska Press, 2024).

15. I have not yet found any judicial file that includes erotic visual materials produced by lesbian women and transgender men. For historical studies on these subjectivities during the Franco regime and the democratic transition, see Matilde Albarracín Soto, "Identidad(es) lésbica(s) en el primer franquismo," in *Mujeres bajo sospecha: Memoria y sexualidad, 1930–1980*, edited by Raquel Osborne (Madrid: Fundamentos, 2012), 69–87; Lucas Platero, "'Su gran placer es usar calzoncillos y calcetines': la represión de la masculinidad femenina bajo la dictadura," in *Mujeres bajo sospecha: Memoria y sexualidad, 1930–1980*, edited by Raquel Osborne (Madrid: Fundamentos, 2012), 175–90; Lucas Platero, "Lesboerotismo y la masculinidad de las mujeres en la España franquista," *Bagoas* 3 (2009): 15–38.

16. *Diccionario de la Real Academia Española*, s.v. "vicio," accessed August 16, 2023, www.rae.es/drae2001/vicio.

17. There is a common slippage between terms such as *obscenity, erotica, pornography,* and *smut.* For different historical definitions of these terms, see Jay A. Gertzman, *Bookleggers and Smuthounds: The Trade in Erotica, 1920–1940* (Philadelphia: University of Pennsylvania Press, 2011), 3; Lynn Hunt, "Introduction: Obscenity and the Origins of Modernity, 1500–1800," in *The Invention of Pornography: Obscenity and the Origins of Modernity, 1500–1800*, ed. Lynn Hunt (New York: Zone Books, 1996), 10; Ronald K. L. Collins and David M. Skover, "The Pornographic State," *Harvard Law Review* 107, no. 6 (1994): 1378; Whitney

Strub, *Perversion for Profit: The Politics of Pornography and the Rise of the New Right* (New York: Columbia University Press, 2013), 4; Elizabeth D. Heineman, *Before Porn Was Legal: The Erotica Empire of Beate Uhse* (Chicago: University of Chicago Press, 2011), 12; Linda Williams, *Hard Core: Power, Pleasure, and the "Frenzy of the Visible"* (London: Pandora, 1990), 6, 22; Sarah L. Leonard, *Fragile Minds and Vulnerable Souls: The Matter of Obscenity in Nineteenth-Century Germany* (Philadelphia: University of Pennsylvania Press, 2015), 2; Kelly Dennis, *Art/Porn: A History of Seeing and Touching* (Oxford: Berg, 2009), 10.

18. Lisa Z. Sigel points out that pornography can be equally encompassing. See Sigel, "Introduction: Issues and Problems in the History of Pornography," in *International Exposure: Perspectives on Modern European Pornography, 1800–2000*, edited by Lisa Z. Sigel (New Brunswick, N.J.: Rutgers University Press, 2005), 7. Eliot Borenstein argues in the same volume that initially "pornography was a subset of obscenity" and that they became autonomous categories in the West as blasphemy ceased to be a primary concern and porn abandoned any artistic pretensions. Borenstein, "Stripping the Nation Bare: Russian Pornography and the Insistence on Meaning," in *International Exposure*, 236. Since neither of these developments consolidated in Spain until the late 1970s, *obscenity* is a more fitting term.

19. On desecration, see Ilan Stavans and Jorge J. E. Gracia, "On Desecration: Andrés Serrano, Piss," *Michigan Quarterly Review* 52, no. 4 (2013); Carolyn J. Dean, "Empathy, Pornography, and Suffering," *Differences* 14 (2003): 102–3; Zeb Tortorici, *Sins against Nature: Sex and Archives in Colonial New Spain* (Durham, N.C.: Duke University Press, 2018).

20. Similar ideas reoccur in other academic works. See Carolyn Dean, *The Frail Social Body: Pornography, Homosexuality, and Other Fantasies in Interwar France* (Berkeley: University of California Press, 2000); Alexander Monea, *The Digital Closet: How the Internet Became Straight* (Cambridge, Mass.: MIT Press, 2022); Paul B. Preciado, *Pornotopia: An Essay on Playboy's Architecture and Biopolitics* (New York: Zone Books, 2019), 40; Natalia Milanesio, *Destape: Sex, Democracy, and Freedom in Postdictatorial Argentina* (Pittsburgh: University of Pittsburgh Press, 2019), 19; Dennis, *Art/Porn*, 96; Sigel, "Introduction," 3.

21. Dennis, *Art/Porn*, 3.

22. Dennis, *Art/Porn*, 2.

23. Preciado, *Pornotopia*, 41. Thomas Waugh presents similar arguments regarding American stag film. See Waugh, "Homosociality in the Classical American Stag Film: Off-Screen, On-Screen," in *Porn Studies*. According to Preciado, *Playboy* maintained a strict separation between the subject and the object of the gaze by not publishing images of male bodies. See Preciado, *Pornotopia*, 43. *Hustler* broke from this tradition by publishing images of erect penises. Dennis, *Art/Porn*, 97–99. As Linda Williams notes, hardcore eventually became defined by the visualization of masculine pleasure, in contraposition with softcore's focus on female nudity. Williams, *Hard Core*.

24. Preciado, *Pornotopia*, 42.

25. Merriam-Webster.com Dictionary, s.v. "peccadillo," accessed August 16, 2023, www.merriam-webster.com/dictionary/peccadillo.

26. Michelle Castañeda, *Disappearing Rooms: The Hidden Theaters of Immigration Law* (Durham, N.C.: Duke University Press, 2023), 1–2.

27. The history of obscenity emerged as an academic field as hardcore films became mainstream during the "porno chic" era, from the late 1960s to the early 1980s. See Williams, *Hard Core*, 9–10. Steven Marcus's *The Other Victorians* (1966) and Walter M. Kendrick's *The Secret Museum* (1987) were groundbreaking works that prefigured some of the field's main concerns: access restrictions, forbidden spaces, and elite males' privileges as historical dynamics that have shaped the meaning of obscenity; the relationship between content, medium, and consumer; and the role of "pornography" in Western modernity. Walter M. Kendrick, *The Secret Museum: The History of Pornography in Literature* (New York: Viking, 1987); Steven Marcus, *The Other Victorians: A Study of Sexuality and Pornography in Mid-Nineteenth-Century England* (London: Routledge, 1966). There is an extensive body of scholarship on liberalism and obscenity, including Leigh Ann Wheeler, *How Sex Became a Civil Liberty* (New York: Oxford University Press, 2013); and Stuart P. Green, *Criminalizing Sex: A Unified Liberal Theory* (New York: Oxford University Press, 2020).

28. Kathleen Lubey, *What Pornography Knows: Sex and Social Protest since the Eighteenth Century* (Stanford: Stanford University Press, 2022).

29. Lynn Hunt argues that pornography as a category took shape "concomitantly with the long-term emergence of Western modernity," through print culture and mass politics. Hunt, "Introduction," 10–11. Recent shifts in obscenity studies have expanded the geographical and thematic scope of the field. See, for instance, Anjali Arondekar, *For the Record: On Sexuality and the Colonial Archive in India* (Durham, N.C.: Duke University Press, 2009); Yvon Wang, *Reinventing Licentiousness: Pornography and Modern China* (Ithaca, N.Y.: Cornell University Press, 2021); Milanesio, *Destape*; Richa Kaul Padte, *Cyber Sexy: Rethinking Pornography* (Gurgaon, India: Penguin Books, 2018). There is a debate among historians of Latin America on whether democratization and sexual permissiveness are correlated. See Milanesio, *Destape*; Pablo Ben and Santiago Joaquín Insausti, "Race and Politics in Peruvian and Argentine Porn under the Transition to Democracy, 1975–1985," *Journal of Latin American Cultural Studies*, forthcoming; Benjamin A. Cowan, *Securing Sex: Morality and Repression in the Making of Cold War Brazil* (Chapel Hill: University of North Carolina Press, 2016).

30. On archival touch and intoxicating affects, see Marika Cifor, "Presence, Absence, and Victoria's Hair: Examining Affect and Embodiment in Trans Archives," *Transgender Studies Quarterly* 2 (2015): 645–47.

31. *Diccionario de la Real Academia Española*, s.v. "tocado," accessed August 16, 2023 https://dle.rae.es/tocado.

32. On "the affective texture of porn," see Strub and Bronstein, "Introduction," 4; On social history methods and the history of vernacular porn's material

culture, see Lisa Z. Sigel, *The People's Porn: A History of Handmade Pornography in America* (London: Reaktion Books, 2020); and Lisa Z. Sigel, "Handmade and Homemade: Vernacular Expressions of American Sexual History," *Journal of the History of Sexuality* 25, no. 3 (2016): 438–43.

33. Walter Benjamin, *The Arcades Project*, trans. Howard Eiland, Kevin MacLaughlin, and Rolf Tiedemann (Cambridge, Mass.: The Belknap Press, 2002), 204–5. On how Benjamin's notion of the collector applies to erotica, see Zeb Tortorici, "Circulating Erotica: Flea Markets, Collections, and Archives in Mexico," *Journal of Popular Culture* 53 (2020): 1339.

34. In addition, vagrancy and dangerousness files generally become accessible to researchers only after fifty years pass from their closing date, which makes it difficult to elaborate reliable statistics on the nationwide implementation of these laws.

35. On the implications of these self-recording techniques, see Javier Fernández-Galeano, "Performing Queer Archives: Argentine and Spanish Policing Files for Unintended Audiences (1950s–1970s)," in *Turning Archival: The Life of the Historical in Queer Studies*, edited by Zeb Tortorici and Daniel Marshall (Durham, N.C.: Duke University Press, 2023).

36. Pamela Radcliff, *Modern Spain, 1808 to the Present* (Hoboken, N.J.: Wiley-Blackwell, 2017), 146–47.

37. On liberalism and obscenity in this period, see Lisa Z. Sigel, "Censorship in Inter-War Britain: Obscenity, Spectacle, and the Workings of the Liberal State," *Journal of Social History* 45, no. 1 (2011): 61–83; Gertzman, *Bookleggers and Smuthounds*, ch. 4; Dean, *Frail Social Body*.

38. On *sicalipsis*, see Jean-Louis Guereña, *Detrás de la cortina: el sexo en España (1790–1950)* (Madrid: Ediciones Cátedra, 2018); Maite Zubiaurre, *Culturas del erotismo en España, 1898–1939* (Madrid: Cátedra, 2015); Lily Litvak, "La novela corta erótica de entreguerras, 1920–1936," in *Los territorios literarios de la historia del placer*, edited by José Blas Vega et al. (Madrid: Huerga & Fierro Editores, 1996); Carmen Cubero Izquierdo, "Procesos contra la pornografía. La construcción del control sobre el erotismo en España: 1880–1936," in *De los controles disciplinarios a los controles securitarios*, edited by Pedro Oliver Olmo and María Carmen Cubero Izquierdo (Cuenca, Spain: Universidad De Castilla-La Mancha, 2020); Gloria G. Durán, *Sicalípticas: el gran libro del cuplé y la sicalipsis* (Madrid: Editorial La Felguera, 2022).

39. Gonzalo Torrente Ballester, "El erotismo en la calle y aledaños," *Triunfo*, 26 September 1970, 45.

40. Gertzman, *Bookleggers and Smuthounds*, 10.

41. Zeb Tortorici argues for Colonial New Spain that "bodies and desires came to be permanently archived through the very attempts of colonial authorities to suppress them." Tortorici, *Sins against Nature*, 24.

42. Dean, *Frail Social Body*, 160.

43. Gloria G. Durán, for instance, argues that the Civil War put an end to *sicalipsis* in Spain. Durán, *Sicalípticas*, 134.

44. Historian Sasha D. Pack argues that there is a direct relationship between international tourism and the relaxation of Spanish mores. See Sasha D. Pack, *Tourism and Dictatorship: Europe's Peaceful Invasion of Franco's Spain* (New York: Palgrave Macmillan, 2006), 146.

45. Maite Zubiaurre traces how in the early decades of the twentieth century, the Spanish intelligentsia (including figures such as Gregorio Marañón and José Ortega y Gasset) situated the purest Spanish masculinity, founded on the values of austerity and self-control, in Castilla and the Basque Country. In contrast, the same intellectuals expressed their concern about Andalusians' ambiguous gender and the corrupting influence that modernization had in metropolitan areas, and most particularly in Barcelona. Zubiaurre, *Cultures of the Erotic in Spain*, 74–75, 91–92.

46. Whitney Strub and Carolyn Bronstein, "Introduction," in *Porno Chic and the Sex Wars: American Sexual Representation in the 1970s*, edited by Whitney Strub and Carolyn Bronstein (Amherst: University of Massachusetts Press, 2017), 1–7.

47. *Procuradores* represented the multiple sociopolitical sectors that supported the regime's status quo, from the fascist party Falange to Catholic bishops, whereas the presence of a "family third [of legislators]" elected by male breadwinners reinforced the façade of "organic democracy." Radcliff, *Modern Spain*, 216–23.

48. Jennifer Evans emphasizes that "queer erotic photographs are particularly frenetic, trafficked from place to place, circulating in tourist and fine art networks, on the boundary between high and low." See Evans, "Seeing Subjectivity: Erotic Photography and the Optics of Desire," *American Historical Review* 118, no. 2 (2013): 460.

49. By the same token, during the Cold War liberal regimes differentiated themselves from the Communist bloc by loosening censorship and considering sexual pleasure's potential social value. Sigel, "Introduction," 16.

50. Germán Labrador defines the *destape* as a "process of mediatic and state construction of a mass erotic culture that suddenly became visible in public spaces." Germán Labrador Méndez, "Una urna puede ser el mejor preservativo: Porno-política y tecno-democracia en la transición española, entre el destape y la Constitución," *Mélanges de la Casa de Velázquez* 50, no. 1 (2020): 85.

51. See, for example, Santiago Fouz-Hernández, ed., *Spanish Erotic Cinema* (Edinburgh: Edinburgh University Press, 2018); Alejandro Melero, *Placeres ocultos. gays y lesbianas en el cine español de la transición* (Madrid: Notorius, 2010); Juli Cáceres García, *El destape del macho Ibérico: masculinidades disidentes en la comedia sexy (celt)Ibérica*, PhD dissertation, Georgetown University, 2008.

Chapter One

1. On these films, see Maite Zubiaurre, *Culturas del erotismo en España, 1898–1939* (Madrid: Cátedra, 2015), 393–94.

2. Ricardo de Baños and Ramón de Baños, *El Ministro* (Royal Films, date unknown). I consulted the copies of these films available for consultation at the València *filmoteca*, which also holds the originals.

3. Mireille Miller-Young, *A Taste for Brown Sugar: Black Women in Pornography* (Durham, N.C.: Duke University Press, 2015), 64.

4. Ricardo de Baños and Ramón de Baños, *Consultorio de señoras* (Royal Films, date unknown).

5. See Francisco Vázquez García, *Pater infamis: genealogía del cura pederasta en España (1880–1912)* (Madrid: Cátedra, 2020).

6. Casto Escópico extemporaneously infers that "the lacking attractiveness of the actors makes us think that they came from marginal environments associated with prostitution," although he cites the testimony of a cameraman who worked in the early porn industry and remembers that there were amateur performers who had not been involved in sex work before. See Casto Escópico, *Sólo para adultos: historia del cine X* (València, Spain: La Máscara, 1996), 32.

7. STS 108/1917, CENDOJ.

8. Durán, *Sicalípticas*, 126.

9. Piro Subrat, *Invertidos y rompepatrias: marxismo, anarquismo y desobediencia sexual y de género en el Estado español (1868–1982)* (Madrid: Imperdible, 2019), 41.

10. Javier Ugarte Pérez, *Las circunstancias obligaban: Homoerotismo, identidad y resistencia* (Barcelona: Egales Editorial, 2011), 201–3.

11. Cubero, "Procesos contra la pornografía," 546.

12. "Real decreto-ley aprobando el proyecto de Código Penal, que se inserta, y disponiendo empiece a regir como Ley del Reino el día 1º de enero de 1929," *Gaceta de Madrid,* 13 September 1928, 1506.

13. "Real Orden Circular," *Gaceta de Madrid,* 22 March 1928, 1812.

14. Subrat, *Invertidos y rompepatrias,* 41–42; Zubiaurre, *Culturas del erotismo,* 63.

15. Tortorici, "Circulating Erotica," 1349.

16. Similarly, in Imperial Russia, "Sexual imagery and naked bodies were deemed acceptable within high culture, but these images became 'obscene' when they were mass-produced and printed on postcards or in the popular press, where they could be accessed by women, youth, and lower-class people." Siobhán Hearne, "An Erotic Revolution? Pornography in the Russian Empire, 1905–1914," *Journal of the History of Sexuality* 30, no. 2 (2021): 196.

17. Y. Yvon Wang similarly traces how in Modern China the boundaries of licentiousness were set depending on who the consumer was. Wang, *Reinventing Licentiousness.*

18. Siobhán Hearne contextualizes the meaning of "pornography" in the early twentieth century, arguing that "pornography was an umbrella term used to describe everything from images of naked women to advertisements for venereal disease cures." Hearne, "An Erotic Revolution?," 200.

19. Cubero, "Procesos contra la pornografía," 542–44.

20. STS 350/1888, CENDOJ.

21. STS 350/1888, CENDOJ.

22. The 1885 events were cited in the decades to come as establishing the need to persecute "serious and transcendental debauchery," as a 1908 memo by the attorney general characterized them. This memo focused on potential indecency in medical advertising but cited as precedent the 1885 case, describing how naked "subjects" begged for divine mercy "in a primitive state." "Circular de la Fiscalia del Tribunal Central," *Gaceta,* 6 May 1908, 630. The language of primitivism points to the dynamics of internal colonialism as the analytical lenses through which some historians have approached the "civilizing mission" taken by European nation-states through their policies in remote rural areas over the course of the nineteenth century. See Eugen Weber, *Peasants into Frenchmen: The Modernization of Rural France, 1870–1914* (Stanford: Stanford University Press, 1988).

23. In one of the cases against Juan Caballero Soriano, for instance, his defense lawyer acknowledged the "pornographic character" of the novelette *La insaciable Margot* (The unsatiable Margot) yet denied that there had been a crime of public scandal, precisely on the grounds that "cultivated people" had the decision-making capacity to avoid those readings that would offend them. Furthermore, the lawyer argued that, while the title and the cover provided enough information to deter modest people from reading the novelette, these elements were not scandalous by themselves. Finally, in addition to these legal defense strategies, the most effective subterfuge was simply to escape the justice system, as Caballero Soriano did by becoming a fugitive (*rebelde*) in multiple trials. Statement by Defense Lawyer Francisco Brualia on 7 August 1926 and Order for Fugitive on 22 September 1926, File 26, Legajo 164, Sala de lo Criminal, Audiencia Provincial de Madrid, Archivo Histórico Nacional, Madrid, Spain (hereafter AHN).

24. Defendant's deposition on 27 July 1932, File 33, Legajo 18, AHN.

25. Deposition on 30 July 1932, File 33.

26. Report by the DGS, File 33.

27. Deposition on 15 November 1932, File 33.

28. Report by the Civilian Government of Madrid, 7 December 1932, File 33.

29. Ruling issued by the jury on 5 February 1935, File 33.

30. Report on 13 June 1935, File 33.

31. Hannah Arendt, *On Violence* (New York: Harcourt, 1969), 81.

32. See, for instance, File 5, Legajo 151, and File 21, Legajo 179, AHN. Jay A. Gertzman argues regarding erotica in the interwar United States that "writers and publishers needed money as badly as almost everyone else." Gertzman, *Bookleggers and Smuthounds,* 11.

33. Report on 19 September 1925, File 14, Legajo 185, AHN.

34. Deposition on 24 September 1925, File 14.

35. Deposition on 26 September 1925, File 14.

36. Deposition on 2 October 1925, File 14.

37. Order for Fugitive on 8 October 1925, File 14.

38. "[S]eré yo el único responsable de todos los efectos que pudieren derivarse de la publicación de tales originales. Igualmente me encargo de tener en mi domicilio la administración de esas publicaciones a los efectos consiguientes." Letter from José De La Mata on 26 June 1926, File 11, Legajo 164, AHN.

39. Letter from Luis Uriarte on 26 November 1926, File 7, Legajo 164, AHN.

40. Deposition on 2 December 1926, File 7.

41. Deposition on 6 December 1926, File 7.

42. The issue of artificial contracts used as cover-up resurfaced in multiple cases, all related to the triad formed by Luis Uriarte, Julian José De La Mata and Segundo Ildefonso Uriarte. See File 18, Legajo 164, AHN, and File 27, Legajo 164, AHN.

43. A previous memo from the attorney general had stipulated that booksellers were to be held fully accountable for the materials they sold, no matter whether they knew their content through reading it. "Circular de la Fiscalía del Tribunal Supremo," *Gaceta de Madrid,* 3 December 1930, 1391.

44. "Decreto," *Gaceta de Madrid,* 16 November 1935, 1316.

45. STS 1335/1885, CENDOJ.

46. Sharon L. Reeves, "La prostitución en Madrid a finales del siglo XIX en la novela naturalista de Eduardo López Bago," in *Madrid en la literatura y las artes*, edited by Jorge H. Valdivieso and L. Teresa Valdivieso (Phoenix: Editorial Orbis Press, 2006), 86.

47. Durán, *Sicalípticas*, 109.

48. Alberto Mira, "After Wilde: Camp Discourse in Hoyos and Retana, or The Dawn of Spanish Gay Culture," *Journal of Spanish Cultural Studies* 5, no. 1 (2004): 29–47.

49. Defense statement by Aquiles Ulrich on 16 December 1925, File 5, Legajo 98, AHN.

50. Ruling issued on 10 February 1926, File 5.

51. "Circular, Fiscalía del Tribunal Supremo," *Gaceta de Madrid,* 17 February 1928, 1153.

52. "Circular, Fiscalía del Tribunal Supremo."

53. There were previous but less centralized precedents for this systematic policy of obliteration. Pura Fernández points out the sort of policies that have made it difficult for scholars to trace the publication and circulation of erotic literature in *fin-de-siècle* Spain. In 1891, for instance, hundreds of "pornographic pamphlets and illustrations" were burned in the headquarters of the Madrid Civilian Government, culminating a "cleansing campaign" supported by the conservative Catholic press, which mostly affected peddlers and small booksellers. Pura Fernández, "Censura y práctica de la transgresión: Los dominios del eros y la moralidad en la literatura española decimonónica," in *Los territorios literarios de la historia del placer*, edited by José Blas Vega et al. (Madrid: Huerga & Fierro Editores, 1996), 72.

54. "Circular Fiscalía del Tribunal Supremo."

55. Likewise, the mayors of some towns had to pay fines for their neglectful implementation of the ordinances regarding pornography and other unseemly behaviors. Cubero, "Procesos contra la pornografía," 545.

56. STS 1387/1929 and STS 474/1929, CENDOJ.

57. "Real Orden," *Gaceta de Madrid,* 26 August 1927, 1143.

58. Ruling issued on 28 October 1926, File 50031/1927, Appeals to the Supreme Court, 69, AHN.

59. Sigel, "Handmade and Homemade," 440.

60. File 15, Legajo 164, AHN.

61. In a case against Octavio Precioso García, his acquittal also entails that the ruling does not include obscene material. The novel under examination, *Más fuerte que el amor* (Stronger than love), does not appear to be preserved at the National Library either. File 16, Legajo 164, AHN.

62. File 25, Legajo 164, AHN.

63. See, for instance, File 30, Legajo 173, AHN.

64. File 20, Legajo 179, AHN.

65. File 20.

66. File 19, Legajo 179, AHN.

67. File 15, Legajo 11, AHN.

68. Zubiaurre, *Cultures of the Erotic,* 326. Similarly, in Gloria G. Durán's interpretation, there was a genre of clandestine popular literature that awakened the "ghost of [sexual] otherness." Durán, *Sicalípticas,* 114.

69. File 21, Legajo 179, AHN.

70. Zubiaurre, *Cultures of the Erotic,* 304.

71. The file includes reports that detail the confiscation and destruction of the copies of the novel that were found when the police searched the publishing company Prensa Moderna. They could not find the originals, which had already been destroyed, according to one employee and the manager. The jury ruled that the author of the novel, Segundo Ildefonso Uriarte de Pujana, had to serve a prison penalty of four months and pay a monetary fine of five hundred pesetas. File 21.

72. Cited in Cubero, "Procesos contra la pornografía," 544.

73. Durán, *Sicalípticas,* 112.

74. Zubiaurre, *Culturas del erotismo,* 132; Cubero "Procesos contra la pornografía," 545; Litvak, "La novela corta," 117–18.

75. File 33, Legajo 18, AHN.

76. Deposition on 27 July 1932, File 33.

77. Litvak, "La novela corta," 115–16.

78. Cited in Litvak, "La novela corta," 119.

79. The same pattern can be traced in a positive critique of Max Hoddan's sexological treaty, lauded for avoiding a pornographic tone (*El Heraldo de Madrid,* 2 January 1936, 6); in a review of Eduardo Zamacois's *La antorcha apagada* that praised the book as nonpornographic, because it warned of those pedagogical styles that drive pupils into homosexuality (*La Libertad,* 9 June 1935, 5); a review

of Gregorio Marañón's *Los estados intersexuales* (*El Heraldo de Madrid*, 5 February 1929, 7); and a review of Pierre Louys's *Afrodita* that characterized the book as realistic but not pornographic (*Nuevo mundo*, 9 September 1927, 6).

80. Richard Cleminson and Francisco Vázquez García, *Los Invisibles: A History of Male Homosexuality in Spain, 1850–1939* (Cardiff: University of Wales Press, 2011), 137–217.

81. Cubero, "Procesos contra la pornografía," 546. Similarly, in Imperial Russia, "reactions to pornography signaled unease with the empire's accelerated path toward 'modernity,' broadly defined as a period of industrialization, urbanization, consumerism." See Hearne, "An Erotic Revolution?," 195.

82. Eduardo Bonilla de la Vega, "El problema sexual ante la medicina," *Revista de especialidades médicas*, 1 July 1916, 533–34.

83. "Ensayo," *El Sol*, 2 April 1931, 2.

84. Ogier Preteceille, "HALL, RADCLYFFE: 'The Well of Loneliness,'" *El Sol*, 7 September 1928, 2.

85. Emilio Carrére, "Retablillo literario," *Madrid cómico*, 30 November 1923, 10.

86. Dennis, *Art/Porn*, 8.

87. Litvak, "La novela corta," 119. According to Gloria G. Durán, Carrere collaborated with state repression as an informer. Durán, *Sicalipticas*, 126.

88. File 52125/1928, Legajo 69, Appeals to the Supreme Court (Tribunal Supremo, Recursos), AHN.

89. "Recurso de casación," File 52125/1928.

90. When I conducted my research at the AHN in 2021 and 2022, the following files related to Retana's career were inaccessible because of material deterioration: File 22/1926, Legajo 180, Audiencia Madrid/Criminal; File 8/1926, Legajo 99, Audiencia Madrid/Criminal, AHN; File 8/1926, Legajo 180, Audiencia Madrid/Criminal.

91. File 51390/1928, Legajo 69, Appeals to the Supreme Court (Tribunal Supremo, Recursos), AHN.

92. File 51390/1928, 8–9.

93. File 51390/1928, 11.

94. File 51390/1928, 12.

95. Cited in Alberto Mira, "After Wilde," 39–40.

96. File 51390/1928, 13.

97. Mira, "After Wilde," 38, 40, 43.

98. Mira, "After Wilde," 45.

99. File 51390/1928.

100. For a close reading of the relationship between Retana's work and his life as performance, see Rafael M. Mérida Jiménez, *Transbarcelonas: cultura, género y sexualidad en la España del siglo XX* (Barcelona: Edicions Bellaterra, 2016), 27–36.

101. Luis Bulffi de Quintana, *¡Huelga de vientres!* (Barcelona: Biblioteca Editorial Salud y Fuerza, 1909).

102. Juan Suriano, *Anarquistas, Cultura y política libertaria en Buenos Aires. 1890–1910* (Buenos Aires: Manantial, 2001), 188, 210.

103. File 17, Legajo 11, AHN.

104. Hugh Thomas, *Historia de la Guerra Civil Española* (Barcelona: Círculo de Lectores, 1976), 88.

105. Miguel Pérez Ferrero, "Adiós a Baldrich," *ABC,* 8 August 1959, 25; Fernando de la Milla, "Nuestros dibujantes," *La Esfera,* 16 October 1926, 10–11.

106. "Las mujeres de Baldrich," *Nuevo Mundo,* 10 August 1928, 14.

107. "Las mujeres de Baldrich."

108. Letter from the bailiff to the judge, 12 April 1928, File 17, Legajo 85, AHN.

109. Letter from the Governor's office on 20 April 1928, File 17.

110. Auto, 30 April 1928, File 17.

111. Paul Preston, *A People Betrayed: A History of Corruption, Political Incompetence, and Social Division in Modern Spain, 1874–2018* (London: William Collins, 2021).

112. "La Filmoteca Valenciana custodia 3 películas porno que encargó Alfonso XIII," *La Vanguardia,* 16 January 2019.

113. Hunt, "Introduction," 12–13.

Chapter Two

An earlier draft of this chapter was published in Spanish. See Javier Fernández-Galeano, "Dildos y lubricantes: La cultura material del erotismo en Torremolinos frente a la retórica del régimen franquista," in *Cruising Torremolinos: Cuerpos, territorio y memoria,* edited by Javier Cuevas del Barrio and Ángelo Néstore (València, Spain: Tirant Humanidades, 2022), 23–48.

1. File 298, Legajo 1362, AGA.

2. Cifor, "Presence," 645–47.

3. Hunt, "Introduction," 30.

4. See Arondekar, *For the Record,* 97–130.

5. "Ley de 22 de abril de 1938, de Prensa (rectificada). Habiéndose padecido error en la publicación de la Ley de este Ministerio, fecha de ayer, 23 de abril," *Boletín Oficial del Estado* 550 (24 April 1938), 6938–6940.

6. Radcliff, *Modern Spain,* 214–18.

7. Julián Casanova y Carlos Gil Andrés, *Twentieth Century Spain: A History* (Cambridge, U.K.: Cambridge University Press, 2014), 239–62.

8. "LEY DE 15 DE JULIO DE 1954 por la que se modifican los artículos 2° y 6° de la Ley de Vagos y Maleantes, de 4 de agosto de 1933," *Boletín Oficial del Estado,* 17 July 1954, 4862.

9. Geoffroy Huard, *Los invertidos: verdad, justicia y reparación para gais y transexuales bajo la dictadura franquista* (Barcelona: Icaria, 2021), 8, 13.

10. As Kyle Frackman notes, in East Germany "censorship and import embargoes made illicit art production and reproduction more likely." Frackman, "Homemade Pornography and the Proliferation of Queer Pleasure in East

Germany," *Radical History Review* 142 (2022): 94. Sigel makes a similar point regarding homemade porn in the United States. Sigel, *People's Porn,* 10.

11. Acta de incautación, 25 June 1958, Brigada de Investigación Criminal, File 298, Legajo 1362, AGA.

12. Tortorici, "Circulating Erotica," 1341–1342.

13. Acta de incautación.

14. Ruling, 8 March 1943, Juzgado de Instrucción de Huelva, Recurso nº 1021/1943 contra la sentencia de la Audiencia Provincial de Huelva sobre escándalo público, Fondo Tribunal Supremo Penal, Legajo 6, File 1021, AGA.

15. Ganaele Langlois and Andrea Slane, "Economies of Reputation: The Case of Revenge Porn," *Communication and Critical/Cultural Studies* 14 (2017): 120.

16. Langlois and Slane, "Economies," 132–33.

17. The defense lawyer appealed the sentence on the grounds that the confiscated materials were for private use, but the magistrates considered that the defendants' intention to sell them was proven. Ruling, 21 June 1947, Recurso no. 234BIS/1946 contra la sentencia pronunciada por la Audiencia de Madrid sobre escándalo público, Fondo Tribunal Supremo Penal, Legajo 86, File 234bis, AGA.

18. Similarly, Kendrick emphasizes that "pruning" the archives was a source of pride for many Victorians who justified their own efforts at cleaning the past because of previous generations' moral flaws. Kendrick, *Secret Museum*, 52.

19. Francisco Franco Bahamonde, "Franco habla a los españoles con motivo del Año Nuevo," *Falange* (Las Palmas de Gran Canaria), 1 January 1957, 2.

20. Hunt, "Introduction," 34.

21. "Sumario, Presidencia de la Junta Técnica del Estado," *Boletín Oficial del Estado,* 24 December 1936, 469.

22. "Órdenes, Presidencia de la Junta Técnica del Estado," *Boletín Oficial del Estado,* 24 December 1936, 471–72.

23. "Órdenes, Presidencia de la Junta Técnica del Estado," *Boletín Oficial del Estado,* 17 September 1937 (page numbers illegible).

24. The minutes of the Salamanca commission are quite indicative in this respect. The members of the commission discussed the "physical impossibility" of carrying out the assigned task in the prescribed period, but they still performed a superficial study of libraries' content and withdrew books from public consultation. The commission exempted some monasteries from further screening, assuming their libraries would not contain subversive nor obscene books. "Libro de actas de la Comisión depuradora de Bibliotecas del Distrito de Salamanca de 1937 a 1938," AUSA_LR, 335, Archivo de la Universidad de Salamanca, Salamanca, Spain.

25. Kendrick, *Secret Museum*, 49.

26. "Comunicación del Ministerio de Educación Nacional, firmada en Vitoria el 8 de Junio de 1938." Legajo 3370. Fondo Antiguo y Archivo Histórico, Biblioteca Rector A. Machado y Núñez, Universidad de Sevilla, Sevilla, Spain.

27. Mercedes del Amo, *Salvador Vila: el rector fusilado en Víznar* (Granada, Spain: Editorial Universidad de Granada, 2005); Ian Gibson, "Salvador Vila Hernández," *El País*, 10 February 2003.

28. Antonio González Bueno, "Juan Casas Fernández," *Real Academia de la Historia / Biografías*, https://dbe.rah.es/biografias/21731/juan-casas-fernandez, accessed on 23 August 2022.

29. "Actas de la Comisión Depuradora de Bibliotecas y Centros de Lectura," Libro 04608, Archivo Universitario de Granada, Granada (Spain).

30. "Actas de la Comisión Depuradora." Other towns, like Colmenar in Málaga, reported that they did not have a single public library or reading room. The reports from small towns and libraries still included stamps with Republican symbology and references to the town halls' loyalty to the Constitution. The mayor of Alpandeire reported on 8 November 1937 that "Marxist hordes" had burned the single public library of the village. "Comunicaciones recibidas por la Comisión Depuradora de Bibliotecas y Centros de Lecturas." Caja 01962/011. Archivo Universitario de Granada.

31. "Documentación sobre las bibliotecas militares de la provincia, 1938," Caja 01882/ 008, Archivo Universitario de Granada.

32. "Libro de Registro de las Obras de las Bibliotecas Escolares de la Capital y Provincia de Valladolid retiradas por la Comisión Reguladora (1938)," Archivo de la Universidad de Valladolid, Valladolid, Spain.

33. Lists of purged books, Archivo Universitario de la Universidad de Zaragoza, Zaragoza, Spain.

34. On the publication of Wilde's work in Spain, see Alberto Lázaro, "La narrativa inglesa de Terror y el terror de la censura española," in *Tiempo de censura. La represión editorial durante el franquismo*, edited by Eduardo Ruíz Bautista (Gijón, Spain: Ediciones TREA, 2008), 193–232.

35. On Wilde and the bohemian cult of art, see William Gaunt, *The Aesthetic Adventure* (London: Sphere Books Ltd., 1975).

36. Ana Martínez Rus, "La política del libro durante la segunda república: socialización de la lectura," PhD dissertation, Universidad Complutense de Madrid, 2000, 63, 143, 476.

37. Peter Pan was purged from public libraries in the Valladolid University district as well. Carmen Diego Pérez, "Un caso paradigmático de represión cultural: depuración de bibliotecas escolares en la provincia de Palencia durante la guerra civil española (2ª parte)," *Represura* 7 (2011).

38. Robert Richmond Ellis, "Looking Queer in *El beso de Peter Pan* of Terenci Moix," *España Contemporánea: Revista de Literatura y Cultura* 9, no. 2 (1996): 15.

39. Leela Gandhi, *Affective Communities: Anticolonial Thought, Fin-De-Siècle Radicalism, and the Politics of Friendship* (Durham, N.C.: Duke University Press, 2006).

40. José Antonio Ramos Arteaga, personal e-mail communication with the author, 6 July 2023.

41. Escritura de fundación, Biblioteca Pública Arús, Barcelona.

42. I was able to conduct this research thanks to the guidance of Zeb Tortorici, Víctor Macías-González, and Teresa Abelló.

43. Juan Pablo Calero Delso, *Celso Gomis Mestre: excursiones por la provincia de Guadalajara* (Ciudad Real, Spain: Centro de Estudios Castilla-La Mancha, 2011).

44. Collection Gomis, volume 1, page 1, Biblioteca Pública Arús.

45. Email communication with Biblioteca Pública Arús, 17 January 2022.

46. Manon Lecaplain, "Political Press, Nude Press, and La Bonne Presse: Amédée Vignola, or an Atypical Career," *Sociétés et Représentations* 47, no. 1 (2019): abstract.

47. Kyle Frackman notes how composition techniques in homemade queer erotica draw attention "toward the near center of the photo—the man's penis." Frackman, "Homemade Pornography," 99.

48. Williams notes that the shift from female nudity to male genitalia signals the emergence of hardcore. Williams, *Hard Core*.

49. Dennis, *Art/Porn*, 100.

50. Paul R. Deslandes, *The Culture of Male Beauty in Britain: From the First Photographs to David Beckham* (Chicago: University of Chicago Press, 2021).

51. Carlos Rufas, "Biblioteca Pública Arús, centro del saber masón en Barcelona," *Metropoli,* 16 July 2017.

52. Kendrick, *Secret Museum,* 13.

53. Benita Sampedro Vizcaya, "Rethinking the Archive and the Colonial Library: Equatorial Guinea," *Journal of Spanish Cultural Studies* 9 (2008): 343.

54. Sampedro, "Rethinking," 346.

55. Sampedro, "Rethinking," 347.

56. *La Guinea Española* (Santa Isabel), 9 June 1940, 192.

57. *Proa* (León), 16 November 1941, 1; *Falange* (Las Palmas de Gran Canaria), 28 November 1941.

58. Sigel, "Introduction," 12.

59. *Sabadell,* 28 May 1957, 7.

60. Jesús Suevos, "La conspiración del silencio," *Falange* (Las Palmas de Gran Canaria), 22 May 1957.

61. "La juventud rusa de hoy es peor que la de los tiempos de Lenin," *Falange* (Las Palmas de Gran Canaria), 30 November 1958.

62. José Ramón Alonso, "ESPAÑA: El más bajo coeficiente de delincuencia infantil," *Diario de Avisos* (Santa Cruz de La Palma), 15 November 1962, 3.

63. Subsecretaría de Turismo, "'España es para usted': Orientaciones para el turista," *El Eco de Canarias,* 17 May 1964, 8.

64. For an in-depth analysis of this corpus, see Javier Cuevas del Barrio, "Soy memoria de hombre. Luego nada. Cultura visual queer y redes afectivas a través de la correspondencia en la Andalucía de los años sesenta," manuscript shared with the author, forthcoming in an edited volume on queer daily life in Franco's Spain.

65. File 44/1966, Signatura 11793, Juzgado Especial de Vagos y Maleantes de Granada, Archivo Histórico Provincia de Málaga, Málaga, Spain.

66. Esperanza Peláez, "Aquel esplendoroso Torremolinos," *El País*, 9 March 2003.

67. Rafael Cáceres Feria y José María Valcuende del Rio, "Turismo y homosexualidad en la España franquista: Torremolinos (1960–1971)," in *Las locas en el archivo. Disidencia sexual bajo el franquismo*, edited by Geoffroy Huard and Javier Fernández-Galeano (Barcelona: Marcial Pons, 2023), 308.

68. David López Frías, "Hijos de Torremolinos: del primer topless de España a emporio gay," *El Español*, 6 August 2017.

69. Police report, File 10/1960, Signatura 8937, Juzgado Especial de Vagos y Maleantes de Málaga, Archivo Histórico Provincial de Sevilla (hereafter AHPS).

70. Javier Fernández-Galeano, "Is He a 'Social Danger'? The Franco Regime's Judicial Prosecution of Homosexuality in Málaga under the Ley de Vagos y Maleantes," *Journal of the History of Sexuality* 25, no. 1 (2016): 1–31.

71. Pack, *Tourism and Dictatorship*, 146.

72. Javier Cuevas del Barrio and Alejandro Martín Rodríguez, "Cruising Torremolinos. Mito, imagen, arquitectura," in *Reimaginar la disidencia sexual en la España de los 70: redes, vidas, archivos*, edited by Alberto Berzosa and Gracia Trujillo (Barcelona: Bellaterra, 2019), 338.

73. Cáceres Feria and Valcuende del Río, "Turismo y homosexualidad," 317.

74. Cuevas del Barrio and Martín Rodríguez, "Cruising Torremolinos," 340.

75. File 6/1964, Signatura 8880, Juzgado Especial de Vagos y Maleantes de Málaga, AHPS.

76. Police report, 19 June 1965, File 12/1965, Signatura 8922, Juzgado Especial de Vagos y Maleantes de Málaga, AHPS.

77. Mary Hartson, *Casting Masculinity in Spanish Film: Negotiating Identity in a Consumer Age* (Lanham, Md.: Lexington Books, 2017), 124.

78. Report by the Málaga Police Chief, 27 January 1966, File 12/1965.

79. Deposition by the defendant, 27 January 1966, File 12/1965.

80. Note published in a local newspaper, File 12/1965.

81. Kendrick, *Secret Museum*.

82. "medicina, antigua y siempre nueva, que se llama la gracia de Dios," note published in a local newspaper, File 12/1965.

83. Ruling, File 12/1965.

84. Police report, File 10/1960, Signatura 8937, Juzgado Especial de Vagos y Maleantes de Málaga, AHPS.

85. Police report, submitted 7 October 1965, File 89/1965, Box 8892, Juzgado Especial de Vagos y Maleantes de Málaga, AHPS.

86. Defendant's deposition in front of the judge, October 9, 1965, File 89/1965. In fact, Norberto handed the photographs over to the court, and they were shown to Carlos in a face-to-face deposition during which Carlos agreed they were not pornographic but suggested there might be other photographs. Face-to-face deposition, October 13, 1965, File 89/1965.

87. Defense plea presented on November 11, 1965, File 89/1965.

88. Dennis suggests that the democratization of access in the nineteenth century changed Renaissance art's meaning through museums' civility norms,

which prioritized sight rather than touch as the dominating sense in common people's reception of canonical art. Dennis, *Art/Porn*, 21. Sexually explicit materials have always existed, but the processes of classification and archiving transform them into pornography. Tim Dean, "Pornography, Technology, Archive," in *Porn Archives*, edited by Tim Dean, Steven Ruszczycky, and David Squires (Durham, N.C.: Duke University Press, 2015), 1–26.

Chapter Three

1. Heineman, *Before Porn*, 2–8.

2. Eric Schaefer, "Introduction. Sex Seen: 1968 and Rise of 'Public' Sex,'" in *Sex Scene: Media and the Sexual Revolution,* edited by Eric Schaefer (Durham, N.C.: Duke University Press, 2014), 15.

3. Schaefer, "Introduction," 3, 13.

4. Schaefer, "Introduction," 14.

5. Kelly Dennis argues that (feminist) antipornography arguments rely on the "fiction that woman is an immutable object." Dennis, *Art/Porn*, 122.

6. Similarly, in the United States, passage of a law in 1842 banning the importation of foreign obscenity fostered domestic production. See Judith Giesberg, *Sex and the Civil War: Soldiers, Pornography, and the Making of American Morality* (Chapel Hill: University of North Carolina Press, 2017), 12.

7. On international discourses on the moral protection of the poor, see Sigel, "Introduction," 12; Hearne, "An Erotic Revolution?," 196, 205.

8. For an overview of the historiographical debate about the causes and consequences of this law, see Elisa Chuliá Rodrigo, "La Ley de Prensa de 1966: La explicación de un cambio institucional arriesgado y de sus efectos virtuosos," *Historia y política: Ideas, procesos y movimientos sociales* 2 (1999): 198–200.

9. "Ley Fundamental de 17 de mayo de 1958 por la que se promulgan los principios del Movimiento Nacional," *Boletín Oficial del Estado* 119 (19 May 1958), 4511.

10. "Decreto por el que se aprueba y promulga el 'Código Penal, texto refundido de 1944,' según la autorización otorgada por la Ley de 19 de julio de 1944," *Boletín Oficial del Estado,* 13 January 1945, 459 (Capítulo V/Art. 428).

11. Jean-Louis Guereña, "La prostitución en el primer franquismo," in *Pobreza, marginación, delincuencia y políticas sociales bajo el franquismo,* edited by Conxita Mir et al. (Lleida, Spain: Edicions de la Univeritat de Lleida, 2005), 167–83.

12. Historian Abel Díaz argues that married and "masculine" men enjoyed lenient treatment from the authorities even when they had occasional sex with other males (as long as they were penetrating the other and not vice versa). Abel Díaz, "Los invertidos: homosexualidad(es) y género en el primer franquismo," *Cuadernos de Historia Contemporánea* 41 (2019): 329.

13. Leonard, *Fragile Minds*, 3.

14. Germán Labrador Méndez demonstrates how the politicization of countercultures before, during, and after the democratic transition shaped the generational experiences of people who came of age in Spain between the late 1960s

and the mid-1980s. Germán Labrador Méndez, *Culpables por la literatura: imaginación política y contracultura en la transición española (1968–1986)* (Madrid: Ediciones Akal, 2017).

15. Schaefer, "Introduction," 12.

16. "PROYECTO DE LEY: De Peligrosidad Social, reformando la de Vagos y Maleantes de 4 de agosto de 1933," Archivo del Congreso de los Diputados, Madrid (Spain).

17. José Manuel Martínez-Pereda Rodríguez, *El delito de escándalo público* (Madrid: Editorial Tecnos, 1970), 172.

18. Martínez-Pereda, *El delito,* 187.

19. Martínez-Pereda, *El delito,* 184–86.

20. Martínez-Pereda, *El delito,* 188.

21. Francisco J. Bastida, *Jueces y franquismo: el pensamiento político del Tribunal Supremo en la dictadura* (Barcelona: Ariel, 1986), 17.

22. Supreme Court case 57/1969, cited in Bastida, *Jueces y franquismo,* 36.

23. Bastida, *Jueces y franquismo,* 37.

24. STS 350/1888, CENDOJ.

25. Supreme Court case 66/1970 and Supreme Court case 74/1970, cited in Bastida, *Jueces y franquismo,* 34–37.

26. Supreme Court case 72/1970 cited in Bastida, *Jueces y franquismo,* 39.

27. Bastida, *Jueces y franquismo,* 35.

28. See STS 2634/1968; STS 2959/1969; STS 2617/1970; STS 2719/1970; STS 482/1971; STS 2419/1971; STS 2455/1971; STS 2455/1971; STS 2460/1971; STS 3380/1972; STS 1355/1973; STS 1029/1975; STS 1277/1975, CENDOJ.

29. The policing of pornography in the U.S. military in the nineteenth century followed a similar pattern. See Giesberg, *Sex and the Civil War.*

30. STS 1428/1950, CENDOJ.

31. STS 1143/1953, CENDOJ.

32. STS 719/1954, CENDOJ.

33. STS 3050/1964, CENDOJ.

34. STS 414/1964, CENDOJ.

35. STS 414/1964, CENDOJ.

36. STS 987/1968, CENDOJ.

37. STS 987/1968, CENDOJ.

38. Thierry Paquot, "Jean-Jacques Pauvert (1926–2014) Éditeur en roue livre . . . ," *Hermès, La Revue* 71 (2015): 311–13; "Mort de Jean-Jacques Pauvert, éditeur de Sade et d'Histoire d'O," *Le Parisien,* 27 September 2014.

39. STS 759/1969, CENDOJ.

40. STS 759/1969.

41. STS 2986/1969, CENDOJ.

42. STS 2986/1969.

43. STS 1207/1973, CENDOJ.

44. Similarly, portraits of women in academic poses were sold as candy wrappers and confiscated by the police as obscenity in 1930s China. Wang emphasizes

that these images would not have been considered obscene if they had been oil paintings. Wang, *Reinventing Licentiousness.*

45. STS 2780/1970, CENDOJ.

46. STS 297/1971, CENDOJ.

47. STS 297/1971, CENDOJ.

48. STS 651/1973, CENDOJ.

49. STS 1532/1974, CENDOJ.

50. STS 387/1975, CENDOJ.

51. STS 1680/1974, CENDOJ.

52. STS 1680/1974.

53. STS 1680/1974.

54. Hunt, "Introduction," 15.

55. STS 2126/1974, CENDOJ.

56. STS 2126/1974.

57. See M. Montserrat Guibernau i Berdún, *Catalan Nationalism: Francoism, Transition, and Democracy* (London: Routledge, 2004).

58. STS 2431/1974, CENDOJ.

59. Translation by the author. The ruling, includes the original poem in Catalan and a Castilian translation. I am not transcribing these versions here because they are already accessible through the CENDOJ database.

60. STS 2431/1974, CENDOJ.

61. Antonio Sabater Tomás, *Peligrosidad social y delincuencia* (Barcelona: Nauta, 1972), 190.

62. Kevin Heffernan, "Prurient (Dis)Interest: The American Release and Reception of *I Am Curious (Yellow),*" in *Sex Scene,* 106–19.

63. Göran Lindgren and Vilgot Sjoman, *Jag Ar nyfiken: ben film i gult (I am curious: yellow)* (Stockholm: Firm, 1967).

64. Gorka Zamarreño Aramendia, *Cine y turismo en la Costa del Sol: retrato de unos colonizados* (Málaga, Spain: Repositorio Institucional de la Universidad de Málaga, 2010).

65. Manuel Rivas Guadilla and Martín Rodríguez Estevan, "INFORME PROYECTO DE LEY: De Peligrosidad Social, reformando la de Vagos y Maleantes de 4 de agosto de 1933," Archivo del Congreso de los Diputados.

66. Sabater Tomás, *Peligrosidad social,* 192.

67. Sabater Tomás, *Peligrosidad social,* 193–96.

68. José María del Moral Pérez de Zayas, Enmienda 28, 5 February 1970, Archivo del Congreso de los Diputados. The amendment presented by José Luis Fernández Cantos also pointed out the system's flaws: "In the face of the current wave of pornography, repression is being credited as insufficient." José Luis Fernández Cantos, Enmienda 52, 9 February 1970, Archivo del Congreso de los Diputados.

69. Manuel Escudero Rueda, Amendment 76, 8 February 1970, Archivo del Congreso de los Diputados.

70. On Escudero Rueda's reformist politics, see Javier Corcuera Atienza, "Manuel Escudero Rueda, procurador en Cortes aperturista," *El País,* 9 January

1998. Similarly, Stanley Payne describes Moral Pérez de Zayas as an "adaptable bureaucrat." Payne, *Franco y José Antonio. El extraño caso del fascismo español* (Barcelona: Planeta, 1997), 617.

71. José María Zaldivar Aranzana, Amendment 73, 8 February 1970, Archivo del Congreso de los Diputados.

72. Agustín Barcena Reus, Amendment 1, 19 January 1970, Archivo del Congreso de los Diputados.

73. In fact, Bárcena resigned in 1977 to protest the democratic transition process. See "Dimite el presidente del Sindicato Nacional de la Pesca," *Arriba*, 6 September 1977.

74. See Cécile Stephanie Stehrenberger, "Bichos raros: los Coros y Danzas de la Sección Femenina en Guinea Ecuatorial," in *Intersecciones: Cuerpos y sexualidades en la encrucijada*, edited by Lucas Platero Méndez (Madrid: Bellaterra, 2012), 301–24.

75. Wayne H. Bowen, "Pilar Primo de Rivera and the Axis Temptation," *The Historian* 67, no. 1 (2005): 62–72.

76. Pilar Primo de Rivera y Sáenz de Heredia, Enmienda 13, 27 January 1970, Archivo del Congreso de los Diputados.

77. Lisa Gitelman, *Always Already New: Media, History, and the Data of Culture* (Cambridge: MIT Press, 2006), 2, 6.

78. "Josefina Veglison Jornet," *ABC*, 19 September 1971.

79. On the particularities of right-wing women's mobilization in support of authoritarianism, see Margaret Power, *Right-Wing Women in Chile: Feminine Power and the Struggle against Allende, 1964–1973* (University Park: Pennsylvania State University Press, 2002).

80. "Ley 16/1970, de 4 de agosto, sobre peligrosidad y rehabilitación social," *Boletín Oficial del Estado,* 6 August 1970.

Chapter Four

1. Dennis, *Art/Porn*, 1.

2. There is a growing corpus of research focused on homosexuality under the Franco regime. See, among others, Arturo Arnalte, *Redada de violetas: la represión de los homosexuales durante el franquismo* (Madrid: Esfera de los Libros, 2003); Fernando Olmeda, *El Látigo y la pluma: Homosexuales en la España de Franco* (Madrid: Oberon, 2004); Gema Pérez-Sánchez, *Queer Transitions in Contemporary Spanish Culture: From Franco to La Movida* (New York: State University of New York Press, 2008); Alberto Mira Nouselles, *De Sodoma a Chueca: una historia cultural de la homosexualidad en España en el siglo XX* (Barcelona: Egales, 2007); Francisco Javier Ugarte Pérez, *Las circunstancias obligaban: Homoerotismo, identidad y resistencia* (Barcelona: Egales Editorial, 2011); Víctor Mora Gaspar, *Al margen de la naturaleza: la persecución de la homosexualidad durante el franquismo, leyes, terapias y condenas* (Barcelona: Debate, 2016); Brice Chamouleau, *Tiran al maricón: los fantasmas "queer" de*

la democracia (1970–1988), una interpretación de las subjetividades gais ante el Estado español (Madrid: Ediciones Akal, 2017); Víctor M. Ramírez Pérez, *Peligrosas y revolucionarias: las disidencias sexuales en Canarias durante el franquismo y la transición* (Las Palmas de Gran Canaria, Spain: Fundación Canaria Tamaimos, 2019); Ramón Martínez, *Lo nuestro sí que es mundial: una introducción a la historia del movimiento LGTB en España* (Barcelona: Editorial Egales, 2018); Geoffroy Huard and Javier Fernández-Galeano, eds., *Las locas en el archivo. Disidencia sexual bajo el franquismo* (Barcelona: Marcial Pons, 2023).

3. On the particularities and abusive uses of "dangerousness" as a legal framework that targeted potential rather than actual criminality, see Juan Terradillos Basoco, *Peligrosidad social y estado de derecho* (Madrid: Akal, 1981); Fernández-Galeano, "Is He a 'Social Danger'?," 1–31; Geoffroy Huard, *Los antisociales: Historia de la homosexualidad en Barcelona y París, 1945–1975* (Madrid: Marcial Pons Historia, 2014).

4. There are no definitive figures, just estimates, because judicial archives have access restrictions that impede the elaboration of full statistics. Jordi M. Monferrer Tomás estimates that there were over three thousand homosexuality files produced by Dangerousness Courts nationwide in the 1970s. Jordi M. Monferrer Tomás, "La construcción de la protesta en el movimiento gay español: La Ley de Peligrosidad Social (1970) como factor precipitante de la acción colectiva," *Revista Española de Investigaciones Sociológicas* 102 (2003): 185–86. In his recent work, Huard emphasizes the difficulties in quantifying the effects of state repression and problematizes the figure of "five thousand" as the most common estimate for files related to homosexuality under the Franco regime. Huard, *Los invertidos*, 86–88.

5. Huard, *Los antisociales*, 100–101. Huard's estimates include cases that ended up in a condemnatory sentence and files without a sentence but not cases that ended up in acquittal.

6. Terenci Moix, *El cine de los sábados* (Barcelona: Plaza & Janés, 1990), 158.

7. Castañeda, *Disappearing Rooms*, 11.

8. Frackman, "Homemade Pornography," 94.

9. Frackman, "Homemade Pornography," 100.

10. Dennis argues that "the fantasy is not sex so much as it is the possibility of fantasy itself." Dennis, *Art/Porn*, 111.

11. Frackman, "Homemade Pornography," 94.

12. By destroying materials confiscated from these defendants, the "physical evidence and memory incarnate of the crime was quite literally erased, rendered absent, and turned into ashes" (unless otherwise lost in the chain of custody) in order "to deaden the memory of the act," as Tortorici notes for a different period and place. Tortorici, *Sins against Nature*, 126, 158.

13. "Miguel Ángel, Rembrandt, Velázquez... Los mayores atentados que han sufrido las grandes obras maestras," *ABC*, 31 May 2022.

14. "El pirómano afirma que es un superhombre, pero incomprendido," *La nueva España*, 29 September 1968, 28.

15. *El Eco de Canarias* published an actual photograph of Antonio along with the identikit on September 29, 1968.

16. *Boletín Oficial del Ministerio del Aire*, 20 July 1967, 1021.

17. Antonio U.T., "Cartas al director. Los enfermos mentales," *El País*, 4 February 1985.

18. The press's interest in gay porn confiscated from thieves resurfaced in a different high-profile case from the Canaries, this time implicating a man accused of forgery with checks. *El eco de Canarias*, 12 May 1976, 32.

19. *La provincia* (Las Palmas de Gran Canaria), 26 November 1972, 27.

20. The argument that pornography led to homosexuality was common currency to justify stringent moral regulation in Spain. Santiago I. Antúnes published an article in 1972 that illustrated the dangers of a "global explosion" of pornography with a photograph of a male wearing a skirt, captioned "public homosexual exhibitionism." Santiago I. Antúnes, "Explosión mundial de la pornografía," *El Correo de Zamora*, 13 June 1972, 11–12.

21. As Frackman points out for queer images in East Germany, "the individuals producing these photos had a range of motivations, including the creation of sexual community (often with reciprocal sharing), personal enjoyment and mementos, artistic expression, or commercial gain through the sale of the images." Frackman, "Homemade Pornography," 97.

22. Dennis, *Art/Porn*, 113. Zubiaurre traces this tradition in Spain through a multiplicity of visual materials included in the chapter "Patriotic Sex: Mantillas, Cigarettes, and Transvestites." Zubiaurre, *Cultures of the Erotic*.

23. File 337/1975, Juzgado de Peligrosidad y Rehabilitación Social Número 1 de Barcelona, Arxiu Central dels Jutjats de la Ciutat de la Justícia, Hospitalet de Llobregat, Spain (hereafter ACJCJ).

24. See also File 44/70, Signatura 11809, Juzgado Especial de Vagos y Maleantes de Granada, Archivo Histórico Provincial de Málaga, Málaga, Spain.

25. Antonio Sabater Sanz, *El test de Szondi en sexuología forense* (Murcia, Spain: Fragua, 1972), 309–10.

26. Structures of stigma have made it difficult for gay people to preserve visual evidence of their intimacy. Stephen Vider studies, for instance, how the photos of a wedding ceremony that a gay couple celebrated in Philadelphia in 1957 were lost to their owners because of homophobia. Stephen Vider, *The Queerness of Home: Gender, Sexuality, and the Politics of Domesticity after World War II* (Chicago: University of Chicago Press, 2021), 35–36.

27. Deposition, 15 September 1965, File 552/1965, Legajo 2192, Juzgado Especial de Vagos y Maleantes de Madrid, AGA.

28. Deposition, 23 September 1965, File 552/1965.

29. Ruling, 4 November 1965, File 552/1965.

30. One decade later, in 1975, the "double life" of a different defendant also led him to destroy personal erotica. Being blackmailed by another man with whom

he had had sex, the defendant decided to tear up and throw out three photographs of a naked man he carried in his wallet before going to the police station to report the blackmailer. File 74/1976, Juzgado de Peligrosidad y Rehabilitación Social de Valencia, Arxiu Històric de la Comunitat Valenciana, València, Spain (hereafter, AHCV).

31. Report, 23 March 1962, File 87/1962, Legajo 2154, Juzgado Especial de Vagos y Maleantes de Madrid, AGA.

32. Ruling on 28 October 1969, File 87/1962.

33. Report by the Cartagena Police on 2 December 1974, File 531/1975, Juzgado de Peligrosidad y Rehabilitación Social de Valencia, AHCV.

34. Report by the Badajoz Prison on 10 June 1976, File 531/1975.

35. Comparecencia in Palma de Mallorca on 24 July 1975, File 275/1972, Juzgado de Peligrosidad y Rehabilitación Social Número 2 de Barcelona, ACJCJ.

36. Deposition on 24 July 1975, File 275/1972.

37. The file of this defendant was not catalogued and preserved in the archive labeled pornography. Instead, we have access to his story through the file of one of the men who was put in jail to secretly record his conversations. It is possible that he was either prosecuted under different charges (such as homosexuality) or released due to his socioeconomic status.

38. Declaration by the complainant on 27 April 1960, File 589/1960, Juzgado Especial de Vagos y Maleantes de Barcelona, L'Arxiu Central dels Jutjats de la Ciutat de la Justícia de Barcelona (ACJCJB).

39. Statement by the defense lawyer on 27 February 1961, File 589/1960.

40. Ruling by Antonio Sabater Tomás issued on 2 March 1961, File 589/1960.

41. Thomas Waugh, *Hard to Imagine: Gay Male Eroticism in Photography and Film from the Beginnings to Stonewall* (New York: Columbia University Press, 1996), 217. James N. Green documents this phenomenon in Brazilian cities as well, where these magazines provided the most accessible images of semi-nude male bodies between the 1940s and 1960s. James Naylor Green, *Beyond Carnival: Male Homosexuality in Twentieth-Century Brazil* (Chicago: University of Chicago Press, 1999), 159–62.

42. Terenci Moix, *El beso de Peter Pan* (Barcelona: Plaza & Janés, 1993), 47, 59.

43. File 155/1965, Juzgado Especial de Vagos y Maleantes de Barcelona, ACJCJB.

44. Robert L. Caserio, "Art and Pornography: At the Limit of Action," in *Porn Archives*, edited by Tim Dean et al. (Durham, N.C.: Duke University Press, 2014), 181.

45. Ruling by Antonio Sabater Tomás issued on 28 May 1965, File 155/1965,

46. Ann Cvetkovich, *An Archive of Feelings: Trauma, Sexuality, and Lesbian Public Cultures* (Durham, N.C.: Duke University Press, 2019), 7.

47. Report submitted on 3 January 1967, File 4/1967, Juzgado Especial de Vagos y Maleantes de Barcelona, ACJCJB.

48. Waugh, *Hard to Imagine*, 158.

49. File 800/1965, Juzgado Especial de Vagos y Maleantes de Barcelona, ACJCJB.

50. Caserio, "Art and Pornography," 181.

51. Ruling by Antonio Sabater Tomás issued on 26 January 1966, File 800/1965.

52. Dennis, *Art/Porn*, 102.

53. Rafael Borrás Pastor, "Estudio médico-legal del expediente de peligrosidad. Análisis de los expedientes sustanciados por el juzgado de peligrosidad y rehabilitación social de Valencia en el quinquenio de 1975–1979," PhD dissertation, Universitat de València, 1982.

54. Borrás Pastor, "Estudio médico-legal."

55. Deposition on 1 June 1973, File 424/1975, Juzgado de Peligrosidad y Rehabilitación Social de Valencia, AHCV.

56. Report by the Guardia Civil on 21 May 1973, File 424/1975.

57. Deposition on 1 June 1973, File 427/1975, Juzgado de Peligrosidad y Rehabilitación Social de Valencia, AHCV.

58. Ruling on 11 December 1973, File 427/1975. Since he was married and the father of three children, had a stable job, was well regarded in his workplace, and did not obtain any profit, his lawyer reckoned that there were grounds for an appeal. However, the appeal court was even more outraged by the defendant's behavior, referring to the movies as "abject and repulsive material," "the clearest exponent of obscenity and eroticism in scenes of the utmost debasement," and "monstruous indecency." Ruling on 23 April 1974, File 427/1975.

59. Report about the screening on 5 June 1973, File 427/1975.

60. Georges Bataille, *Erotism: Death and Sensuality*, translated by Mary Dalwood (San Francisco: City Lights Books, 1986), 16.

61. Bataille, *Erotism*, 40–41.

62. Mariah Larsson, "Oh Paris! The Journeys of Lasse Braun's 8mm Pornography," *JCMS: Journal of Cinema and Media Studies* 58 (2018): 161.

63. Larsson, "Oh Paris!," 160.

64. Larsson, "Oh Paris!," 158, 163.

65. Cited in Mariah Larsson, "Lasse Braun, Rape Scenarios, and Swedish Censorship: A Case Study of Two 8-mm Porn Films Featuring Rape," *Porn Studies* 4 (2017): 29.

66. Larsson, "Lasse Braun," 29.

67. Larsson, "Lasse Braun," 30–31.

68. "Un matrimonio iraní, distribuidores de folletos y películas," *El Eco de Canarias,* 18 November 1969, 3.

69. Interrogation by the Lloret del Mar Guardia Civil, 4 May 1972, File 31/1972, Juzgado de Peligrosidad y Rehabilitación Social de Barcelona, ACJCJB. Furthermore, in a later deposition, the defendant clarified that when he was arrested, he was carrying only the socialist pamphlet, while the porn and the marijuana were added to the report by the police officers to make sure that the charges went through. Deposition, 30 May 1972, File 31/1972.

70. See, for instance, "Secretaría general/Sanciones," *Falange,* 23 May 1951, 2; "Sanciones gubernativas," *Diario de Las Palmas,* 29 January 1963, 7. A newspaper in Soria, a city at the heart of Castilla, reported in 1964 that "foreign pornographic magazines" had been found and confiscated in a small stationery business in Barcelona. "Fuerte sanción," *Soria, hogar y pueblo,* 18 November 1964, 1.

71. "Cuatro detenidos, acusados de tráfico y exhibición de material pornográfico." *La nueva España,* 27 March 1969, 2. On Barcelona's central role in porn distribution, see also "Intervención de dieciséis mil ejemplares de novelas pornográficas en Barcelona," *El Correo de Zamora,* 24 January 1965, 2.

72. Two individuals arrested in 1974 for selling pornographic magazines in an esplanade close to the port in Las Palmas de Gran Canaria declared that they were sailors who had bought the magazines in South Africa, which they had visited while working on container ships. *La provincia* (Las Palmas de Gran Canaria), 12 November 1974, 28. Likewise, in 1976, 158 films and 175 magazines were confiscated from a defendant who had bought these materials from a Polish sailor and was planning to sell them clandestinely. "Pornografía: intervenidas 158 películas y 175 revistas," *El eco de Canarias,* 29 January 1976, 32.

73. Report by the Sagunto Guardia Civil on 30 October 1975, File 962/1975, Juzgado de Peligrosidad y Rehabilitación Social de Valencia, AHCV.

74. The defendant insisted that he had never shared his porn with anyone and that it was locked away and inaccessible, so it did not disturb his "marvelous" domestic life. Deposition on 31 October 1975 and Deposition on 11 November 1975, File 963 de 1975, Juzgado de Peligrosidad y Rehabilitación Social de Valencia, AHCV. The ruling indicates that the defendant's peccadilloes were considered excusable, as long as they did not detract from his breadwinner role, respectable appearance, and domestic life. Ruling on 6 December 1975, File 963/1975.

75. Report by the Sagunto Police Department on 18 November 1975, File 962/1975.

76. Report about the screening on 29 January 1976, File 962/1975.

77. Ruling on 23 Septembre 1976, File 962/1975.

78. Appraisal of costs on 11 October 1976, File 962/1975.

79. Deposition on 21 April 1975, File 581/1975, Juzgado de Peligrosidad y Rehabilitación Social de Valencia, AHCV.

80. Ruling issued on 10 May 1975, File 581/1975.

81. Report by the Castellón Police on 20 October 1971, File 8/1975, Juzgado de Peligrosidad y Rehabilitación Social de Valencia, AHCV.

82. Interrogation on 20 October 1971, File 8/1975.

83. Deposition on 25 October 1971, File 8/1975.

84. Sentence issued on 7 October 1972, File 8/1975.

85. Files 151/1976, 113/1974, and 519/1976, Juzgados de Peligrosidad y Rehabilitación Social de Barcelona, ACJCJB.

86. Files 265/1975, 375/1976, and 518/1976, Juzgados de Peligrosidad y Rehabilitación Social de Barcelona, ACJCJB.

87. Addendum to the delivery report [ampliación de diligencia de entrega] issued on 28 June 1972, File 552/1972, Juzgado de Peligrosidad y Rehabilitación Social de Barcelona, ACJCJB.

88. Like archives in the paradigm centered on evidence and the "natural residue" of power structures, the chain of custody provides contextual validity to records. On this paradigm, see Terry Cook, "Evidence, Memory, Identity, and Community: Four Shifting Archival Paradigms," *Archival Science: International Journal on Recorded Information* 13, no. 2–3 (2013): 101–2, 105. However, police and court officers mediated the chain of custody through their desire to privately enjoy the "evidence" (or, quite literally, touch themselves with it to generate sexual excitement).

89. The 1956 French comedy *En effeuillant la marguerite* (Plucking the daisy), starring Brigitte Bardot, was released in the United States with the same title of *Mademoiselle Striptease*. However, the depositions of some of the women who had attended the screening of the movie at the defendant's house suggest that they saw fragments from the 1957 movie directed by Foucaud, since they described scenes of five naked women in a French cabaret.

90. Eric Schaefer, "'I'll Take Sweden': The Shifting Discourse of the 'Sexy Nation' in Sexploitation Films," in *Sex Scene,* 210.

91. Gitelman, *Always Already New,* 4.

92. Schaefer, "'I'll Take Sweden,'" 212–13.

93. Dennis, *Art/Porn*, 21–22.

94. Cited in Dennis, *Art/Porn*, 15.

95. Dennis, *Art/Porn*, 26–31.

96. As Leonard notes, "representations welcome in one geographical or social location may be threatening or arousing (or both) in another space." Leonard, *Fragile Minds*, 3.

97. Deposition on 7 September 1975, File 385/1975, Juzgado de Peligrosidad y Rehabilitación Social de Barcelona, ACJCJB.

98. Robert S. Nelson, "The Slide Lecture, or the Work of Art 'History' in the Age of Mechanical Reproduction," *Critical Inquiry* 26 (2000): 417–22.

99. Ruling issued on 29 January 1976, File 385/1975.

100. Deposition on 18 February 1975, File 733/1974, Juzgado de Peligrosidad y Rehabilitación Social de Barcelona, ACJCJB.

101. Prosecution's opinion on 13 May 1975 and Ruling issued on 17 May 1975, File 733/1974.

102. On this filmic genre, see Cáceres García, *El destape*.

103. Pack, *Tourism and Dictatorship*, 145–48.

104. Deposition on 19 December 1975, File 713/1975, Juzgado de Peligrosidad y Rehabilitación Social de Barcelona, ACJCJB.

105. Statement by the defense lawyer on 13 May 1976, File 713/1975.

106. Ruling on 12 July 1976, File 713/1975. He appealed and the Court of Appeals of Madrid reversed the ruling in 1977, concluding that there was not enough evidence of the defendant trafficking porn on a regular basis. Ruling issued on

10 May 1977, File 713/1975. Raising the standard of evidence and the degree of involvement in pornography trafficking was one of the ways in which the judicial authorities adjusted their rulings to the post-dictatorship social reality.

Chapter Five

See Javier Fernández-Galeano, "Running Mascara: The Hermeneutics of Trans Visual Archives in Late Franco-Era Spain," *Radical History Review,* no. 142, 72–92. Copyright 2022, MARHO: The Radical Historians' Organization, Inc. All rights reserved. Republished by permission of the publisher. www.dukeupress.edu.

1. File 279/1968, Legajo 1465, Juzgado Especial de Vagos y Maleantes de Madrid, Archivo General de la Administración (AGA).

2. Emmett Harsin Drager, "Looking After Mrs. G: Approaches and Methods for Reading Transsexual Clinical Case Files," in *Turning Archival*; Fernández-Galeano, "Performing Queer Archives"; Zeb Tortorici, "Decolonial Archival Imaginaries: On Losing, Performing, and Finding Juana Aguilar," in *Turning Archival*.

3. Lucas Platero and María Rosón, "Una genealogía trans*: siglo XX," in *Trans*: diversidad de identidades y roles de género*, edited by Niurka Gibaja Yábar and Andrés Gutiérrez Usillos (Madrid: Ministerio de Educación, Cultura y Deporte, 2017), 135.

4. Lucas Platero, *Por un chato de vino. Historias de travestismo y masculinidad femenina* (Barcelona: Bellaterra, 2015).

5. Lucas Platero, "'Su gran placer es usar calzoncillos y calcetines': la represión de la masculinidad femenina bajo la dictadura," in *Mujeres bajo sospecha: Memoria y sexualidad, 1930–1980*, edited by Raquel Osborne (Madrid: Fundamentos, 2012), 175–90. Similarly, Raúl Solís identifies "joy, irreverence, and naughtiness" as the traits that allowed trans women to carve their own spaces of survival. Raúl Solís Galván, *La doble transición* (Madrid: Libros.com, 2019), 20–22.

6. Norma Mejía, *Transgenerismos: una experiencia transexual desde la perspectiva antropológica* (Barcelona: Bellaterra, 2006), 16.

7. Mejía, *Transgenerismos*, 21–22.

8. Mérida Jiménez also argues that in the 1970s most trans women employed in the Barcelona show business came from a working-class background. The police targeted these visible, working-class trans women—labeled *mariconas*—and spared affluent trans women. Mérida Jiménez, *Transbarcelonas*, 68–69, 79.

9. Ferran Imedio, "Los recuerdos de Carmen de Mairena," *El Periódico*, 29 January 2016.

10. Tatiana Sentamans [O.R.G.I.A.], "Redes transfeministas y nuevas políticas de representación sexual (I). Diagramas de flujos," in *Transfeminismos: epistemes, fricciones y flujos*, edited by Miriam Solà and Elena Urko (Tafalla, Spain: Txalaparta, 2013), 36–37.

11. Cyle Metzger and Kirstin Ringelberg, "Prismatic Views: A Look at the Growing Field of Transgender Art and Visual Culture Studies," *Journal of Visual Culture* 19, no. 2 (2020): 162.

12. Lucas Platero, "Críticas al capacitismo heteronormativo," in *Transfeminismos*, 220, 333.

13. Reina Gossett, Eric A. Stanley, and Johanna Burton, "Known Unknowns: An Introduction to Trap Door," in *Trap Door: Trans Cultural Production and the Politics of Visibility*, edited by Reina Gossett, Eric A. Stanley, and Johanna Burton (Cambridge: MIT Press, 2017), xv–xvi.

14. Singer, "From the Medical Gaze to Sublime Mutations," 601.

15. This aligns with the insistence "on pleasure, self-care, beauty, fantasy, and dreaming as elements key to sustained radical change." Gossett, Stanley, and Burton, "Known Unknowns," xxiv.

16. Elizabeth Edwards, "Photography and the Material Performance of the Past," *History and Theory* 48, no. 4 (2009): 130–36.

17. Tina M. Campt, *Listening to Images* (Durham, N.C.: Duke University Press, 2017), 1–5.

18. Campt, *Listening to Images*, 8.

19. Campt, *Listening to Images*, 5.

20. I borrow this definition of cameras as hermeneutic devices from Edwards, who argues that "the camera, photographs, and archive, and the spaces between them, become sites where things are made readable." Hence, following Edwards, we ought to focus our attention on how "material practices make photographs adequate to the historical desires that enmesh them." Edwards, "Photography and the Material Performance of the Past," 137.

21. "Ley Orgánica 15/1999, de 13 de diciembre, de Protección de Datos de Carácter Personal," *Boletín Oficial del Estado* 298.

22. Jordi Terrasa Mateu, "Control, represión y reeducación de los homosexuales durante el franquismo y el inicio de la transición," PhD dissertation, University of Barcelona, 2016, 512–16.

23. "Ley Orgánica 15/1999."

24. María Elena Martínez, "Archives, Bodies, and Imagination: The Case of Juana Aguilar and Queer Approaches to History, Sexuality, and Politics," *Radical History Review* 120 (2014): 159–82.

25. I am indebted to transgender studies scholar Cole Rizki for pointing out the intricacies of this ethical choice and providing me with resources to critically think about it.

26. Singer, "From the Medical Gaze to Sublime Mutations," 602.

27. Singer, "From the Medical Gaze to Sublime Mutations," 604–6, 611.

28. Singer, "From the Medical Gaze to Sublime Mutations," 602.

29. File 279/1968, Juzgado Especial de Vagos y Maleantes de Madrid, AGA.

30. According to Mérida Jiménez, trans people imprisoned and interviewed by psychiatrists and other medical experts described their transitioning as a fundamental step to escape repressive mechanisms and formalize their relationships with their partners. Mérida Jiménez, *Transbarcelonas*, 91.

31. Deposition of Daniela in front of the court of first instance on 5 April 1968, File 279/1968.

32. Report by the Guardia Civil of Aranjuez on 5 April 1968, File 279/1968.

33. Rizki presents a similar analysis of the crossing out of the "heterosexual" from reports on HIV by the Buenos Aires police. Cole Rizki, "'No State Apparatus Goes to Bed Genocidal Then Wakes Up Democratic': Fascist Ideology and Transgender Politics in Post-dictatorship Argentina," *Radical History Review* 138 (2020): 89.

34. Forensic report, 8 April 1968, File 279/1968.

35. Susan Stryker, *Transgender History* (Berkeley: Seal Press, 2008).

36. Ruling on 24 May 1968, File 279/1968.

37. Report by the police of San Sebastian, 7 October 1968, File 192/1968 from the Vagrancy Court of Bilbao, included in File 279/1968.

38. Police report, 6 May 1972, File 279/1968.

39. Jun Zubillaga-Pow, "'In the Raw': Posing, Photography, and Trans*Aesthetics," *Transgender Studies Quarterly* 5, no. 3 (2018): 447–49.

40. Campt, *Listening to Images*, 6.

41. Nancy Scheper-Hughes, *Death without Weeping: The Violence of Everyday Life in Brazil* (Berkeley: University of California Press, 1993), 135.

42. Police report, 6 April 1974, File 279/1968.

43. Police report, 6 April 1974, File 279/1968.

44. Gossett, Stanley, and Burton, "Known Unknowns," xvi.

45. For instance, in 1968 the District Attorney of València shared his concern about young men prostituting themselves to access a consumer culture centered on fashion trends, describing: "jumbled gatherings of long-haired Yé-yé, hippie, and beatnik [individuals] wearing all kinds of extravagant clothing, in oppressively narrow alleyways." Cited in Víctor Ramírez Pérez, "Franquismo y disidencia sexual. La visión del Ministerio Fiscal de la época," *Aposta: Revista de Ciencias Sociales* 77 (2018): 158.

46. Gabriela Cano, "Unconcealable Realities of Desire: Amelio Robles's (Transgender) Masculinity in the Mexican Revolution," in *Sex in Revolution: Gender, Politics, and Power in Modern Mexico*, edited by Jocelyn Olcott, Mary K. Vaughan, and Gabriela Cano (Durham, N.C.: Duke University Press, 2006), 38.

47. Marcia Ochoa, *Queen for a Day: Transformistas, Beauty Queens, and the Performance of Femininity in Venezuela* (Durham, N.C.: Duke University Press, 2014), 157–58, 161.

48. Tonia Sutherland, "Reading Gesture: Katherine Dunham, the Dunham Technique, and the Vocabulary of Dance as Decolonizing Archival Praxis," *Archival Science: International Journal on Recorded Information* 19 (2019): 167.

49. Sutherland, "Reading Gesture," 181.

50. Arrest report, 20 June 1974, File 416/1974, Juzgado Especial de Vagos y Maleantes de Barcelona, ACJCJ.

51. Deposition in front of the judge, 20 June 1974, File 416/1974.

52. Ruling on 16 October 1974, File 416/1974.

53. Deposition by Carla's mother, 21 February 1975, File 416/1974.

54. Police report, 19 March 1975, File 416/1974.

55. Report by the Guardia Civil of Sabadell, 23 May 1975, File 416/1974.

56. File 416/1974.

57. Huard, *Los invertidos*, 89.

58. As Tina Campt highlights, the "seeming insignificance" of these everyday practices of visibility obscures that the trivial and mundane are essential in the lives of the dispossessed. Campt, *Listening to Images,* 4, 7–8.

59. Edwards, "Photography and the Material Performance of the Past," 148.

60. Report by the Guardia Civil of Sabadell, 23 May 1975, File 416/1974.

61. Report by the Guardia Civil of Sabadell, 23 June 1974, File 442/1974, Juzgado Especial de Vagos y Maleantes de Barcelona, ACJCJ.

62. Kate Eichhorn, "Late Print Culture's Social Media Revolution: Authorship, Collaboration, and Copy Machines," *Authorship* 2 (2018): 5.

63. Merriam-Webster.com Dictionary, s.v. "photocopy," accessed August 16, 2023, www.merriam-webster.com/dictionary/photocopy.

64. Cole Rizki, "Familiar Grammars of Loss and Belonging: Curating Trans Kinship in Post-Dictatorship Argentina," *Journal of Visual Culture* 19, no. 2 (2020): 201.

65. Singer, "From the Medical Gaze to Sublime Mutations," 607.

66. Between 11 and 15 May 2022, Tania stayed with me in València, and we recorded approximately four hours of interviews about her experiences. I cite these interviews as a single audio file dated in May 2022. Tania Navarro Amo, interviews with the author, València, Spain, May 2022.

67. Meeting among DGAIA, Tania Navarro Amo, and the author, 20 June 2022, Arxiu Central dels Jutjats de la Ciutat de la Justícia.

68. An official report included in Tania's file exemplifies the prejudices against single mothers by blaming Tania's lack of a "basic education" on her mother being separated from her father. Report by the Hospitalet City Hall, 12 June 1972, File 435/1972, Juzgado de Peligrosidad y Rehabilitación Social Número 2 de Barcelona, ACJCJB.

69. Tania Navarro Amo, *La infancia de una transexual en la dictadura* (Barcelona: Planeta, 2021),

70. Juana Navarro Amo's declaration, 7 April 1975, File 435/1972.

71. Tania Navarro Amo's declaration, 23 April 1975, File 435/1972.

72. Navarro Amo, *La infancia*, 57.

73. Navarro Amo, interviews, May 2022.

74. Police report, 27 March 1969. Tania has kept a copy of this document, which was provided to her by the government when she applied for reparations. She did not keep photocopies in their original order, and for that reason I do not know to which of her files this report belonged.

75. Navarro Amo, *La infancia.*

76. Huard, *Los invertidos*, 111.

77. Navarro Amo, *La infancia*, 42–43.

78. Police report, 24 May 1972; Tania's declaration, 26 May 1972, File 435/1972.

79. Forensic report, 6 June 1972, File 435/1972.

80. Report by the Hospitalet City Hall, 17 November 1972; Report by the Guardia Civil, 30 May 72, File 435/1972.

81. Ruling by Judge Antonio Sabater Tomás, 1 December 1972, File 435/1972.

82. Navarro Amo, *La infancia.*

83. Navarro Amo, interviews, May 2022.

84. Tania Navarro Amo, phone interview with the author, 18 September 2022.

85. For more on Coccinelle's international impact, see Ana Álvarez, "Coccinelle: entre el cabaret y la pantalla grande," *Moléculas Malucas* (June 2021), www.moleculasmalucas.com/post/coccinelle-entre-el-cabaret-y-la-pantalla, accessed on August 16, 2023.

86. Tania's declaration, 19 March 1975, File 435/1972. On Casablanca as a place of "pilgrimage" for sex change, see Daniela Ferrández, "Voces desde el gueto: vidas trans, oportunidades de supervivencia y esperanzas de cambio en el Vigo de la transición," *Cuadernos de Historia Contemporánea* 46 (2024).

87. Valeria Vegas, "La mujer transexual que desafió a Franco y hoy tiene una calle," *Vanity Fair,* 27 June 2020.

88. Navarro Amo, interview, 18 September 2022.

89. Tania's declaration, 1 June 1976, File 435/1972.

90. Navarro Amo, interviews, May 2022.

91. Forensic report, 1 June 1976, File 435/1972.

92. Navarro Amo, interview, 18 September 2022.

93. Navarro Amo, interviews, May 2022.

94. Mercè Picornell, "¿De una España viril a una España travesti? Transgresión transgénero y subversión del poder franquista en la transición española hacia la democracia," *Feminismo/s* 16 (2010): 283.

95. Picornell, "¿De una España viril a una España travesti?," 285.

96. Lluís Fernàndez, *El anarquista desnudo* (Barcelona: Anagrama, 1979), 90–91.

97. Lluís Fernàndez, "Valencia puede ofrecer un tipo de literatura picaresca que entroncaría con el siglo XVI," by Amparo Tuñón, *El País*, 10 September 1978.

98. Picornell, "¿De una España viril a una España travesti?," 290; see also Pérez-Sánchez, *Queer Transitions,* 95, 137.

99. Subrat, *Invertidos y rompepatrias,* 477–78.

100. Navarro Amo, interviews, May 2022.

101. File 98/1981, Juzgado de Peligrosidad y Rehabilitación Social Número 1 de Barcelona, ACJCJB.

102. Navarro Amo, interviews, May 2022.

Chapter Six

1. File 145/1978, Juzgado de Peligrosidad y Rehabilitación Social Número 1 de Barcelona, ACJCJB.

2. Report on 22 December 1978, File 145/1978.

3. Report on 18 December 1978, File 145/1978.

4. Inquiry on 28 December 1978, File 145/1978; Report on 28 February 1979, File 145/1978.

5. Statement by the defendant on 29 March 1979, File 145/1978.

6. Statement by the prosecutor on 7 May 1979, Ruling on 7 May 1979, File 145/1978.

7. "Ley 77/1978, de 26 de diciembre, de modificación de la Ley de Peligrosidad y Rehabilitación Social y de su Reglamento," *Boletín Oficial del Estado,* 11 January 1979, 658–59.

8. The Ley de Peligrosidad was repealed in 1995. Since then, only child pornography is typified in the penal code. "Ley Orgánica 10/1995, de 23 de noviembre, del Código Penal," *Boletín Oficial del Estado,* 24 November 1995.

9. Armand de Fluvià, "Letter to Héctor Anabitarte Rivas on 8 February 1976," Unit 132, Moviment Gai collection, Arxiu Nacional de Catalunya, Sant Cugat del Vallès, Spain.

10. Francisco Fernández de Alba, *Sex, Drugs, and Fashion in 1970s Madrid* (Toronto: University of Toronto Press, 2020), 42–68.

11. "El erotismo en España," *Triunfo,* 26 September 1970, 24.

12. Jeffrey Escoffier, *Sex, Society, and the Making of Pornography: The Pornographic Object of Knowledge* (New Brunswick, N.J.: Rutgers University Press, 2021), 2.

13. "El erotismo en España," 24.

14. Torrente Ballester, "El erotismo," 46.

15. Labrador, "Una urna," 92–97.

16. Alberto Elena, "La puerta del infierno: tres notas sobre la circulación del cine pornográfico," PhD dissertation, Universidad Autónoma de Madrid, 2000, 7.

17. Elena, "La puerta del infierno," 8–9.

18. "To a significant degree, then, the history of erotic and pornographic photography is 'French.'" Dennis, *Art/Porn,* 95.

19. "Asalto de la pornografía a las salas de cine," *Blanco y negro,* 5 July 1975, 75.

20. Jean Cau, "La Ola erótica," *ABC,* 14 February 1971.

21. "El papa contra la pornografía," *ABC,* 14 February 1971.

22. Amy C. Whipple, "Speaking for Whom? The 1971 Festival of Light and the Search for the 'Silent Majority,'" *Contemporary British History* 24, no. 3 (2010): 319–39.

23. Ben Strassfeld, "The Blight of Indecency: Antiporn Politics and the Urban Crisis in Early 1970s Detroit," *Journal of the History of Sexuality* 27 (2018): 421.

24. Strassfeld, "Blight of Indecency," 422–23.

25. Alfonso Barra, "Los jóvenes, contra la pornografía," *ABC,* 30 January 1972.

26. Whipple, "Speaking for Whom?," 320, 325–26.

27. Barra, "Los jóvenes."

28. Barra, "Los jóvenes."

29. Andy Campbell, "Myra Breckinridge Was an Agent of Doom for the American Male," *Garage,* 17 July 2018.

30. Barra, "Los jóvenes."

31. Hunt points out that, since the early modern period, moralists have been aware of "the contradiction implicit in openly discussing pornographic literature," thus giving it publicity. Hunt, "Introduction," 15.

32. Barra, "Los jóvenes."

33. Elena, "La puerta del infierno," 10. Historian Dan Callwood has studied how "pornography combined a number of fears floating in the French imagination in 1975, namely, economic uncertainty, American influence, and the specter of sexual liberation." Callwood, "Anxiety and Desire in France's Gay Pornographic Film Boom, 1974–1983," *Journal of the History of Sexuality* 26 (2017): 26.

34. Callwood, "Anxiety and Desire," 31–33.

35. Callwood, "Anxiety and Desire," 35.

36. Callwood, "Anxiety and Desire," 39, 50.

37. Antonio Colón, "La marea 'porno' en el cine europeo," *ABC*, 8 July 1975, 89.

38. "Orden de 19 de febrero de 1975 por la que se establecen normas de calificación cinematográfica," *Boletín Oficial del Estado*, 1 March 1975, 4313–4314.

39. "Orden de 19 de febrero de 1975."

40. "DECRETO 2998/1974 de 29 de octubre, por el que se dispone el cese de don Pío Cabanillas Gallas como Ministro de Información y Turismo," *Boletín Oficial del Estado*, 30 October 1974, 22129.

41. Lorenzo López Sancho, "Truculencia demostrativa en 'las adolescentes,'" *ABC*, 11 October 1975, 79.

42. José Antonio Valverde and Adolfo Abril, *Las españolas en secreto: comportamiento sexual de la mujer española* (Madrid: Sedmay, 1975), 178–80.

43. Report, 5 March 1975, Censorship File 4063/1975, AGA.

44. Report on 12 May 1976, Censorship File 5567/1976, AGA.

45. Censorship File 5567/1976, AGA.

46. "Tarancón: un no al 'papanatismo' del impudor," *Blanco y negro*, 22 November 1975, 90.

47. Alberto Cardín and Federico Jiménez Losantos, "Introducción. Un nuevo objeto cultural," in *La revolución teórica de la pornografía*, edited by Alberto Cardín and Federico Jiménez Losantos (Barcelona: Iniciativas Editoriales, 1978), 10.

48. Cardín and Jiménez Losantos, "Introducción," 14.

49. Cardín and Jiménez Losantos, "Introducción," 17–21.

50. Labrador, "Una urna," 98, 104.

51. Jorge Marí, "Desnudos, vivos y muertos: La transición erótico-política y/ en la crítica cultural de Vázquez Montalbán," in *Manuel Vázquez Montalbán: el compromiso con la memoria*, edited by José F. Colmeiro (Woodbridge, U.K.: Tamesis, 2007), 129–30.

52. Carlos Santos, *333 historias de la Transición: chaquetas de pana, tetas al aire, ruido de sables, suspiros, algaradas y consenso* (Madrid: La esfera de los

libros, 2015), 283; Carlos Santos, "La transición también se hizo en las camas," *La Razón,* 22 December 2015.

53. Santos, *333 historias,* 283–85.

54. Santos, *333 historias,* 286.

55. Labrador, "Una urna," 109–10.

56. *Interviú,* April 1982.

57. Navarro Amo, interviews, May 2022.

58. Statement by the defense lawyer on 13 December 1976, File 322/1976, Juzgado de Peligrosidad y Rehabilitación Social Número 1 de Barcelona, ACJCJB.

59. "Real Decreto 2716/1976, de 18 de octubre, por el que se regula la aplicación en materia de Prensa e Imprenta del Real Decreto-ley 10/1976, de 30 de julio," *Boletín Oficial del Estado,* 27 November 1976, 23648.

60. "Real Decreto-ley 24/1977, de 1 de abril, sobre libertad de expresión," *Boletín Oficial del Estado,* 12 April 1977, 7928–7929.

61. Justino Sinova, "La libertad de expresión también le debe a Adolfo Suárez," *El Mundo,* 25 March 2014.

62. Judge's decision on 14 March 1978, File 322/1976.

63. Report on 23 April 1976, File 151/1976, Juzgado de Peligrosidad y Rehabilitación Social Número 2 de Barcelona, ACJCJB.

64. Ruling on 7 January 1977, File 151/1976.

65. Appeal on 30 June 1977, File 151/1976.

66. Ruling by the Sala Especial de Peligrosidad y Rehabilitación Social de la Audiencia Nacional on 27 January 1978, File 151/1976.

67. "Iglesia y Estado contra la 'porno,'" *Blanco y negro,* 14 February 1976, 70–72.

68. "Cartas al director," *Blanco y negro,* 21 February 1976, 12.

69. "La mayoría de los españoles son partidarios de la desaparición de la censura," *Ya,* 10 November 1976.

70. Pablo Sánchez León, "Desclasamiento y desencanto. La representación de las clases medias como eje de una relectura generacional de la transición española," *Kamchatka: Revista de Análisis Cultural* 4 (2014): 63–89.

71. Report issued on 4 May 1976, File 519/1976, Juzgado de Peligrosidad y Rehabilitación Social de Barcelona, ACJCJB.

72. Ruling issued on 3 October 1977, File 519/1976.

73. Report on 10 June 1976, File 309/1976, Juzgado de Peligrosidad y Rehabilitación Social Número 1 de Barcelona, ACJCJB, underlined in the original.

74. Deposition by the defendant on 8 July 1976, File 309/1976.

75. "Decreto 619/1976, de 18 de marzo, por el que se fija el salario mínimo interprofesional," *Boletín Oficial del Estado,* 27 March 1976, 6200–6201.

76. Prosecutor's statement on 8 February 1977, File 309/1976.

77. Communication between courts on 7 February 1977, File 309/1976.

78. Prosecutor's statement on 21 February 1978, Judge's ruling on 9 March 1978, File 309/1976.

79. Report by the Granollers Court of Instruction on 6 June 1979, Proceedings 166/1979, Juzgado de Peligrosidad y Rehabilitación Social Número 2 de Barcelona, ACJCJB.

80. Report on 5 June 1979, Proceedings 166/1979.

81. Judge's decision on 10 December 1985, Proceedings 166/1979.

82. "Real Decreto-ley 24/1977."

83. Daniel Gozalbo Gimeno, "Historia archivística de los expedientes de censura editorial (1942–2017)," *Creneida: Anuario de Literaturas Hispánicas* 5 (2017): 33.

84. Santos, *333 historias*, 308.

85. Eloy de la Iglesia (interview with J. M. Amilibia), "Censura, no; homosexualidad, sí," *Interviú,* 24 February 1977.

86. Personal communication with the author, 20 July 2022.

87. Censorship File 1177/1979, Signatura73/06866, AGA.

88. On Tom of Finland's iconography, see Martti Lahti, "Dressing Up in Power: Tom of Finland and Gay Male Body Politics," *Journal of Homosexuality* 35, no. 3 (1998): 185–90.

89. Gitelman, *Always Already New*, 20–21.

90. *La perla, colección de lecturas sicalípticas sarcásticas y voluptuosas. Número 16* (Madrid: Ediciones Pole, 1978).

91. Report on 22 December 1977, File 14527/1977, Signatura 73/06417, AGA.

92. "Puerta abierta a la homosexualidad," *Hip* 8, File 14527/1977.

93. "CAPÍTULO VIII. Artículo 240. Decreto 3096/1973, de 14 de septiembre, por el que se publica el Código Penal, texto refundido conforme a la Ley 44/1971, de 15 de noviembre," *Boletín Oficial del Estado,* 12 December 1973. This penal code remained in force until 1995.

94. Censors' reports on 4 April 1978, File 03762, Signatura 73/06550, AGA.

95. Manuel Soriano Gil, *Homosexualidad y represión: iniciación al estudio de la homofilia* (Madrid: Zero, 1978), 68.

96. Marí, "Desnudos," 137. Labrador highlights that Enrique Tierno Galván advocated for "sexual restraint" during the democratic transition and was quite critical of the movements for sexual liberation. Labrador, "Una urna," 102.

97. Susana Estrada's interview with Valeria Vegas, "Quise que los socialistas me explicaran por qué me quitaron el derecho al voto," *Vanity Fair,* 14 February 2018.

98. Estrada and Vegas, "Quise."

99. Iván Tubau, *"Playboy* en España: demasiado tarde, demasiado pronto," *ANÀLISI: Quaderns de comunicaciò i cultur* 2 (1980): 40–41.

100. Tubau, *"Playboy* en España," 40.

101. For a critique of the transition's consensus politics, see Germán Labrador Méndez, "They Called It Democracy? The Aesthetic Politics of the Spanish Transition to Democracy and Some Collective Hijackings of History after the 15M Movement," *Historein* 15, no. 1 (2015): 117–54.

102. Similarly, according to Eliot Borenstein, when the "Russian edition of *Playboy* appeared in 1995, its rhetoric of sexual revolution seemed decidedly dated." Borenstein, "Stripping the Nation Bare," 238–39.

103. Tubau, "*Playboy*," 35–44.

104. Preciado, *Pornotopia*, 40.

105. Verónica Giordano, "Revolución, sexo y política en Brasil en los años setenta. Un análisis desde las notas sobre comida en la revista *Homem* (*Playboy*)," *Cordis: História e Literatura* 10 (2013): 177–207.

106. Tubau, "*Playboy* en España," 43.

107. Dennis, *Art/Porn*, 98–99.

108. *Interviú*'s former director suggests that readers were attracted to the stripping or unveiling of both eroticized nudity and political corruption. Marí, "Desnudos," 134.

109. Marí, "Desnudos," 136.

110. Tubau, "*Playboy*," 36.

111. Cited in Marí, "Desnudos," 134.

112. Ben and Insausti, "Race and Politics."

113. Borenstein, "Stripping the Nation Bare," 242.

114. Dennis similarly traces *Hustler*'s success to its focus on the materiality of the body rather than its idealization. Dennis, *Art/Porn*, 114.

115. Bastida, *Jueces y franquismo*, 13.

116. "Ley 1/1982, de 24 de febrero, por la que se regulan las Salas Especiales de Exhibición cinematográfica, la Filmoteca Española y las tarifas de las tasas por licencia de doblaje," *Boletín Oficial del Estado,* 27 February 1982, 5184–5186; Elena, "La puerta del infierno," 12.

117. As art historian Kelly Dennis notes, "pornography is indissociable from sexual 'norms,'" it belongs to the realm of "normal" sexuality as one of its perversions. Dennis, *Art/Porn*, 120. For historian Lynn Hunt, pornography reveals how "gender differentiations" develop in modern culture. Hunt, "Introduction," 11.

118. Preciado, *Pornotopía*.

119. Mercè Picornell argues that the male body was the object of "both exaltation and vigilance" as the locus of racial regeneration and family/political stability through Franco's fatherly authority. See Picornell, "¿De una España viril a una España travesti?," 286. Likewise, Mary Vincent points out that male authority was predicated on men's sexed body and their capacity to resist its "corruption and decay." Vincent, "La reafirmación de la masculinidad en la cruzada franquista," *Cuadernos de Historia Contemporánea* 28 (2006): 139.

120. The Francoist authorities' way of handing sexual matters reveals that masculinity, national pride, and the relations with the West were among their main concerns. Similar concerns shaped the debates on obscenity in post-soviet Russia, in contrast with nineteenth-century Germany, where subjects' interiority was the main concern driving antiobscenity interventions. Borenstein, "Stripping the Nation Bare," 234; Leonard, *Fragile Minds,* 4–8.

BIBLIOGRAPHY

Archives

Arxiu Central dels Jutjats de la Ciutat de la Justícia
Archivo del Congreso de los Diputados
Archivo General de la Administración
Arxiu Històric de la Comunitat Valenciana
Archivo Histórico Nacional
Archivo Histórico Provincial de Las Palmas
Archivo Histórico Provincial de Málaga
Archivo Histórico Provincial de Sevilla
Arxiu Nacional de Catalunya
Archivo Universitario, Universidad de Granada
Archivo Universitario, Universidad de Valladolid
Archivo Universitario, Universidad de Salamanca
Archivo Universitario, Universidad de Zaragoza
Biblioteca Pública Arús
Centro de Documentación Cinematográfica de València
Fondo Antiguo y Archivo Histórico, Biblioteca Rector A. Machado y Núñez, Universidad de Sevilla, Sevilla
Histórico del Tribunal Supremo/Centro de Documentación Judicial

Interviews
Interviews with Tania Navarro Amo, May and September 2022

Periodicals
Boletín Oficial del Estado
Gaceta de Madrid
Boletín Oficial del Ministerio del Aire
Interviú
Blanco y negro
Soria, hogar y pueblo
Diario de Las Palmas
El Correo de Zamora
La provincia
El Eco de Canarias
Diario de avisos
Sabadell
Madrid cómico
El Sol
El Heraldo de Madrid
La Libertad
La Esfera
Triunfo
Falange (Las Palmas de Gran Canaria)
Nuevo mundo
Revista de especialidades médicas
La Vanguardia
El País
El Español
ABC
Garage
Arriba
La Guinea Española
Proa (León)
Le Parisien
La nueva España
El Mundo
Ya
Vanity Fair
Metropoli
El Periódico

Films
Lindgren, Göran, and Vilgot Sjoman. *Jag ar nyfiken: ben film i gult (I am curious: yellow)*. Stockholm: Firm, 1967.

References

Albarracín Soto, Matilde. "Identidad(es) lésbica(s) en el primer franquismo." In *Mujeres bajo sospecha: Memoria y sexualidad, 1930–1980*, edited by Raquel Osborne, 69–87. Madrid: Fundamentos, 2012.

Álvarez, Ana. "Coccinelle: entre el cabaret y la pantalla grande." *Moléculas Malucas* (June 2021). www.moleculasmalucas.com/post/coccinelle-entre-el -cabaret-y-la-pantalla.

Arendt, Hannah. *On Violence*. New York: Harcourt, 1969.

Arnalte, Arturo. *Redada de violetas: la represión de los homosexuales durante el franquismo*. Madrid: Esfera de los Libros, 2003.

Arondekar, Anjali. *For the Record: On Sexuality and the Colonial Archive in India*. Durham, N.C.: Duke University Press, 2009.

Bastida, Francisco J. *Jueces y franquismo: el pensamiento político del Tribunal Supremo en la dictadura*. Barcelona: Ariel, 1986.

Bataille, Georges. *Erotism: Death and Sensuality*. Translated by Mary Dalwood. San Francisco: City Lights Books, 1986.

Ben, Pablo, and Santiago Joaquín Insausti. "Race and Politics in Peruvian and Argentine Porn under the Transition to Democracy, 1975–1985." *Journal of Latin American Cultural Studies*, forthcoming.

Benjamin, Walter. *The Arcades Project*. Translated by Howard Eiland, Kevin MacLaughlin, and Rolf Tiedemann. Cambridge: The Belknap Press, 2002.

Borenstein, Eliot. "Stripping the Nation Bare: Russian Pornography and the Insistence on Meaning." In *International Exposure: Perspectives on Modern European Pornography, 1800–2000*, edited by Lisa Z. Sigel, 232–54. New Brunswick, N.J.: Rutgers University Press, 2005.

Borrás Pastor, Rafael. "Estudio médico-legal del expediente de peligrosidad. Análisis de los expedientes sustanciados por el juzgado de peligrosidad y rehabilitación social de Valencia en el quinquenio de 1975–1979." PhD dissertation, Universitat de València, 1982.

Bourdieu, Pierre. *Science of Science and Reflexivity*. Translated by Richard Nice. Chicago: University of Chicago Press, 2004.

Bowen, Wayne H. "Pilar Primo de Rivera and the Axis Temptation." *The Historian* 67, no. 1 (2005): 62–72.

Bulffi de Quintana, Luis. *¡Huelga de vientres!* Barcelona: Biblioteca Editorial Salud y Fuerza, 1909.

Cáceres Feria, Rafael, and José María Valcuende Del Río. "Turismo y homosexualidad en la España franquista: Torremolinos (1960–1971)." In *Las locas en el archivo. Disidencia sexual bajo el franquismo*, edited by Geoffroy Huard and Javier Fernández-Galeano, 305–27. Barcelona: Marcial Pons, 2023.

Cáceres García, Juli. *El destape del macho Ibérico: masculinidades disidentes en la comedia sexy (celt)Ibérica*. PhD dissertation, Georgetown University, 2008.

Callwood, Dan. "Anxiety and Desire in France's Gay Pornographic Film Boom, 1974–1983." *Journal of the History of Sexuality* 26 (2017): 26–52.

Campt, Tina M. *Listening to Images*. Durham, N.C.: Duke University Press, 2017.

Cano, Gabriela. "Unconcealable Realities of Desire: Amelio Robles's (Transgender) Masculinity in the Mexican Revolution." In *Sex in Revolution: Gender, Politics, and Power in Modern Mexico*, edited by Jocelyn Olcott, Mary K. Vaughan, and Gabriela Cano, 35–56. Durham, N.C.: Duke University Press, 2006.

Casanova, Julián, and Carlos Gil Andrés. *Twentieth-Century Spain: A History*. Cambridge, U.K.: Cambridge University Press, 2014.

Caserio, Robert L. "Art and Pornography: At the Limit of Action." In *Porn Archives*, edited by Tim Dean, Steven Ruszczycky, and David Squires, 163–82. Durham, N.C.: Duke University Press, 2014.

Castañeda, Michelle. *Disappearing Rooms: The Hidden Theaters of Immigration Law*. Durham, N.C.: Duke University Press, 2023.

Chamouleau, Brice. *Tiran al maricón: los fantasmas "queer" de la democracia (1970–1988)*. Madrid: Ediciones Akal, 2017.

Chuliá Rodrigo, Elisa. "La Ley de Prensa de 1966: La explicación de un cambio institucional arriesgado y de sus efectos virtuosos." *Historia y política: Ideas, procesos y movimientos sociales* 2 (1999): 197–220.

Cleminson, Richard, and Francisco Vázquez García. *Los Invisibles: A History of Male Homosexuality in Spain, 1850–1939*. Cardiff: University of Wales Press, 2011.

Collins, Ronald K. L., and David M. Skover. "The Pornographic State." *Harvard Law Review* 107, no. 6 (1994): 1374–1399.

Cook, Terry. "Evidence, Memory, Identity, and Community: Four Shifting Archival Paradigms." *Archival Science: International Journal on Recorded Information* 13, no. 2–3 (2013): 95–120.

Cowan, Benjamin A. *Securing Sex: Morality and Repression in the Making of Cold War Brazil*. Chapel Hill: University of North Carolina Press, 2016.

Cubero Izquierdo, Carmen. "Procesos contra la pornografía. La construcción del control sobre el erotismo en España: 1880–1936." In *De los controles disciplinarios a los controles securitarios*, edited by Pedro Oliver Olmo and María Carmen Cubero Izquierdo, 541–54. Cuenca, Spain: Universidad De Castilla-La Mancha, 2020.

Cuevas del Barrio, Javier, and Alejandro Martín Rodríguez. "Cruising Torremolinos. Mito, imagen, arquitectura." In *Reimaginar la disidencia sexual en la España de los 70: redes, vidas, archivos*, edited by Alberto Berzosa and Gracia Trujillo, 337–53. Barcelona: Bellaterra, 2019.

Cvetkovich, Ann. *An Archive of Feelings: Trauma, Sexuality, and Lesbian Public Cultures*. Durham, N.C.: Duke University Press, 2019.

Dean, Carolyn. "Empathy, Pornography, and Suffering." *Differences* 14, no. 1 (2003): 88–124.

——. *The Frail Social Body: Pornography, Homosexuality, and Other Fantasies in Interwar France*. Berkeley: University of California Press, 2000.

Dean, Tim. "Pornography, Technology, Archive." In *Porn Archives*, edited by Tim Dean, Steven Ruszczycky, and David Squires, 1–26. Durham, N.C.: Duke University Press, 2015.

Del Amo, Mercedes. *Salvador Vila: el rector fusilado en Víznar.* Granada, Spain: Editorial Universidad de Granada, 2005.

Delso, Juan Pablo Calero. *Celso Gomis Mestre: excursiones por la provincia de Guadalajara.* Ciudad Real, Spain: Centro de estudios de Castilla-La Mancha, 2011.

Dennis, Kelly. *Art/Porn: A History of Seeing and Touching.* Oxford: Berg, 2009.

Deslandes, Paul R. *The Culture of Male Beauty in Britain: From the First Photographs to David Beckham.* Chicago: University of Chicago Press, 2021.

Díaz, Abel. "Los invertidos: homosexualidad(es) y género en el primer franquismo." *Cuadernos de Historia Contemporánea* 41 (2019): 329–49.

Diego Pérez, Carmen. "Un caso paradigmático de represión cultural: depuración de bibliotecas escolares en la provincia de Palencia durante la guerra civil española (2ª parte)." *Represura* 7 (2011).

Drager, Emmett Harsin. "Looking After Mrs. G: Approaches and Methods for Reading Transsexual Clinical Case Files." In *Turning Archival: The Life of the Historical in Queer Studies,* edited by Zeb Tortorici and Daniel Marshall, 165–84. Durham, N.C.: Duke University Press, 2023.

Durán, Gloria G. *Sicalípticas: el gran libro del cuplé y la sicalipsis.* Madrid: Editorial La Felguera, 2022.

Edwards, Elizabeth. "Photography and the Material Performance of the Past." *History and Theory* 48, no. 4 (2009): 130–50.

Elena, Alberto. *La puerta del infierno: tres notas sobre la circulación del cine pornográfico.* Madrid: Universidad Autónoma de Madrid, 2000.

Ellis, Robert Richmond. "Looking Queer in *El beso de Peter Pan* of Terenci Moix." *España Contemporánea: Revista de Literatura y Cultura* 9, no. 2 (1996): 7–24.

Escoffier, Jeffrey. *Sex, Society, and the Making of Pornography: The Pornographic Object of Knowledge.* New Brunswick, N.J.: Rutgers University Press, 2021.

Escópico, Casto. *Sólo para adultos: historia del cine X.* València, Spain: La Máscara, 1996.

Evans, Jennifer V. "Seeing Subjectivity: Erotic Photography and the Optics of Desire." *American Historical Review* 118, no. 2 (2013): 430–62.

Fernández, Pura. "Censura y práctica de la transgresión: Los dominios del eros y la moralidad en la literatura española decimonónica." In *Los territorios literarios de la historia del placer,* edited by José Blas Vega et al., 71–89. Madrid: Huerga & Fierro Editores, 1996.

Fernández de Alba, Francisco. *Sex, Drugs, and Fashion in 1970s Madrid.* Toronto: University of Toronto Press, 2020.

Fernández-Galeano, Javier. "Dildos y lubricantes: La cultura material del erotismo en Torremolinos frente a la retórica del régimen franquista." In *Cruising Torremolinos: Cuerpos, territorio y memoria,* edited by Javier Cuevas del Barrio and Ángelo Néstore, 23–48. València, Spain: Tirant Humanidades, 2022.

Fernández-Galeano, Javier. *Maricas: Queer Cultures and State Violence in Argentina and Spain, 1942–1982.* Lincoln: University of Nebraska Press, 2024.

Fernández-Galeano, Javier, and Mir Yarfitz. "Serious Maricas and Their Male Concubines: Seeking Trans History and Intimacy in Argentine Police and Prison Records, 1921–1945." *Hispanic American Historical Review* 103, no. 4 (2023): 651–78.

Fernández-Galeano, Javier. "'Is He a 'Social Danger'? The Franco Regime's Judicial Prosecution of Homosexuality in Málaga under the Ley de Vagos y Maleantes." *Journal of the History of Sexuality* 25, no. 1 (2016): 1–31.

———. "Performing Queer Archives: Argentine and Spanish Policing Files for Unintended Audiences (1950s–1970s)." In *Turning Archival: The Life of the Historical in Queer Studies*, edited by Zeb Tortorici and Daniel Marshall, 141–64. Durham, N.C.: Duke University Press, 2022.

Ferrández, Daniela. "Voces desde el gueto: vidas trans, oportunidades de supervivencia y esperanzas de cambio en el Vigo de la transición." *Cuadernos de Historia Contemporánea* 46 (2024).

Frackman, Kyle. "Homemade Pornography and the Proliferation of Queer Pleasure in East Germany." *Radical History Review* 142 (2022): 93–109.

Gandhi, Leela. *Affective Communities: Anticolonial Thought, Fin-De-Siècle Radicalism, and the Politics of Friendship*. Durham, N.C.: Duke University Press, 2006.

Gaunt, William. *The Aesthetic Adventure*. London: Sphere Books Ltd., 1975.

Gertzman, Jay A. *Bookleggers and Smuthounds: The Trade in Erotica, 1920–1940*. Philadelphia: University of Pennsylvania Press, 2011.

Giesberg, Judith. *Sex and the Civil War: Soldiers, Pornography, and the Making of American Morality*. Chapel Hill: University of North Carolina Press, 2017.

Giordano, Verónica. "Revolución, sexo y política en Brasil en los años setenta. Un análisis desde las notas sobre comida en la revista *Homem* (*Playboy*)." *Cordis: História e Literatura* 10 (2013): 177–207.

Gitelman, Lisa. *Always Already New: Media, History, and the Data of Culture*. Cambridge, Mass.: MIT Press, 2006.

Gossett, Reina, Eric A. Stanley, and Johanna Burton. "Known Unknowns: An Introduction to Trap Door." In *Trap Door: Trans Cultural Production and the Politics of Visibility*, edited by Reina Gossett, Eric A. Stanley, and Johanna Burton, xv–xvi. Cambridge, Mass.: MIT Press, 2017.

Gozalbo Gimeno, Daniel. "Historia archivística de los expedientes de censura editorial (1942–2017)." *Creneida: Anuario de Literaturas Hispánicas* 5 (2017): 8–34.

Green, James Naylor. *Beyond Carnival: Male Homosexuality in Twentieth-Century Brazil*. Chicago: University of Chicago Press, 1999.

Green, Stuart P. *Criminalizing Sex: A Unified Liberal Theory*. New York: Oxford University Press, 2020.

Guereña, Jean-Louis. *Detrás de la cortina: el sexo en España (1790–1950)*. Madrid: Ediciones Cátedra, 2018.

———. "La prostitución en el primer franquismo." In *Pobreza, marginación, delincuencia y políticas sociales bajo el franquismo*, edited by Conxita Mir et al., 167–83. Lleida, Spain: Edicions de la Universitat de Lleida, 2005.

Guibernau i Berdún, Montserrat. *Catalan Nationalism: Francoism, Transition, and Democracy.* London: Routledge, 2004.

Hartson, Mary. *Casting Masculinity in Spanish Film: Negotiating Identity in a Consumer Age.* Lanham, Md.: Lexington Books, 2017.

Hearne, Siobhán. "An Erotic Revolution? Pornography in the Russian Empire, 1905–1914." *Journal of the History of Sexuality* 30, no. 2 (2021): 195–224.

Heffernan, Kevin. "Prurient (Dis)Interest: The American Release and Reception of *I Am Curious (Yellow).*" In *Sex Scene: Media and the Sexual Revolution*, edited by Eric Schaefer, 105–25. Durham, N.C.: Duke University Press, 2014.

Heineman, Elizabeth D. *Before Porn Was Legal: The Erotica Empire of Beate Uhse.* Chicago: University of Chicago Press, 2011.

Houlbrook, Matt, *Queer London: Perils and Pleasures in the Sexual Metropolis, 1918–1957.* Chicago: University of Chicago Press, 2020.

Huard, Geoffroy. *Los antisociales: Historia de la homosexualidad en Barcelona y París, 1945–1975.* Madrid: Marcial Pons Historia, 2014.

——. *Los invertidos: Verdad, justicia y reparación para gais y transexuales bajo la dictadura franquista.* Barcelona: Icaria, 2021.

Hunt, Lynn. "Introduction: Obscenity and the Origins of Modernity, 1500–1800." In *The Invention of Pornography: Obscenity and the Origins of Modernity, 1500–1800*, edited by Lynn Hunt, 9–48. New York: Zone Books, 1996.

Kendrick, Walter M. *The Secret Museum: The History of Pornography in Literature.* New York: Viking, 1987.

Labrador Méndez, Germán. *Culpables por la literatura: imaginación política y contracultura en la transición española (1968–1986).* Madrid: Ediciones Akal, 2017.

——. "They Called It Democracy? The Aesthetic Politics of the Spanish Transition to Democracy and Some Collective Hijackings of History after the 15M Movement." *Historein* 15, no. 1 (2015): 117–54.

——. "Una urna puede ser el mejor preservativo: Porno-política y tecno-democracia en la transición española, entre el destape y la Constitución." *Mélanges de la Casa de Velázquez* 50, no. 1 (2020): 85–114.

Lahti, Martti. "Dressing Up in Power: Tom of Finland and Gay Male Body Politics." *Journal of Homosexuality* 35, no. 3 (1998): 185–205.

Langlois, Ganaele, and Andrea Slane. "Economies of Reputation: The Case of Revenge Porn." *Communication and Critical/Cultural Studies* 14, no. 2 (2017): 120–38.

Larsson, Mariah. "Lasse Braun, Rape Scenarios, and Swedish Censorship: A Case Study of Two 8-mm Porn Films Featuring Rape." *Porn Studies* 4, no. 1 (2017): 23–34.

——. "Oh Paris! The Journeys of Lasse Braun's 8mm Pornography." *JCMS: Journal of Cinema and Media Studies* 58, no. 1 (2018): 158–63.

Lázaro, Alberto. "La narrativa inglesa de terror y el terror de la censura española." In *Tiempo de censura. La represión editorial durante el franquismo*, edited by Eduardo Ruíz Bautista, 193–232. Gijón, Spain: Ediciones TREA, 2008.

Lecaplain, Manon. "Political Press, Nude Press, and La Bonne Presse: Amédée Vignola, or an Atypical Career." *Sociétés et Représentations* 47, no. 1 (2019): 157–75.

Leonard, Sarah L. *Fragile Minds and Vulnerable Souls: The Matter of Obscenity in Nineteenth-Century Germany*. Philadelphia: University of Pennsylvania Press, 2015.

Litvak, Lily. "La novela corta erótica de entreguerras, 1920–1936." In *Los territorios literarios de la historia del placer*, edited by José Blas Vega et al., 115–31. Madrid: Huerga & Fierro Editores, 1996.

Lubey, Kathleen. *What Pornography Knows: Sex and Social Protest since the Eighteenth Century*. Stanford: Stanford University Press, 2022.

Marcus, Steven. *The Other Victorians: A Study of Sexuality and Pornography in Mid-Nineteenth-Century England*. London: Routledge, 1966.

Marí, Jorge. "Desnudos, vivos y muertos: La transición erótico-política y/en la crítica cultural de Vázquez Montalbán." In *Manuel Vázquez Montalbán: el compromiso con la memoria*, edited by José F. Colmeiro, 129–42. Woodbridge, U.K.: Tamesis, 2007.

Martínez, María Elena. "Archives, Bodies, and Imagination: The Case of Juana Aguilar and Queer Approaches to History, Sexuality, and Politics." *Radical History Review* 120 (2014): 159–82.

Martínez, Ramón. *Lo nuestro sí que es mundial: una introducción a la historia del movimiento LGTB en España*. Barcelona: Editorial Egales, 2018.

Martínez-Pereda Rodríguez, José Manuel. *El delito de escándalo público*. Madrid: Editorial Tecnos, 1970.

Mejía, Norma. *Transgenerismos: una experiencia transexual desde la perspectiva antropológica*. Barcelona: Bellaterra, 2006.

Melero, Alejandro. *Placeres ocultos: gays y lesbianas en el cine español de la transición*. Madrid: Notorius, 2010.

Mérida Jiménez, Rafael. *Transbarcelonas: cultura, género y sexualidad en la España del siglo XX*. Barcelona: Bellaterra, 2016.

Metzger, Cyle, and Kirstin Ringelberg. "Prismatic Views: A Look at the Growing Field of Transgender Art and Visual Culture Studies." *Journal of Visual Culture* 19, no. 2 (2020): 159–70.

Milanesio, Natalia. *Destape: Sex, Democracy, and Freedom in Postdictatorial Argentina*. Pittsburgh: University of Pittsburgh Press, 2019.

Miller-Young, Mireille. *A Taste for Brown Sugar: Black Women in Pornography*. Durham, N.C.: Duke University Press, 2015.

Mira Nouselles, Alberto. *De Sodoma a Chueca: una historia cultural de la homosexualidad en España en el siglo XX*. Barcelona: Egales, 2007.

Mira Nouselles, Alberto. "After Wilde: Camp Discourse in Hoyos and Retana, or the Dawn of Spanish Gay Culture." *Journal of Spanish Cultural Studies* 5, no. 1 (2004): 29–47.

Moix, Terenci. *El beso de Peter Pan*. Barcelona: Plaza & Janés, 1993.

———. *El cine de los sábados*. Barcelona: Plaza & Janés, 1990.

Monea, Alexander. *The Digital Closet: How the Internet Became Straight.* Cambridge, Mass.: MIT Press, 2022.

Monferrer Tomás, Jordi M. "La construcción de la protesta en el movimiento gay español: La Ley de Peligrosidad Social (1970) como factor precipitante de la acción colectiva." *Revista Española de Investigaciones Sociológicas* 102 (2003): 171–204.

Mora Gaspar, Víctor. *Al margen de la naturaleza: la persecución de la homosexualidad durante el franquismo, leyes, terapias y condenas.* Barcelona: Debate, 2016.

Navarro Amo, Tania. *La infancia de una transexual en la dictadura.* Barcelona: Planeta, 2021.

Ochoa, Marcia. *Queen for a Day: Transformistas, Beauty Queens, and the Performance of Femininity in Venezuela.* Durham, N.C.: Duke University Press, 2014.

Olmeda, Fernando. *El Látigo y la pluma: Homosexuales en la España de Franco.* Madrid: Oberon, 2004.

Pack, Sasha. *Tourism and Dictatorship: Europe's Peaceful Invasion of Franco's Spain.* New York: Palgrave Macmillan, 2011.

Padte, Richa Kaul. *Cyber Sexy: Rethinking Pornography.* Gurgaon, India: Penguin Books, 2018.

Paquot, Thierry. "Jean-Jacques Pauvert (1926–2014) Éditeur en roue livre . . ." *Hermès, La Revue* 71 (2015): 311–13.

Payne, Stanley G. *Franco y José Antonio. El extraño caso del fascismo español.* Barcelona: Planeta, 1997.

Pérez, Jorge. "Undressing Opus Dei: Reframing the Political Currency of Destape Films." In *Spanish Erotic Cinema*, edited by Santiago Fouz-Hernández, 92–108. Edinburgh: Edinburgh University Press, 2017.

Pérez-Sánchez, Gema. *Queer Transitions in Contemporary Spanish Culture: From Franco to La Movida.* New York: State University of New York Press, 2008.

Picornell, Mercè. "¿De una España viril a una España travesti? Transgresión transgénero y subversión del poder franquista en la transición española hacia la democracia." *Feminismo/s* 16 (2010): 281–304.

Platero, Lucas. "Críticas al capacitismo heteronormativo: queer crips." In *Transfeminismos: epistemes, fricciones y flujos*, edited by Miriam Solà and Elena Urko, 211–24. Tafalla, Spain: Txalaparta, 2013.

———. "Lesboerotismo y la masculinidad de las mujeres en la España franquista." *Bagoas* 3 (2009): 15–38.

———. *Por un chato de vino. Historias de travestismo y masculinidad femenina.* Barcelona: Bellaterra, 2015.

———. "'Su gran placer es usar calzoncillos y calcetines': la represión de la masculinidad femenina bajo la dictadura." In *Mujeres bajo sospecha: Memoria y sexualidad, 1930–1980*, edited by Raquel Osborne, 175–90. Madrid: Fundamentos, 2012.

Platero, R. Lucas, and María Rosón. "Una genealogía trans*: siglo XX." In *Trans*: diversidad de identidades y roles de género*, edited by Niurka Gibaja Yábar and Andrés Gutiérrez Usillos, 134–41. Madrid: Ministerio de Educación, Cultura y Deporte, 2017.

Power, Margaret. *Right-Wing Women in Chile: Feminine Power and the Struggle against Allende, 1964–1973*. University Park: Pennsylvania State University Press, 2002.

Preciado, Paul B. *Pornotopia: An Essay on Playboy's Architecture and Biopolitics*. New York: Zone Books, 2019.

Preston, Paul. *A People Betrayed: A History of Corruption, Political Incompetence, and Social Division in Modern Spain, 1874–2018*. London: William Collins, 2021.

Radcliff, Pamela. *Modern Spain, 1808 to the Present*. Hoboken, N.J.: Wiley-Blackwell, 2017.

Ramírez Pérez, Víctor M. "Franquismo y disidencia sexual. La visión del Ministerio Fiscal de la época." *Aposta: Revista de Ciencias Sociales* 77 (2018): 132–76.

———. *Peligrosas y revolucionarias: las disidencias sexuales en Canarias durante el franquismo y la transición*. Las Palmas de Gran Canaria, Spain: Fundación Canaria Tamaimos, 2019.

Reeves, Sharon L. "La prostitución en Madrid a finales del siglo XIX en la novela naturalista de Eduardo López Bago." In *Madrid en la literatura y las artes*, edited by Jorge H. Valdivieso and L. Teresa Valdivieso, 85–94. Phoenix: Editorial Orbis Press, 2006.

Rizki, Cole. "Familiar Grammars of Loss and Belonging: Curating Trans Kinship in Post-Dictatorship Argentina." *Journal of Visual Culture* 19, no. 2 (2020): 197–211.

———. "'No State Apparatus Goes to Bed Genocidal Then Wakes Up Democratic': Fascist Ideology and Transgender Politics in Post-dictatorship Argentina." *Radical History Review* 138 (2020): 82–107.

Sabater Sanz, Antonio. *El test de Szondi en sexuología forense*. Murcia, Spain: Fragua, 1972.

Sabater Tomás, Antonio. *Peligrosidad social y delincuencia*. Barcelona: Nauta, 1972.

Sampedro Vizcaya, Benita. "Rethinking the Archive and the Colonial Library: Equatorial Guinea." *Journal of Spanish Cultural Studies* 9, no. 3 (2008): 341–63.

Sánchez León, Pablo. "Desclasamiento y desencanto. La representación de las clases medias como eje de una relectura generacional de la transición española." *Kamchatka: Revista de Análisis Cultural* 4 (2014): 63–89.

Santos, Carlos. *333 historias de la Transición: chaquetas de pana, tetas al aire, ruido de sables, suspiros, algaradas y consenso*. Madrid: La esfera de los libros, 2015.

Schaefer, Eric. "'I'll Take Sweden': The Shifting Discourse of the 'Sexy Nation' in Sexploitation Films." In *Sex Scene: Media and the Sexual Revolution*, edited by Eric Schaefer, 207–34. Durham, N.C.: Duke University Press, 2014.

———. "Introduction. Sex Seen: 1968 and Rise of 'Public' Sex." In *Sex Scene: Media and the Sexual Revolution*, edited by Eric Schaefer, 1–22. Durham, N.C.: Duke University Press, 2014.

Scheper-Hughes, Nancy. *Death without Weeping: The Violence of Everyday Life in Brazil.* Berkeley: University of California Press, 1993.

Sentamans, Tatiana [O.R.G.I.A.]. "Redes transfeministas y nuevas políticas de representación sexual (I). Diagramas de flujos." In *Transfeminismos: epistemes, fricciones y flujos*, edited by Miriam Solà and Elena Urko, 31–44. Tafalla, Spain: Txalaparta, 2013.

Sigel, Lisa Z. "Censorship in Inter-War Britain: Obscenity, Spectacle, and the Workings of the Liberal State." *Journal of Social History* 45, no. 1 (2011): 61–83.

———. "Handmade and Homemade: Vernacular Expressions of American Sexual History." *Journal of the History of Sexuality* 25, no. 3 (2016): 437–62.

———. "Introduction: Issues and Problems in the History of Pornography." In *International Exposure: Perspectives on Modern European Pornography, 1800–2000*, edited by Lisa Z. Sigel. New Brunswick, N.J.: Rutgers University Press, 2005.

———. *The People's Porn: A History of Handmade Pornography in America.* London: Reaktion Books, 2020.

Singer, T. Benjamin. "From the Medical Gaze to Sublime Mutations: The Ethics of (Re)Viewing Non-normative Body Images." In *The Transgender Studies Reader*, edited by Susan Stryker and Stephen Whittle, 601–20. London: Routledge, 2013.

Solís Galván, Raúl. *La doble transición.* Madrid: Libros.com, 2019.

Soriano Gil, Manuel. *Homosexualidad y represión: iniciación al estudio de la homofilia.* Madrid: Zero, 1978.

Stavans, Ilan, and Jorge J. E. Gracia. "On Desecration: Andrés Serrano, Piss." *Michigan Quarterly Review* 52, no. 4 (2013): 582–94.

Stehrenberger, Cécile Stephanie. "Bichos raros: los Coros y Danzas de la Sección Femenina en Guinea Ecuatorial." In *Intersecciones: Cuerpos y sexualidades en la encrucijada,* edited by Lucas Platero Méndez, 301–24. Madrid: Bellaterra, 2012.

Steiner, George. "Ten (Possible) Reasons for the Sadness of Thought." *Salmagundi* no. 146/147 (2005): 3–32.

Strassfeld, Ben. "The Blight of Indecency: Antiporn Politics and the Urban Crisis in Early 1970s Detroit." *Journal of the History of Sexuality* 27 (2018): 420–41.

Strub, Whitney. *Perversion for Profit: The Politics of Pornography and the Rise of the New Right.* New York: Columbia University Press, 2013.

Strub, Whitney, and Carolyn Bronstein. "Introduction." In *Porno Chic and the Sex Wars: American Sexual Representation in the 1970s*, edited by Whitney Strub and Carolyn Bronstein, 1–24. Amherst: University of Massachusetts Press, 2017.

Stryker, Susan. *Transgender History.* Berkeley: Seal Press, 2008.

Subrat, Piro. *Invertidos y rompepatrias: marxismo, anarquismo y desobediencia sexual y de género en el Estado español (1868–1982).* Madrid: Imperdible, 2019.

Suriano, Juan. *Anarquistas, Cultura y política libertaria en Buenos Aires. 1890–1910*. Buenos Aires: Manantial, 2001.

Terradillos Basoco, Juan. *Peligrosidad social y estado de derecho*. Madrid: Akal, 1981.

Terrasa Mateu, Jordi. "Control, represión y reeducación de los homosexuales durante el franquismo y el inicio de la transición." PhD dissertation, University of Barcelona, 2016.

Thomas, Hugh. *Historia de la Guerra Civil Española*. Barcelona: Círculo de Lectores, 1976.

Tortorici, Zeb. "Circulating Erotica: Flea Markets, Collections, and Archives in Mexico." *The Journal of Popular Culture* 53, no. 6 (2020): 1335–1357.

——. "Decolonial Archival Imaginaries: On Losing, Performing, and Finding Juana Aguilar." In *Turning Archival: The Life of the Historical in Queer Studies*, edited by Zeb Tortorici and Daniel Marshall, 63–92. Durham, N.C.: Duke University Press, 2022.

——. *Sins against Nature: Sex and Archives in Colonial New Spain*. Durham, N.C.: Duke University Press, 2018.

Tubau, Iván. "Playboy en España: demasiado tarde, demasiado pronto." *ANÀLISI: Quaderns de comunicaciò i cultur* 2 (1980): 33–46.

Ugarte Pérez, Francisco Javier. *Las circunstancias obligaban: Homoerotismo, identidad y resistencia*. Barcelona: Egales Editorial, 2011.

Valentine, David. *Imagining Transgender: An Ethnography of a Category*. Durham, N.C.: Duke University Press, 2007.

Valverde, José Antonio, and Adolfo Abril. *Las españolas en secreto: comportamiento sexual de la mujer española*. Madrid: Sedmay, 1975.

Vázquez García, Francisco. *Pater infamis: genealogía del cura pederasta en España (1880–1912)*. Madrid: Cátedra, 2020.

Vider, Stephen. *The Queerness of Home: Gender, Sexuality, and the Politics of Domesticity after World War II*. Chicago: University of Chicago Press, 2021.

Vincent, Mary. "La reafirmación de la masculinidad en la cruzada franquista." *Cuadernos de Historia Contemporánea* 28 (2006): 135–51.

Vivas Marzal, Luis. "Contemplación jurídico-penal de la homosexualidad. Discurso de ingreso en la Academia Valenciana de Jurisprudencia y Legislación." *Publicaciones de la Academia Valenciana de Jurisprudencia y Legislación* 53 (1963): 5–24.

Wang, Yvon. *Reinventing Licentiousness: Pornography and Modern China*. Ithaca, N.Y.: Cornell University Press, 2021.

Waugh, Thomas. *Hard to Imagine: Gay Male Eroticism in Photography and Film from the Beginnings to Stonewall*. New York: Columbia University Press, 1996.

——. "Homosociality in the Classical American Stag Film: Off-Screen, On-Screen." In *Porn Studies*, edited by Linda Williams, 127–41. Durham, N.C.: Duke University Press, 2004.

Weber, Eugen. *Peasants into Frenchmen: The Modernization of Rural France, 1870–1914*. Stanford: Stanford University Press, 1988.

Wheeler, Leigh Ann. *How Sex Became a Civil Liberty.* New York: Oxford University Press, 2013.

Whipple, Amy C. "Speaking for Whom? The 1971 Festival of Light and the Search for the 'Silent Majority.'" *Contemporary British History* 24, no. 3 (2010): 319–39.

Williams, Linda. *Hard Core: Power, Pleasure and the "Frenzy of the Visible."* London: Pandora, 1990.

——. "Porn Studies: Proliferating Pornographies on/scene: An Introduction." In *Porn Studies,* edited by Linda Williams, 1–26. Durham, N.C.: Duke University Press, 2004.

Zamarreño Aramendia, Gorka. *Cine y turismo en la Costa del Sol. Retrato de un colonizado.* Málaga, Spain: Repositorio Institucional de la Universidad de Málaga, 2010.

Zubiaurre, Maite. *Cultures of the Erotic in Spain, 1898–1939.* Nashville: Vanderbilt University Press, 2012.

Zubillaga-Pow, Jun. "'In the Raw': Posing, Photography, and Trans*Aesthetics." *Transgender Studies Quarterly* 5, no. 3 (2018): 443–55.

INDEX

Note: Page entries listed in *italics* indicate figures.

ABC (newspaper), 177–78, 186–87, 180

abortion, 69, 81–82, 180

Abril, Adolfo, 181

abuse, sexual, 18, 115, 166, 184, 191

activism, homosexual, 104

adultery, 32, 84, 180

aesthetics, 109, 145, 151–52, 156, 157, 159

affects, queer, 9, 69, 70, 150

agency, 12, 18, 35, 148, 150, 153–54, 196

AHN. *See* Archivo Histórico Nacional (AHN)

Alfonso XIII (king of Spain), 10, 17–19, 45–46

Álvarez Cruz, Enrique, 185

Amor a la española (Merino), 103

Anabitarte, Héctor, 174

anal sex, images of, 2–3, *3*, 120, *123*, 195

anilingus, 17

anonymity, 111, 120, 124, 173

anonymization, 149–50, 161

antiporn activism, 15, 106, 108, 177–78, 187

antisemitism, 75–76

antisocial behaviors, 3, 85, 104, 110, 113–14, 138

Antúnes, Santiago I., 226n20

aphrodisiacs, 12, 119

archival materials, 9, 112, 117, 136–37, 154

archives: access to, 9, 39; aims of, 2, 8; in evidence paradigm, 230n88; and inconsistent handling of erotica and porn, 110–11; and performance, 109; preservation of obscene materials in, 5, 20, 29, 32, 42, 45, 181; queering of, 7, 136–37;

archives (*continued*)
and state violence, 56, 68, 71, 146;
trans women in, 14–15, 147–50. *See
also* curatorial practices
Archivo Histórico Nacional (AHN), 9,
11, 21, 22, 32, 39, 45, 215n90
Arendt, Hannah, 25
Arondekar, Anjali, 48
art: destruction of, 14, 113; disentangle pornography and, 85, 93–94,
100, 104, 210n49; erotization of,
138–41, *139*, *140*; and homosexuality, 121; and pornography embracing each other, 120
Arús y Arderiu, Rosendo, 60
authorities. *See* state agents
authors, literary, 20, 26–27, 28, 37, 38,
40–41

Balzac, Honoré de, 58
Baños, Ramón de, 19
Baños, Ricardo de, 19
Barcelona: and illegal importation
of porn, 132; migration of queer
people to, 164, 165; nightlife
in, 172; porn normalization in,
173–74; porn produced in, 17, 18,
44; as prone to embracing foreign
trends, 74, 210n45; queer protests
in, 169
Bárcena y Reus, Agustín de la, 105,
224n73
Bardot, Brigitte, 71, 230n89
Barra, Alfonso, 177–79
Barrie, James Matthew, 58–59
Bars, 72, 117, 171
Basque Country, 210n45
Bataille, George, 129
BDSM, 115–16, 197
Ben, Pablo, 200
Benjamin, Walter, 9
Bergman, Ingmar, 102
Biblioteca Arús, 59–60, 62, 64, *63*
Biblioteca Nacional, 10, 32, 214n61

birth control, 42. *See also*
contraception
bisexuality, 34, 68, 195
Blasco Ibáñez, Vicente, 58
blasphemy, 13, 108, 114, 129, 131,
207n18
Blue Division, 75–76
boarding house, 81, 95–96, 116,
121 153
Boccaccio, Giovanni, 19
bodies: and gender self-determination, 145, 151–52, 154–55; of
models, 62, 197–98, 199, 227n41,
240n114; and modern era, 84; in
porn films, 18–19, 129; and the
state's perspective on masculinity,
110, 240n119; and trans women
visibility, 158, *160*, 184
bodybuilding, 120, 227n41
book reviews, 37–38, 214n79
booksellers, 55, 91, 213n43, 213n53
bookstores, 50, 52, 87, 92, 132
border, Spanish: and illegal importation of pornography, 95, 110, 136;
policing on the, 52–54, 67; porousness of, 134; Spaniards' porn
consumption crossing the, 179
Borenstein, Eliot, 207n18, 240n102
Borras Pastor, Rafael, 126
Botticelli, Sandro, 109
Bourdeille Brantóme, Pierre de, 50
Bourdieu, Pierre, 1
Braun, Lasse. *See* Ferro, Alberto
brothels, 12, 18, 84, 85, 176
Bulffi de Quintana, Avelino Luis, 42

Caballero Soriano, Juan, 26, 212n23
Cabanillas, Pío, 180
cabarets, 21, 43–44
calendars, nude, 188
Callwood, Dan, 237n33
Camilo Bolas (comic book), 193
camp (style), 28, 41–42, 68
Campt, Tina, 148, 153, 158, 234n58

Canary Islands, 114, 132, 164, 226n18, 229n72

Cano, Gabriela, 155

Caprichos de lesbiana (Uriarte Pujana), 34–35

Cardín, Alberto, 182–83

Carrere Moreno, Emilio, 38–39, 215n87

Casas Fernández, Juan, 56

Caserio, Robert L., 120, 124

Castañeda, Michelle, 7

Castilla, 210n45

Catalonian nationalism, 20, 98

Catholic Church, 55, 56–57, 98, 167, 186, 201

Catholicism, 6, 13, 49, 66, 68

Cau, Jean, 177

celebrities, 97–98, 199

censorship, 97; in artistic works, 35–36, 41–42, 110, 141; changes in legal framework of, 83, 168, 180; clergy's role in, 45, 49, 56–57; and Communist regimes, 85, 210n49; defense of, 179; effects of, 38, 189, 196, 193, 216n10; end of, 174–75, 187, 190–91; failures in, 103, 105; in judicial files, 29–32; of parish bulletins, 98–100; and state violence, 59, 183

Center for Courses by Correspondence (CCC), 135

Centro de Documentación Cinematográfica (Valencia), 10, 17

chastity, 181

Chekhov, Anton, 58

Cheng, Wou-chan, 94

Chevalier, Denys, 90

childhood, 59. *See also* minors

China, 94, 211n17

cinemas. *See* theaters

citizens, 58–59, 86, 104, 143, 183

civil servants, 24, 190, 191, 195

Civil War, Spanish, 11, 49, 55, 79, 187–88

classicism, 14, 62, 111

Cleminson, Richard, 37

Coccinelle. *See* Dufresnoy, Jacqueline Charlotte

cohabitation, 84, 90–91

Colección Pompadour, 36

Colón, Antonio, 180

colonialism, 12, 48, 64–66, 78

Color (magazine), 44–45

Commission on Culture and Education, 54, 55

Communist regimes, 13, 15, 85, 101, 105–6, 126, 210n49

communities, sexual, 121, 146, 149, 172

Constitution, Spanish, 82, 182, 185

Consultorio de señoras (Baños brothers), 18

contraception, 12, 21, 22, 42, 74, 181, 190

conversion therapy, 166

Convivencia (magazine), 181

Córdoba, Ernesto de, 50–51

Cortes (Francoist legislative body), 100–101, 103–5, 107

countercultures, young: experimentation in, 84, 174–75; moral panic about, 105, 181; policing of, 94, 101

courtrooms, 7; moral exceptionalism in, 8, 112, 143; obscene content displayed in, 10–11, 28, 33, 39–40, 111; racism in, 72. *See also specific courts*

covers: nudes in, 43, 183–84, 193, 199; sex act images in, 195; sexual undertone images in, 32, 90, 97

Crueldades del amor (Retana), 39–40

Cuadernos para el diálogo, 175

Cuba, 78–79

Cubero Izquierdo, Carmen, 22, 35

cultures, sexual: and friendship, 124; of *maricas*, 41, 116, 126, 186; materiality of, 48, 73–74; queer visual codes of, 136

curatorial practices, 5, 146, 148, 158, 161. *See also* archives
currency, foreign, 72
custody, chain of, 136, 189, 230n88
customs, 84, 87, 98, 101, 105, 141, 182. *See also* mores, traditional
Cvetkovich, Ann, 121
cypher, 52, *53*

dangerousness, 101–1, 225n3
Dangerousness Law. *See* Social Dangerousness and Rehabilitation Law
Darwin, Charles, 58
David, Jacques-Louis, 62
decency, 15, 33, 67, 100, 130, 179. *See also* modesty
decorum. *See* decency
Deep Throat (Damiano), 176, 179, 210n50
de la Mata, Julián José, 26–27
democracy, 15, 147, 168, 174, 182, 183–84, 185
democratic transition: iconography of, 168, *194*, 196; political paradoxes of, 199; pornography during, 195, 200–201; sexuality during, 16, 176, 174–75, 182–90
Denmark, 126, 131, 132, 176
Dennis, Kelly, 61, 109, 114, 124, 139, 240n114, 240n117
desires: and gaze, 158, 191; and queer erotica, 111, 120, 121; violence of, 129; visibility of, 70, 116–17
Deslandes, Paul R., 62
destape, 15, 210n50; iconography of, *194*, 196; intensification of, 100, 126, 168, 193; political readings of, 183–84, 199
deviance, 111, 112–14, 119, 148, 172, 202
Dewey, John, 58
Dickens, Charles, 58
dildos, 9, 12, 48, 31, 96

Direcció General d'Atenció a la infàn-cia i l'Adolèscencia (DGAIA), 164
Direction of General Security (DGS), 24, 30
Doll, Dora, 137
dolls, 47, 48, *192*
Dostoevsky, Fyodor, 58
double standards, moral: between mainstream and transgressive materials, 21–22, 184, 191; in porn films' narratives, 19; regarding youth corruption, 76–77; in sentences of public scandal, 93
Drager, Emmet H., 145
drawings, erotic, 8, 50, 68, 87, 120, 191. *See also* illustrations, erotic
drugs: as its association with homo-sexuality, 114, 119; and its associ-ation with pornography, 104, 131, 177; as banned subject, 180; and youngsters, 84, 105
Dufresnoy, Jacqueline Charlotte (pseud. Coccinelle), 167, 168
Duran, Alfonso, 25
Durán, Gloria G., 20, 28, 35, 214n68, 215n87

Edwards, Elizabeth, 148, 158
Eichhorn, Kate, 159
El beso de Peter Pan (Moix), 59
El confesor (Baños brothers), 18
electoral rights, 25, 196
Elena, Alberto, 177
Elías Cabanzón, Luis, 30
Ellis, Robert. R., 59
El mal amor de María Teresa (Uriarte de Pujana), 33–34
El Ministro (Baños brothers), 17–18
El País (newspaper), 196
Engels, Friedrich, 58
Enrique y Tarancón, Vicente, 182
ephebes, 61
erotica, 5–6, 139; circulation of, 50, 52, 118; destroying one's, 2, 111, 116,

226n30; as intellectual tradition, 69; in other countries, 61, 212n32, 226n21; penis centrality in, 219n47; policing of, 55, 81, 141; preservation and curation of, 13, 43, 99, 109–10; uses of, 115, 114, 124

erotism: as citizens' right, 142–43; conservative discourses regarding, 177, 186; and its difference with pornography, 197; as a privilege of wealthy classes, 175; state agents' perspectives on, 82, 129, 133

Erotologie de la Chine (Cheng), 94

Escoffier, Jeffrey, 175

Escópico, Casto, 211n6

Escudero Rueda, Manuel, 105

Espronceda, José de, 58

Estévez, Enrique, 32

Estrada, Susana, 196–97

ethics, 14, 101, 147–50, 152, 158

euphemisms, 38, 72, 78, 96

Europe: and erotica exchange with Latin America, 50; modern integration with, 95; new experience of sex in, 48; sexual excess in, 112, 119, 126, 132, 177, 182

Evans, Jennifer, 210n48

evidence, judicial: archival practices on, 117, 230n88; and defendants' privacy, 68, 71, 119, 159; queer visual cultures as, 136–37

Exhibition (Davy), 179

exile, 49, 72, 100, 110, 152, 157

Fabiola (Blasetti), 110

Falange (fascist party), 55, 56, 74, 104, 106, 210n47

families: as chosen, 165; and control over youth, 94, 100; and exile sentences, 157; as Spanish national value, 21, 79, 84–85; traditional model of, 107, 164, 180, 198

fantasies, 48–49, 59, 66, 131, 138, 191, 199

fashion, 43, 68–69, 94, 154

femininity, 34, 155

feminism, 44, 45

Fernández, Lluís, 168–69, 183

Fernández, Pura, 213n53

Fernández Cantos, José Luis, 223n68

Fernández Palomero, Manuel, 50–51

Ferro, Alberto (pseud. Braun, Lasse), 128

Fidalgo, Manuel, 56

films, erotic / pornographic: during the democratic transition, 15, 180–81; judicial authorities access to, 109, 118–19, 127–29; made in Spain, 17–20, 130; moral panic about, 228n58; from other countries, 95, 138; preservation of, 45–46; screening of, 132, 137, 176, 187, 189. *See also specifics films*

fines, monetary, 21, 22, 25, 190, 157, 214n71

Fini, Leonor, 182

flamenco, 68

flapper girls, 44

Flaubert, Gustave, 58

Flores González, Josefa (pseud. Pepa Flores), 183–84

Fluvià, Armand de, 174–75

foreigners, 13–14, 131–32. *See also* tourists, international

forensic doctors, 2, 115–16, 151–52

forensic reports, 151–52, 166, 168

Foucaud, Pierre, 137, 230n89

Frackman, Kyle, 111, 216n10, 219n47, 226n21

Fraga Iribarne, Manuel, 83

France: and border with Catalonia, 95, 110, 136; erotic movies in, 137–38; hardcore in, 141–42, 177, 179–80

Franco, Francisco, 49; death of, 15, 126, 168, 174, 179, 182, 183, 200; friends of, 62; photographs of, 103; speeches of, 54

Franco regime, 49; and antipornography consensus, 15, 55; archiving practices of, 14, 112, 148–49; censorship apparatus of the, 45, 59, 67, 99–100, 103, 105, 138–39, 189, 190; and family-centered national values, 64–66, 83–84, 107, 240n120; modernization of, 72, 174–75, 182; political adversaries of, 11, 52, 54, 98; and tourism-related permissiveness, 71

freedom, sexual. *See* sexual liberation

freedom of expression, 49, 75, 86, 90, 174–75, 185, 190

Freud, Sigmund, 58, 177

friendship, 68–69, 70–71, 118, 124

Gaceta de Madrid (newspaper), 30–31

Gandhi, Leela, 59

García y García de Castro, Rafael, 56, 57

gender, 38, 120, 151

gender affirmation surgery, 167

gender nonconformity. *See* gender transgressions

gender roles, 43, 77, 138

gender/sexual identities: hierarchies between, 82; and porn consumption, 13, 92–93; and portraits, 155–56, 158; questioning rigid schemes of, 195; and self-determination, 145

gender transgressions: and archival recording, 158–59, 161, 187; arrests on account of, 146, 151, 157, 167; as foreign to Spain, 131; in literature, 37, 38; and queer bonds, 70; and visibility, 2, 5, 36, 169–70, 175

genitals, 61, 151, 191, 193

Germany, 10, 57, 76, 216n10, 226n21, 240n120

Gertzman, Jay A., 212n32

gestural documents, 156

gestures, facial, 18, 61, 115, 153

Gilda (Vidor), 196–97

Giordano, Verónica, 199

Giscard d'Estaing, Valéry, 179

Gitelman, Lisa, 138

Goethe, Johann Wolfgang von, 58

Gomis, Celso, 60–62, *64*, *65*

Good Hot Stuff (DeSimone & Deveau), 179

gossip columns, 97–98

Granada, 57

Green, James N., 227n41

Guardia Civil, 87, 127, 133, 189, 195–96. *See also* police

Guinea Equatorial, 64–66

Hall, Radclyffe, 37

hardcore porn, 207n23; and the attempt to legally ban it, 186–87; boundary between softcore and, 61; normalization of, 12–13, 104, 179–80, 176; selling of, 188. *See also* pornography

Hayworth, Rita, 196

Hearne, Siobhán, 211n18

hedonism, 35, 120, 198

Hefner, Hugh, 197–98, 199

Hernández Redondo, Tomás, 56

heterosexuality, 41, 181

hierarchies: of accountability, 27; in archival praxis, 137; between sexual and gender identities, 12–13, 39, 77, 82, 138

Historias de striptease (theater show)

Historie d'O (Reáge), 90

Hoddan, Max, 214n79

Hollywood movies, 68, 110, 178

homosexuality: authorities' valorization of, 72, 86, 121; effects of obscene content in, 199, 214n79, 226n20; in erotic publications, 91–92, 195; in forensic reports, 166; and handling confiscated materials, 136; legal framework for the prosecution of, 2, 20, 49–50,

93, 109–10, 174–75; as obscenity,
3–4, 37–39, 111, 113–14, 190–91;
prosecution of, 115, 118; tensions
regarding positive representation
of, 36, 41, 178, 186
hospital, psychiatric, 113, 166
hospitality, 78–79
Houlbrook, Matt, 205n5
Hoyos, Antonio de, 36
Huard, Geoffroy, 165, 191, 225n4–5
¡Huelga de vientres! (Bulffi de Quintana), 42
Hunt, Lynn, 48, 97, 237n31
Hustler (magazine), 199, 207n23,
240n114

I Am Curious (Yellow) (Sjöman),
102–3
Ibsen, Henrik, 58
Iglesia, Eloy de la, 190–91
illustrations, erotic, 32, 36, 43, 52, 56,
94, 191
images, erotic, 14, 35, 52, 82–83,
141, 193
imprisonment: for obscenity distribution, 21, 22, 107; recurrent cycle
of, 154, 167; as a security measure,
49, 72, 100, 110, 152–53; shaving
defendants' heads after, 171
Insausti, Joaquín, 200
intellectuals, 58, 169, 175, 182–83,
196, 210n45. *See also specifics
intellectuals*
International Workers Association:
local anarchist branches of, 60
Interviú (Magazine), 183–84, 199–200,
240n108
intimacy: defendants' strategies to
protect their, 116, 119–20, 146; and
modern era, 84; violation of, 1,
68, 118, 154, 162; visual language
of, 52, 121, 148, 156, 163. *See also*
privacy
Italy, 130

Jiménez Losantos, Federico, 182–83
journalists: and antiporn activism,
177–79, 180; under Franco regime,
49, 185; and obscenity boundaries,
37, 44; and sensationalism, 184
joy, 15, 121, 148, 156, 163, 167
judges: and their failure to protect
society from obscenity, 107, 111;
and obscene content in their
sentences, 11, 29, 31–32; and porn
consumption, 12–13, 128–29;
and porn normalization, 108,
135–36, 185–86, 189–90; and their
positions in democracy, 201; and
prosecution of homosexuality, 4,
91, 97. *See also specific judges*
judicial files: access to, 9, 209n34,
225n4; anonymization in, 149, 161;
critical reading of, 7; as derivate
form of obscenity, 2, 10–11, 21,
28–29, 35; personal photography in,
78; and state agents' double standards, 72, 96–97, 184; trans women
in, 151–52, 154, 158–59, 163

Kant, Immanuel, 58
Kendrick, Walter M., 56, 62–64, 75
King, Martin Luther, 75, 102
kinship, 69, 157

Laaksonen, Touko Valio (pseud. Tom
of Finland), 191
La Boquilla (bar), 72
Labrador, Germán, 176, 183–84,
210n50
La ciudad del vicio (Elías Cabanzón),
30
La Fontaine, Jean de, 58
La Hoja del Lunes (newspaper), 74–75
*La infancia de una transexual en la
dictadura* (Navarro Amo), 146
La insaciable Margot (Caballero
Soriano), 212n23
Langloisa, Ganaele, 51–52

La pálida (López Bago), 28

Larra, Mariano José de, 58

Las adolescentes (Masó), 180–81

Las españolas en secreto (Valverde & Abril), 181

Las primeras armas (Uriarte de Pujana), 33–34

Latin America, 50

¡Lavó su honra! (Precioso), 32

law, Spanish: and guardianship of women and minors, 66, 84, 112, 138; inconsistencies in, 7, 126, 103–4, 185; and policing obscenity, 11–12, 142; and purity of Spaniards' moral, 134; reforming of, 171. *See also specific laws*

Law for the Protection of Personal Data, 149

Law on the National Movement's Principles, 83

Lennon, John, 71

Leonard, Sarah L., 230n96

lesbianism: and boarding schools, 37; in magazines, 95, 180–81, 195; male fetishization of, 18; in sicaliptic fiction, 34–35, 38, 40

letters, 26–27, 68–71, 134–35, 143, 161

Ley de Peligrosidad y Rehabilitación Social. See Social Dangerousness and Rehabilitation Law

liability, 25–27, 45, 115, 188

libertinage, 54, 71, 76

libraries, public, 11–12, 52, 54–64, 217n24, 218n27

lifestyles, 4, 43, 76, 131, 198–99

Litvak, Lili, 35

Llaugé, Félix, 191

London, England, 177

López Bago, Eduardo, 28

Lorde, Audre, 169

Los placeres ocultos (Iglesia), 190–91

Louys, Pierre, 50, 214n79

Luna, Pablo, 50–51

Machado, Antonio, 58

Mademoiselle Striptease (Foucaud), 137

Madrid, 34, 35, 40, 52, 131

magazines, erotic: clandestine importation of, 91, 95, 131, 134, 229n72; confiscation of, 50, 75, 87, 113, 132, 186, 188, 229n70; in the democratic transition, 15, 174, *194*, 194–95, 197–201; models in, 90, 120; and modernization, 74, 107; and preservation in archives, 45. *See also specific magazines*

magistrates. *See* judges

Mairena, Carmen de, 147

makeup, 154, 159

Manuel Castán dance company, 167

Marañón, Gregorio, 92–93, 210n45, 214n79

Marcuse, Herbert, 177

Marí, Jorge, 183, 196, 199

maricas, 5; and personal erotica, 6, 14, 110; and pornography, 82, 168–69, 187; as subject of desire, 195; transgressive lifestyle of, 71, 77, 186

Marín Ocete, Antonio, 56

marriage, 77, 84, 91, 97–98, 180

Martínez, María Elena, 149

Martínez Anido, Severiano, 43

Martínez Baldrich, Roberto, 43–45

Más allá del vicio (Caballero Soriano), 26

masculinity: and extra-marital sex, 91; family paradigm of, 14, 59, 66, 112, 164, 199; as national value, 49, 210n45, 240n120; and porn consumption, 2, 6, 13, 82, 92–93, 133; undermining of, 124, 129, 131, 179; and working-class, 193

masochism, 90, 115

mass media: coverage of the "Madrid arsonist" in, 112–13; homosexuality in, 111; and loosing up moral controls, 84, 100; and pornography,

107, 169, 174; and sexual liberation, 82, 183, 176. *See also* press

masturbation: in art works, 18, 33–34, 139; inducing young people to, 37, 92; as a sign of arrested development, 82; with youngsters, 115. *See also* onanism

material culture, 10–12, 74, 97, 124, 137

Mateu y Pla, Miguel, 62

Matosas, Francisco, 200

McCarthy, Joseph, 67

Mejía, Norma, 147

memory, social, 11, 147, 149

Mendès, Catulle, 19

Mérida Jiménez, Rafael, 147, 232n30

Metaphysique du striptease (Chevalier), 90

Metzger, Cyle, 147–48

Mexico, 50, 75, 136

Michelangelo, 109

middle class, 23, 36, 174–75, 187, 199

Miller-Young, Mireille, 18

Ministry of Culture, 190, 195

Ministry of Governance, 24–25, 26, 36

Ministry of Information and tourism, 181, 185, 190

Ministry of National Education, 55

Ministry of the Interior, 173

minors: arrests of, 156, 165; and exposition to obscene content, 93, 100, 116, 141, 188, 189, 193; guardianship of, 14, 112; porn commercialization by, 135. *See also* childhood; youngsters

Mira, Alberto, 28, 41

models: in academic art, 60–62, *64*, *65*; in erotic magazines, 16, 197–98, 199–200; in homemade erotica, 50, 88–90, 120–24

modernization, 35, 72, 98, 101, 178, 180, 182

modesty: abstract concept of, 23–24; offence against, 4, 82, 85, 88,

91–92, 93–94; protection of, 89, 100. *See also* decency

Moix, Terenci, 59, 110

Monaco, 130

Mona the Virgin Nymph (Benveniste & Ziehm), 176

Monferrer Tomas, Jordi M., 225n4

morality: and its effects in gay lives, 190; and Francoist policymakers, 101, 182; and scandal criteria, 82; state protection of, 66, 83–84, 100; undermining of, 4, 21, 72, 97, 141; women in debates on, 107

moral panic, 15, 72, 77, 105, 133, 179

Moral Pérez de Zayas, José María del, 105

mores, traditional: and censorship, 181; and homosexuality, 3, 72; protection of, 101, 104–5, 153; shaping public narratives on, 29–30, 52–54; undermining of, 67–68, 78, 84–85. *See also* customs

Morocco, 64, 167

movements, corporal, 34, 127, 129

museums, 46, 83, 93, 113, 139

Musset, Alfred de, 50

National Library, 10, 32, 214n61

Nationwide Festival of Lights, 177–78

Navarro Amo, Tania, 146, 163–71, *170*, 184, 234n66–68, 234n74

Nazism, 52, 75–76, 106

neighborhood, 133, 165

neoliberalism, 179–80

Netherlands, 132

newspapers, 37–38, 49, 75, 132. *See also specifics newspapers*

newsstand owners: commercialization of obscenity, 35–36, 42, 52, 92, 107, 132–33; and delivery of obscenity to authorities, 55; and state permissiveness, 188–89

Nietzsche, Friederich, 58

Nigeria, 205n6

night shows, 167

nonreproductive sexualities, 42, 180–81, 190, 195

novelette. *See* novels, erotic

novels, erotic: censorship of, 28, 51–52; commercialization of, 36–38, 66; confiscation / destruction of, 24–26, 50–51, 214n71; and its fragmentation in courtroom, 33–34; moral effects of, 55; as pornography, 35, 39–40. *See also specific novels*

nudist beach, 196

nudity: for medical training, 56; normalization of, 180–81, 191, 193, 196, 199; as obscenity, 104; in visual arts, 60, 111, 121, 138–39

nuns, 114

obscenity, 6, 109; archival recording of, 29–32, 35, 40; art as alibi for, 94, 138–41, 177; and clandestine circulation, 12, 132; commercialization of, 19, 111; conservative valorizations of, 13, 74, 90; and elite individuals, 10–11, 22, 42–46, 127; history of, 7–8, 113, 193; as homemade, 48, 50; and homosexuality, 3–4, 104, 169; legal framework for the persecution of, 16, 20–21, 23, 86, 91, 185; and masculinity, 82, 112; spread of, 95, 100, 200; subterfuges in causes of, 24–28

Ochoa, Marcia, 155

onanism, 37, 95, 129. *See also* masturbation

Oppelt García, José, 29

oral sex, 2–3, 4, 17, 18, 195

orgasm, 18, 34–35, 128–29

orgy, 77, 194

Pack, Sasha D., 72, 210n44

paintings, 62, 93, 139–41, *140*, 182

Palacios Ruíz de Almodóvar, Diego, 56

Papini, Giovanni, 57

Pardo Bazán, Emilia, 58

Pardo López, María, 56

parish bulletin, Catholic, 81, 95, 98–100

parole (judiciary system), 121, 124, 152

pasear (strolling), 14–15, 146, 157–59

Patronato de Protección a la Mujer, 66

Paul VI (pope), 177

Pauvert, Jean-Jacques, 90, 94

Pearl, The (erotic tales), 192–93

Peláez, Alberto, 75–76

Peligrosidad social y delicuencia (Sabater Tomás), 101

penises, 4, 51, 61, 124, 131, 195, 219n47

Penthouse, 200

Pepa Flores. *See* Flores González, Josefa

Pérez Galdós, Benito, 58

Pérez Mendoza, Amadeo, 50

performances, artistic, 41, 169, *170*

permissiveness, state: boundaries of, 184; and international tourism, 67–68, 71; with male consumers of mainstream porn, 7, 21, 132, 174; and newsstands owners, 188–89

Perpignan, France, 136, 141, 188, *192*

Perversion—Cerimony (Braun), 128–31

Peter Pan (Barrie), 58–59, 218n37

photocopying, 146, 159, 161

photographs, daily life, 150, 155–56, 158–61, *160*, 163, 171

photographs, erotic: of BDSM scenarios, 115; destroying one's, 116, 118, 119–20; as homemade, 2–3, *3*, 4–5, 51–52, 111, 205n6; as material performances, 14–15, 145; models in, 59–62, *64*, *65*, 87–88, 120–24,

122, *123*, *125*; in personal letters, 68, 69
Picornell, Mercè, 168, 169
Platero, Lucas, 147
Playboy: confiscation of, 91, 93; and gaze, 6–7, 207n23; in other countries, 75, 240n102; and sexual populism, 193; Spanish edition of, 16, 174, 197–200
pleasure: and criteria defining pornography, 93, 139; gestures of, 18, 34, 129; images producing, 6–7, 52; politicization of, 42, 183; and women, 35, 181
pluralism, sexual, 101, 195
Poe, Edgar Alan, 58
poems, 81, 98–100, 146, 161–62
Polen editions, 192–93
police: and its archival practices, 5, 9; banning denounces of abuses by, 190, 195; and defendants' fashion description, 153–54, 158–59; and gender hierarchies, 12, 77; intrusion in people intimacy by, 118, 162; and material sexual cultures, 47–48; and policing of obscenity, 24, 25, 34, 36, 113; searching conducted by, 52, 75, 88–89, 96, 114, 115; and sting operations, 117–18; targeting trans women and *maricas* by, 145–46, 164–66, 195–96; and youth corruption, 72, 76. *See also* Guardia Civil
police reports, 47–48, 50, 73–74, 77–78, 96–97, 159
policies, state: inconsistencies in, 24–25, 173, 191; against obscenity, 29, 50, 55–56, 101, 110, 138–39; of porn normalization, 182, 185–86
political radicalism, 10, 55, 58, 102–3, 176, 177
Pompeii, secret museum of, 64
Por favor (Magazine), 183

porn consumers: anonymity of, 173; hypocrisy of, *192*; legitimate and illegitimate types of, 6, 15, 112, 126, 174, 180, 182, 191; lenient treatment given to, 13, 124
pornification, 13, 66, 100, 104, 112, 126, 136
pornographers: France as reference for, 177; legal liability of, 13; *maricas* as, 187; perceptions of, 38, 67, 104; state agents as, 2, 46
pornographic business: amateur performers in, 211n6; during democratic transition, 180, 189, 197; and film global market, 176, 180; foreign people in, 131–32; and separation with public sphere, 88, 173; undermining of, 105, 126
pornography, 22, 75, 79, 93–94, 133, 211n18; and colonialism, 48, 66; commercial distribution of, 10, 50, 91–92, 117, 185–86; confiscation and/or destruction of, 29, 56, 64, 81, 87, 96, 213n53; and differences with erotica and erotism, 6, 14, 109, 139, 197; effects of, 54–55, 113–14, 138, 177–78, 183, 226n20; and handling differences between mainstream and transgressive content, 13, 110–11, 126, 137; history of, 7–8, 62–64, 207n18; illegal importation of, 67, 95, 127, 131, 132–33, 136; legal and judicial frameworks for prosecution of, 16, 27, 82–83, 84–85, 85–87, 100–107, 142; legalization of, 179–82, 201; literature as, 35–42; as a male rite, 13, 93, 120; normalization of, 174, 189, 199, 200; self-representation among holders of, 74, 134, 141, 184; and sociopolitical contexts, 19–20, 22, 129–30; and trans and *marica* subjectivities, 168
Por qué engañan ellas (Precioso), 28

port cities, 132

portraits, 60, 121, 155, 158

posing, 15, 88, 98, 148, 155–56

Postal Service, 26–27, 43, 135

power, 17–18, 64, 154

Prado Museum, 113

Preciado, Paul, 6–7, 198–99, 207n23

Precioso, Artemio, 28, 32

Precioso García, Octavio, 214n61

press: and coverage of obscenity, 13–14, 105, 131, 226n18; disclosing defendants' names in, 132; freedom of, 67, 175, 185; as serving the Franco regime, 44, 49. *See also* mass media

Press Law, 185

Preston, Paul, 45

Preteceille, Ogier, 37–38

Primo de Rivera, Miguel, 20, 21

Primo de Rivera, Pilar, 13, 106–7, 197–98

Primo de Rivera regime, 8, 10, 11, 20–21, 42–43

print culture, 7–8, 159

privacy: and archives public access, 149–50; as citizens' right, 76, 143; as a privilege, 93, 133; violation of, 1, 68, 118, 159. *See also* intimacy

procuradores, 13, 103–6, 108

promiscuity, 34, 71, 91, 105, 177

prostitution, 50, 84, 85, 147, 180. *See also* sex work; transactional sex

protests, 77, 169–70, 177–78

psychoanalysis, 101, 179

psychosis, 104, 113, 133; pornography as cause of, 104, 113, 133

publications: illegal importation of, 48–49, 88; as left-wing oriented, NA; non-normative sexual content in, 91

public opinion, 49, 174, 178, 187

public / private boundaries, 82, 85, 168, 183; and pornography, 183

public scandal, 4, 42; criteria of, 11, 23–24, 82, 87–94, 96–97, 212n23; and elite individuals, 43, 77; homosexuality as, 20, 109; and literature, 33–35, 81; under ordinary criminal law, 22, 176, 185, 190, 201; pornography as, 85–86; prosecution of, 7, 26, 39, 51–52, 73, 190, 196; and state inconsistencies, 21

publishers, 20, 26–27, 36, 37, 55, 186

publishing houses. *See* publishers

purging commissions, 56–58, 217n24

racism: and ideas about degeneration, 37, 38; in pornographic films, 130; and racialized others as a threat, 72–73, 132; and sexual predators, 78, 180–81; in Spain, 75–76

Ramos Arteaga, José A., 59

rape, 130, 166, 181

Reáge, Pauline, 90

reformatories, 165–66

Reguera Guajardo, Andrés, 185

Retana, Álvaro, 28, 36, 38–42, 215n90

revenge porn, 51–52

Ringelberg, Kirstin, 148

Rizki, Cole, 163, 233n33

Roaring Twenties, 43

Rousseau, Jean–Jacques, 58

Rubens, Pedro Pable, 141

Russia, 57, 200, 211n16, 215n81, 240n120

Sábater Sanz, Antonio, 115

Sabater Tomás, Antonio, 101–4, 119, 121, 124, 166

Sade, Marquis de, 90

sadism, 90, 95, 115–16

Sagunto, port of, 132

sailors, 111, 120, 124, 132–33, 229n72

Sampedro, Benita, 64

Santos, Carlos, 183–84, 190

Sartre, Paul, 177

Saumench Gimeno, Domingo, 166
scandal, public. *See* public scandal
Scandinavia, 57
Schaefer, Eric, 137
Scheper-Hugues, Nancy, 153
Schlesinger, Martin Ludwig, 57
scientific writings, 56, 191–93
Second Republic: erasing traces of, 66;
    and obscenity, 11, 53, 54–55; *Peter
    Pan* during, 59; supporters of, 49,
    91, 187
Second Vatican Council, 98
secularization, 54
security measures, 72, 100, 110, 115,
    152–53, 189
Sentamans, Tatiana, 147
sexology, 11, 191
sex shops, 173–74, 184
sex toys, 9, 13, 48, 96
sexual liberation: and democratic
    transition, 175, 182–83, 196–97,
    201; as a distant phenomenon, 138;
    as global transition, 106, 176–79;
    for males, 199; and political radi-
    calism, 102–3; racialization of, 181
Sexual Revolution, 12, 111–12, 138,
    183, 202
sex work: arrests on account of,
    95–96, 117, 171; as banned subject,
    180; and international tourism,
    72; publicity of, 50; and trans
    women, 156, 153, 165, 167. *See also*
    prostitution; sex work
sicalipsis, 10, 20, 35, 193. *See also*
    novels, erotic
Sigel, Lisa Z., 207n18
Sinatra, Frank, 71
Singer, T. Benjamin, 149–50, 163
sisterhood, 15, 148, 155, 157, 163, 165
Sjöman, Vilgot, 102–3
Slane, Andrea, 51–52
Social Dangerousness and Reha-
    bilitation Law: approbation of,
13, 104–5, 107; and overlapping
    with other laws, 103, 185; protests
    against, 169; reparations for
    victims of, 184; as a response to
    sex's visibility, 84–85, 101
Social Dangerousness Courts, 14, 110,
    149, 176, 185–86, 189–90, 225n4
soft-core porn, 207n23; boundaries
    of, 188; normalization of, 16, 180,
    185–86; in other countries, 75, 104,
    176–77, 199; and penis erection, 61.
    See also pornography
Soriano Gil, Manuel Ángel, 195
South Africa, 229n72
Spain: conservative national values
    in, 3, 6, 13, 133; and its enemies,
    54, 56, 98; films produced in, 103,
    142; geopolitical positioning of, 12,
    48–49, 71, 75–76, 85, 101; LGTBQ+
    movements in, 169; literature
    in, 18, 35, 59; male prerogatives
    in, 199; moral regulation in, 67,
    135–36, 226n20
state agents: and archive curation
    of transgressive materials, 2–3,
    3, 7–9, 46, 96–97, 119, 158, 161;
    and double standard between
    mainstream and transgressive ma-
    terials, 184, 191; and homosexual
    lifestyle, 72, 126; and negotiation
    of obscenity boundaries, 20; porn
    consumption by, 129, 133, 136,
    189; and purging public libraries,
    11–12, 55; and sympathy for naive
    masculine men, 142–43; and
    violation of intimacy, 1, 116, 118.
    *See also authorities of specific
    institutions*
status quo, 108, 111, 112, 169
stigma, 8, 84, 109, 111, 158, *192*
Strassfeld, Ben, 178
striptease, 196
strolling (*pasear*), 14–15, 146, 157–59

Suárez administration, 174, 185
Subrat, Piro, 20, 21, 170, 193
Suevos, Jesús, 67
suicides, 68, 69, 70, 104, 166, 180
Supreme Court: appeals to the, 39, 41,
    97, 200; and jurisprudence on por-
    nography, 22–24, 28, 37, 83, 85–87,
    92, 93; obscene content in the
    rulings of the, 29–32; and policing
    obscenity, 1–2, 3–4, 7, 19–20, 87, 95,
    98; and public scandal criteria, 11,
    82; response to porn's visibility by,
    12, 99–100; and treatment given to
    obscene materials, 81; and young
    countercultures, 94
surveillance: and intimacy, 118; as a
    security measure, 72, 100, 107, 110,
    201; and sexual revolution, 143; of
    trans women, 157, 172
Sutherland, Tonia, 156
Sweden, 130

tales, erotic, 192–93
theaters: bookstores as, 50, 132;
    children in, 37; cruising in, 70;
    in other countries, 177, 179; and
    porn normalization, 175, 186, 201;
    women in, 35
Tierno Galván, Enrique, 196
Tintoré, Fernando, 133
Tintoretto, 109, 141
Titian, 139
Tolstoy, León, 58
Tom of Finland. See Laaksonen,
    Touko Valio
Torremolinos, 12, 68, 71–74, 164
Torrente Ballester, Gonzalo, 10, 175
Tortorici, Zeb, 50, 145, 209n41
touching: and homoerotic bonds,
    124; and sight in obscene content,
    138–39; by transgressive content,
    2, 6, 8–9, 109, 112
tourism: economic model based on,
    12, 49; effects of, 68, 101, 118,

    210n44; and loosing up moral
    controls, 67, 84; in Torremolinos,
    71–74
tourists, international: and corruption
    of youth, 76; and denunciations
    of the Franco regime, 102–3; and
    leaving Spain by force, 72, 76; and
    moral exceptionalism, 73, 80, 142;
    and moral policing, 67. See also
    foreigners
transactional sex, 71, 154, 190. See
    also prostitution; sex work
transgender men, 206n15
transgressions: in artistic fields,
    41–42, 168; and definition of
    mainstream pornography, 124; and
    documentation practices, 117, 119,
    143; in pornography, 14, 108, 187;
    visibility of, 2
trans women: in films, 178–79, 184;
    life conditions of, 147, 157; and
    state violence, 150–55; visibility
    of, 169–71, 178–79, 184; visual
    archives of, 15, 145–46, 148–50,
    155–56, 158–61, 160
Treasury, archive of the, 55
Triunfo, 175
Tubau, Iván, 174, 197–98
Tuñón, Amparo, 168–69
Twain, Mark, 139, 139

Umbral, Francisco, 199
Unamuno, Miguel de, 58, 66
United Kingdom, 10, 15, 205n6
United States: and Franco regime,
    12, 49, 101; freedom of the press
    in, 67; obscenity in, 10, 31–32, 82;
    pornography in, 74, 75, 85, 102, 176
upper class, 23, 174–75, 187
Uriarte Pujana, Segundo Ildefonso,
    27, 33–35, 213n42, 214n71
Uriarte Rodríguez, Luis, 26–27, 41,
    213n42
utopia, 58–59, 176, 199

Vagrancy Courts, 13, 110, 149, 296n11

Vagrancy Law, 49–50; implementation of, 12; prosecution of homosexuality under, 109–10; replacement of, 13, 84, 101

Valera, Juan, 58

Valverde Rodríguez, José Antonio, 181

Vázquez García, Francisco, 37

Veglison, Josefina, 107

Velázquez, Diego, 141

Venus of Urbino (Titian), 139, *139*

vice. See *vicio*

vicio, 5; as foreign to Spain, 86, 119, 132; in literature, 28, 36, 40–41; in Torremolinos, 71

victims, 66, 76, 82, 89–90, 96, 184

Victor Hugo, 58

Vidor, Charles, 196–97

Vignola, Amédée, 60–61

Vila Hernández, Salvador, 56

Vincent, Mary, 240n119

violence, sexual, 51–52, 129, 181, 184, 195–96

violence, state: as act of intrusion in trans people's life, 154, 162, 166; and archives, 71, 146, 149, 159; and censorship, 183–84; within the context of book purges, 56–57

virility: and Spanish values, 3

visibility, 148; of BDSM culture, 197; of homosexuality, 36, 190, 195; of pornography, 13, 16, 25, 85, 175, 188; of transgressions, 2, 143; of trans women, 14, 146–47, 156, 158, 163, 167, 170, 184, 234n58

Vivas Marzal, Luis, 3–5

voyeurism: legitimation of, 2; in novels or films, 69, 137–38; and state agents, 118, 119, 196; and voters, 184

Wang, Yvon, 211n17

Waugh, Thomas, 120, 207n23

Weel of Loneliness, The (Hall), 37–38

welfare, material, 101

Whitehouse, Mary, 178

Wilde, Oscar, 38, 58

women: and activism against porn, 106–7, 176; emancipation of, 35, 42, 78, 142, 146, 181; fetishization of, 50, 198; and male moral guardianship, 66, 84, 112, 188; modesty of, 82–83, 88–89; and subversion of power hierarchies, 76–77

work camp, 49, 72, 100, 110

working class, 42, 36, 193

youngsters: as antiporn activism, 178; and countercultures, 84, 94, 105; as exposed to explicit images, 83, 100, 107; and sex work, 117; showing obscene materials to, 92, 114, 131, 139; taking photos of, 115. *See also* minors

Zaldivar Aranzana, José María, 105

Zamacois, Eduardo, 214n79

Zaragoza, 58

Zubiaurre, Maite, 21, 35, 210n45, 226n22

Zubillaga-Pow, Jun, 153

Printed and bound by CPI Group (UK) Ltd, Croydon, CR0 4YY

19/11/2024

14595754-0002